Homilies and Recreations

Homilies and Recreations

HOMILIES AND RECREATIONS

By

John Buchan

First published September 1926

Thomas Nelson and Sons, Ltd.
London, Edinburgh, Paris, and New York

First published September 1926

PRINTED IN GREAT BRITAIN AT
THE PRESS OF THE PUBLISHERS

CONTENTS

CONTENTS

I

SIR WALTER SCOTT

HOMILIES AND RECREATIONS

SIR WALTER SCOTT [1]

IN the spring of 1917 I was compelled, for reasons not unconnected with public affairs, to spend a considerable time in bed, and, in the pleasant idle weeks of convalescence, I amused myself with carrying out a plan which I had long contemplated. I had been in the habit of reading some of the Waverley Novels every year, but on this occasion I re-read carefully what I considered the best—*Waverley, Old Mortality, Guy Mannering, The Antiquary, Rob Roy, The Bride of Lammermoor, The Heart of Midlothian,* and *Redgauntlet.* Then I read my favourites among the voluminous works of Alexandre Dumas, the Valois and D'Artagnan cycles ; then Victor Hugo's *Nôtre Dame* and *Les Misérables* ; and I concluded with half a dozen of Balzac. After that I tried to marshal my thoughts, and one very clear conviction stood out in my mind. Obviously each of those four masters of fiction had special qualities in which he excelled the others ; Dumas in glitter and speed, Victor Hugo in an imaginative intensity akin to poetry, Balzac in his disentangling of the web of

[1] A paper read to the English Association, October 26, 1923.

human society. But I had a clear conviction that Scott was the greatest ; he left upon me more than the others the impression which the great classical writers leave, of seeing things on a grander scale, of clarifying life, of observing justly and interpreting nobly, of possessing that " stellar and undiminishable something " which was Emerson's definition of greatness. I am in many ways abundantly prejudiced, and as a fellow-Borderer I am altogether prejudiced in favour of Sir Walter the man ; but I hope I am willing to judge Sir Walter the writer with an impartial mind. So for what it is worth I present you with this conclusion.

Others have thought the same, but not many have attempted a reasoned justification of their preference. I could wish that some of our younger scholars would turn their admirable critical talent to the prose of Sir Walter Scott. He has been far too much taken for granted, as if he were a statue in a public place. I well understand that to a modern critic there may be more engaging topics than a reputed classic, and that he may prefer to study writers who have a definite effect of attraction or repulsion upon contemporary work. But after all a critic can only show his true mettle in dealing with masterpieces, and when they have said their say about Shakespeare I would like to see them turning to Scott. I believe that criticism to-day in this country is in a healthy state, for it eschews both anarchy and formalism and labours to find a just canon. I believe that with such a critical mood Scott would fare well, and that at his best he will stand the test of the most searching examination and the most austere standards.

It is curious how rarely he has been made the subject

of serious criticism. His encomiasts have been eloquent and sincere like Ruskin, his detractors have been boisterous and bitter like George Borrow, but he has been praised and blamed in a spirit of rhetoric rather than of science. The really penetrating criticism of Scott could be collected in a very slim volume. The best is perhaps his own, or Lockhart's ; or his friend Lady Louisa Stuart's ; admirable, too, is that of a contemporary, J. L. Adolphus, whose *Letters to Richard Heber on the Waverley Novels*, published by Mr. Murray in 1821, deserve to be better known. Walter Bagehot wrote of him with his customary acumen and strong good sense; but for the rest—with rare exceptions— we have only warm appreciations by writers who are too much in love with the man to look judicially upon his work, or essays in belittlement by adherents of some minor coterie. An exception is the late A. W. Verrall—*clarum et venerabile nomen*—whose study of Scott's prose style is a model of what I mean by impartial and penetrating criticism—such criticism as Shakespeare has had for a hundred years. I want to see Dr. Verrall's method applied to all the aspects of Scott's genius, for only thus can justice be done to him.

This short paper is not an attempt to meet that need. I have no claim to speak with authority as a critic. I propose only to consider one or two of the more serious charges which have been advanced against the Waverley Novels, and to offer one or two pleas in defence. I will take criticisms which go to the heart of the matter —which, if admitted, must make us question Scott's right to a place in the highest rank of letters. The three I have selected are the charge against his verbal style, the charge against the form and construction of the tales, and the complaint of a lack of that quality which the Greeks called σπουδαῖον—of a shallow and conventional conception of human life. I offer my remarks in the hope that some among you, who are better equipped than myself, may be induced to take the matter further.

I

The complaint as to his style needs to be exactly stated. Obviously we cannot expect to find in him anything esoteric in the use of words, any delicate exercises in verbal dry-point, any of what Professor Elton has called " those false associations of painful, choice, and fastidious language that have gathered for half a century round the word *art*." I do not say that these refinements have not their beauty and value in their proper place, when the subject admits of them— in Sir Thomas Browne, in Charles Lamb, in Walter Pater, in some of the essays of Stevenson. But in Scott's type of work they are manifestly out of keeping. There is a passage in his *Journal*, written in 1826, where he makes a revealing confession. " I am sensible, that if there be anything good about my poetry or my prose either, it is a hurried frankness of composition, which pleases soldiers, sailors, and young people of bold and active disposition. I have been no sigher in shades." Had Scott indulged in the *finesse* of language he would have been guilty of a grave fault of craftsmanship, and the result would have been as preposterous as the insertion of point lace in a buff coat. Any complaint on this score may be discarded as irrelevant, and left to that not very important class whom Stevenson has described as " the young gentlemen who cant about

Art." I find it impossible to dissociate style from matter, and to admire a form which is not an organic part of the substance. Mere juggling with words for their own sake seems to me a foolish trifling, and I do not understand a manner of saying something which has merit independent of the thing said. I have heard of a short-sighted and somewhat affected lady who one day at a Scottish railway station ran up to a porter and wailed, " What *am* I to do ? I have lost all my luggage and I cannot find a porter." The man regarded her gravely and replied : " Twa verra serious losses. But if ye've lost all your luggage, ye'll no need a porter." We can apply the moral. What use is a porter to those who have no luggage ?

The real charge is a more serious affair. It is that Scott, from carelessness or ineptitude in the use of words, spoiled the artistic effect of his narrative ; that his tools were so blunt and cumbrous that they often fail to do their work ; that his extreme facility kept him always on the edge, and sometimes led him over the edge, of banality ; and that he attains his great moments by a kind of happy accident in defiance of his style. The charge has been made by Stevenson, an admirer and follower, in his " Gossip on Romance," and it has been made in uncompromising terms. " His characters . . . will be wading forward with an un-grammatical and undramatic rigmarole of words." . . . " He could . . . often fob us off with languid, in-articulate twaddle." . . . " He conjured up the ro-mantic with delight, but he had hardly patience to describe it." . . . " He was a great day-dreamer . . . but hardly a great artist ; hardly, in the manful sense, an artist at all."

That is a solemn bill of attainder, but is it just? Well, in the first place I cannot agree with the critic about the example he selects in justification of his charge. It is the famous " recognition " scene in *Guy Mannering*, when Harry Bertram lands at Ellangowan and hears the tune on the flageolet. It is true that it contains a sentence somewhat clumsily interpolated, but the romantic pitch is so high, the drama so intense, that to me, at least, the clumsiness seems negligible. But I do not wish to found on one instance, and I am prepared to make concessions to the critics. Scott is sometimes ungrammatical, as the faithful Lockhart was never tired of telling him. He is sometimes so careless that one sentence trips on the heels of another. He could fall into that jargon which in his time was believed to be polite English, and speak of " the superb monarch of the feathered tribes," when he meant an eagle, and allow Helen Macgregor in *Rob Roy* and Norna in *The Pirate* to talk like a governess from Miss Pinkerton's Academy, and—unpardonable crime—make the adorable Di Vernon thus address Rashleigh Osbaldistone : " Dismiss from your company the false archimage, Dissimulation, and it will better ensure your free access to our classical consultations." Let us grant that he could write abominably. But is there any great writer, especially any great novelist, who does not sometimes nod ? Dickens has appalling lapses of style ; so has Thackeray ; so has George Meredith, though his habit of twisted language often disguises their feebleness.

The truth is that any man whose business it is to portray life in action and who is caught up in the white heat of his task, is certain at times to seize the first phrase which comes to his hand, and jar on his more

(2,709)

fastidious readers. Scott in his careless moments fell into the fault of " polite English," but was it worse than the desiccated quasi-scientific phrases which disfigure the work of even our best to-day ? Was it a worse cloak for laziness and slackness of thought than, say, the chatter of psycho-analysis, with its " complexes " and " reactions " and " inhibitions " ? Does it jar more than the pompous inanities of philosophy which intrude into other men's prose ? I will give you one example from a very great modern. To my mind the most beautiful passage written in our day by any novelist is the last two paragraphs of Mr. Hardy's *Woodlanders*. It is so beautiful that I am almost ashamed to pick a hole in it. You remember how it goes : " As this solitary and silent girl stood there in the moonlight, a straight slim figure, clothed in a plaitless gown, the contours of womanhood so undeveloped as to be scarcely perceptible in her, the marks of poverty and toil effaced by the misty hour, she touched sublimity at points." Could anything be better ? But it goes on: "and looked almost like a being who had rejected with indifference the attribute of sex for the loftier quality of abstract humanism." Could anything be much worse ? It sounds like a sentence from an oration delivered over some deceased Positivist.

This, I grant, is only a plea in extenuation. But I submit further that Scott was a very great artist in words, playing with them as a musician plays with the notes of music, and weaving harmonies as subtle and moving as you will find in the whole range of English prose. On a certain level his gifts are admitted by all. He was a master of easy, swift, interesting narrative ; he was a master of dialogue, especially that of humble folk ;

(2,709)   2

he invented a mode of speech for the figures of past ages, which is at once romantic and natural. But on the highest levels, where alone he is to be judged, he is more wonderful still. When the drama quickens and the stage darkens he attains to a style as perfect and unforgettable as Shakespeare's, and it is most subtly compounded. Dr. Verrall has analysed the speech of Meg Merrilees to the laird of Ellangowan, and has shown with what extraordinary cunning and justice the soft vowels and the harsh consonants are used, how repetition is artfully employed to enhance the majesty of the indictment, how each particular object mentioned, each adjective, plays its part in the total impression. Professor Elton has done the same thing with Claverhouse's speech to Morton in *Old Mortality*. That is the kind of criticism of Scott's style which is worth making—careful, patient, imaginative analysis such as we give to a chorus of Æschylus, and his work is great enough to justify it. The method might well be applied to the closing scene of *Redgauntlet*, or the last chapters of *The Bride of Lammermoor*, and above all to " Wandering Willie's Tale," in which hardly a word fails of its exact adequate effect. If it be urged that this was done by instinct, not by conscious art, I reply that I do not care. Scott wrote hurriedly, and so did Shakespeare ; the divine fire was there and we are not concerned with how it was lit.

One other word in this connection. Scott, as he said, was no sigher in shades, and there are certain qualities of style which we do not look for in romances of active bustling life. But now and then comes another mood, when the sense of the transience of things steals over him and touches his prose with a strange wistful-

ness, as if the strong and self-contained soul at last
found utterance. You will find the mood occasionally
in his novels, but it is in every page of the *Journal*.
There you have the tenderness which keeps watch over
man's mortality and neither quails nor complains—a
language as universal as the Gospel of St. John. Whatever of his work may be forgotten, the *Journal* will
surely remain to comfort the weary and the sorely
tried.

II

The second charge is more important, and touches
the ordering and shaping of his tales, their alleged lack
of proportion, their often huddled and hasty conclusions.
Here again it is necessary to make frank admissions.
Scott's habit was to take a great mass of life and show
it in all its infinite variety. He did not write with a
thesis, and therefore he is loath to discard what interests him, even if its relevance is not very clear. His
affections were so actively engaged with his characters
and their doings that he is apt to linger with them in
side-walks. The architecture of his novels is certainly
not their strong point. Only *Old Mortality* and *The
Bride of Lammermoor*, I think, are really well constructed; and, of course, the short stories like "Wandering Willie's Tale" and "The Two Drovers." I admit
that *Waverley* is disjointed, that *The Heart of Midlothian*
ends anyhow, that he allowed the plot of *St. Ronan's
Well*, a fine tragic theme, to be mauled by the prudery
of his publisher.

But there are two things to remember. One is that,
when he began to write, the tradition of the novel was
picaresque, a rambling, often inconsequent, adventure,

not adapted for the exposition of a single *motif*. The second is that, while a novel as a whole may be badly arranged, the main episodes are almost always perfectly managed. When we judge Scott's architecture I think that we should consider rather the main drama, which is not always coterminous with the whole story. If we take that as the unit we shall find little to complain of. The essence of *The Heart of Midlothian* is the self-sacrificing sisterly love of Jeanie Deans, and the record of that has no flaw in it; of *Redgauntlet*, the tragic irony of a forlorn loyalty surviving into a world of prose; and could there be a more perfect culmination than when on the Solway shore a Campbell speaks the noble and chivalrous epitaph of Jacobitism? There may be padding and fumbling in the minor episodes, but the great dramatic moment arrives and Scott rises to it with the ease and certainty of genius. The list is endless—Fergus MacIvor passing to death under the archway; Caleb Balderstone, picking up the Master's feather and placing it in his bosom; the end of Sergeant Bothwell; Morton's flight from Burley; the recognition scene in *Guy Mannering*; the scene between Elizabeth and Leicester in the grotto at Kenilworth; the meeting of Jeanie Deans and Queen Caroline; the sudden martial ardour of Bailie Nicol Jarvie at the Clachan of Aberfoyle; the gathering in Neil Blane's public-house at the beginning of *Old Mortality*; the whole episode of Elspeth of the Craigburnfoot in *The Antiquary*. These things are great drama, for they proceed from the clash of character, but they are also epic, for they show the conflicts of history sublimated and focussed by a triumphant imagination, and they stir the blood like wine and trumpets.

I will take one last illustration from what seems to
me to be on the whole one of the lesser novels, *Ivanhoe*—
the scene at the tournament at Ashby, when Locksley
is shooting at the butts. Up till then it has all been
excellent vivid narrative—the jousting and the archery,
the pleasantries of Wamba, the jealousy of Saxon and
Norman ; and then suddenly comes something different.—" And now," said Locksley, " I will crave your
Grace's permission to plant such a mark as is used in
the North Country." What has happened ? The horns
of Elfland are blowing. What we have had before has
been the good stock machinery of romance, but now
the horizon is suddenly enlarged to embrace the greenwood, and Old England is summoned to the rescue.
Can we wonder that such a note should appeal to youth ?
Scott judged his audience rightly, and in that lies one
secret of his permanence, for the literature of the middle-
aged has its modes and changes, but the fashion of
youth is eternal.

In connection with this question of construction let
us glance at a complaint often made against the novels—
their *longueurs* and excessive padding, and the flat
monotony of most of the heroes and heroines. We
have Scott's own defence of his padding in his review of
Miss Austen.

" Let any one cut out from the *Iliad* or from Shakespeare's
plays everything . . . which is absolutely devoid of importance or interest *in itself* ; and he will find that what
is left will have lost more than half its charms. We are
convinced that some writers have diminished the effect of
their works by being scrupulous to admit nothing into them
which had not some absolute, intrinsic, and independent
merit. They have acted like those who strip off the leaves
of a fruit-tree, as being of themselves good for nothing, with

the view of securing more nourishment to the fruit, which in fact cannot attain its full maturity and flower without them."

It sounds as if there might be reason in that. His padding, antiquarian and otherwise, is intended as a relief, to provide a rest for the mind in the midst of exciting action. Something of the same kind may be said about his stockish heroes and heroines. They are passive people for the most part, creatures of the average world, not majestic men and women of destiny. But they are not unreal ; the earth is full of them ; they are all the more natural for being undistinguished. They seem to me on the whole to play a very vital and artistic part, for there is such a thing as having too stimulating fare. They form a solid background, a kind of Greek chorus, repeating all the accepted platitudes, and keeping the drama, which might otherwise become fantastic, within reach of our prosaic life.

The point is worth developing further, for it is bound up with the meaning of romance. It is one of Scott's characteristics that, though sympathizing in every fibre with the coloured side of life, with men's exaltations and agonies, he feels bound to let common sense put in its word now and then, to let the voice be heard of the normal, pedestrian world. Coventry Patmore in his *Principle in Art* has pointed out that in a great painting there is always some prosaic object which provides a point of rest for the eye, and without which the whole value of the picture would be altered. This duty is performed in literature by the ordinary man, by Kent in *Lear*, by Horatio in *Hamlet*, by Banquo in *Macbeth*—they are, so to speak, the " eye " of the storm which rages about them, and serve to measure the departure of the others from sanity, moderation, virtue, or merely normal conduct. " Each of these characters," he says, " is a peaceful focus radiating the calm of moral solution throughout all the difficulties and disasters of surrounding fate ; a vital centre, which, like that of a great wheel, has little motion in itself, but which at once transmits and controls the fierce revolution of the circumference." Mr. Patmore calls this point of rest the *Punctum indifferens* ; it has also been called the *Punctum immobile* ; it is the quiet anchorage of good sense from which we are able to watch with a balanced mind the storm without. I am inclined to think that no great art is without it, and that the absence of it prevents certain writers such as Dostoievski from being in the highest class. Scott never loses his head ; he never forgets the " main march of the human affections " ; and the artistic value is as undeniable as the moral value. The fantastic, the supernatural, the quixotic are heightened in their effect by being shown against this quiet background ; moreover, they are made credible by being thus linked to our ordinary world. Behind all the extravagance we hear a voice like Dr. Johnson's, reminding us that somewhere order reigns, that Prometheus may be a fine fellow, but that Zeus is still king of gods and men. Compare Scott with Victor Hugo and you will understand the difference which the lack of this quality makes. In the great Frenchman there is no slackening of the rein, no lowering of the top-note, till the steed faints from exhaustion and the strident voice ceases to impress our dulled ears.

This quality in Scott's work is closely related to a characteristic of the man which is perhaps best described as common sense—the sense of the commonalty. He is always of the centre, walking on the broad main road of humanity, keeping, in the immortal words of Davie Deans, " the middle and straight path, on the ridge of a hill where wind and water shears, avoiding right-hand snares and extremes and left-hand way-slidings, like Johnny Dodds of Farthings Acre, and ae man mair that shall be nameless." An episode in his career, one of the best-known episodes in the history of literature, illustrates the character of the man. Scott, you remember, woke up one morning at the close of 1825, when he was fifty-four years of age, to find himself ruined—saddled with an enormous burden of debt, for the most part the result of his own carelessness and grandiose ambitions. He refused to seek the refuge of bankruptcy ; he set himself to pay off his creditors in full ; for the rest of his days he toiled unceasingly at the task ; he succeeded, but he died of it. To you and me that seems a noble and splendid action, not quixotic or fantastic, but simply the carrying out faithfully of the highest standards of plain human honour.

Now listen to Thomas Carlyle on the subject : " It was a hard trial. He met it proudly, bravely—like a brave, proud man of the world. Perhaps there had been a prouder way still ; to have owned honestly that he *was* unsuccessful then, all bankrupt, broken, in the world's goods and repute ; and to have turned elsewhere for some refuge. Refuge did lie elsewhere ; but it was not Scott's course or fashion of mind to seek it there."

These words were written, it is true, before Scott's *Journal* was published and the spiritual history of those tragic years given to the world. But, as they stand, what do they mean ? No doubt such a renunciation and retirement would have been what is called in the jargon of to-day, a striking "gesture," and we can imagine the eulogies which later sentimentalists would have expended on this *gran rifiuto*. But it would have meant that his creditors would not have been paid, that innocent people would have suffered for the consequences of his own folly. I am the last man to underrate Thomas Carlyle, but of all great Scotsmen he was the one who lived most exclusively in the world of books. He praised the man of action, but his own days were spent in a library, and he was curiously remote from the rough-and-tumble of life. The course he would have had Scott follow would have been picturesque from a literary standpoint, but it would have been a shirking of a plain duty and repugnant to Sir Walter's manly good sense. He had made a blunder, and his business was to atone for it; had he robed himself in his literary mantle and retired to a shieling among the hills to meditate on the transience of human glory, there would have been no atonement.

That is an extreme instance of the fundamental quality of his character which I have called common sense. It is a mistake, I think, to assume that he had any snobbish contempt for the profession of letters; his whole life showed that he held it in the highest esteem, and he gave to it the best interests and powers of his mind. But he saw that an art is degraded if its practitioners demand privileges in matters of conduct beyond other men. He himself had no vanity or peevishness. He thought that most of his contemporaries wrote better than he did, and that the simplest soldier who carried a gun for his country was a sounder fellow than he was. He refused to indulge in false

heroics about his craft or to think that the possession
of great gifts released him from the humblest human
obligation. He could not see that rules of morality
which held in the case of the soldier, the merchant, and
the country labourer should be slackened for the artist,
or that an imaginative temperament and a creative
mind gave a plenary indulgence to transgress. He
ranked himself with the plain man, and because he
ranked himself with him he understood him.

A consequence of this quality is Scott's skill in cunning anti-climax, which, like the " falling close " in a
lyric, does not weaken but increases the effect. Like
the Gifted Gilfillan in *Waverley*, he can pass easily and
naturally from the New Jerusalem of the Saints to the
price of beasts at Mauchline Fair. The gravedigger
Mortsheugh in *The Bride of Lammermoor* has his petty
grumble amid the shadows of high tragedy : Mause
Headrigg, caught up in religious ecstasy, begs her son
not to " sully the marriage garment," and Cuddie
replies : " Awa, awa, Mither, never fear me . . . ye're
bleezing awa about marriage, and the job is how we
are to win by hanging ; " Alick Polwarth, after the
fine tragic scene of Fergus MacIvor's death, brings us
to earth with information about which gate his head
will be fixed on ; and old Haagen in *The Pirate* dashes
Minna's sentiment about Montrose by expounding with
inexorable logic the superior wisdom of running away.
It is a breaking in upon romance of a voice from the
common world ; it does not weaken the heroic, it
brings it home.

I am willing to go further and argue that, without
some such salt of the pedestrian, romance becomes
only a fairy tale and tragedy a high-heeled strutting.

The kernel of romance is contrast, beauty and valour flowering in unlikely places, the heavenly rubbing shoulders with the earthly. The true romantic is not the Byronic hero ; he is the British soldier whose idea of a *beau geste* is to dribble a football into the enemy's trenches ; he is some such type as the Georgian sea-captains who wore woollen underclothing, and loved food and wine and the solid comforts of the hearth when they were not about their business of fighting ; or some warrior like old Sir Andrew Agnew at the battle of Dettingen, who thus exhorted his regiment : " My lads, ye see these loons on yon hill there ; weel, if ye dinna kill them, they'll kill you." All romance, all tragedy, must be within hailing distance of our humdrum lives, and anti-climax is a necessary adjunct to climax. You will find it in the Ballads—this startling note of common sense linking fact and dream. You will find it in Shakespeare, who can make Cleopatra pass from banter with a peasant to the loftiest of human soliloquies—" Hast thou the pretty worm of Nilus there ? . . . Those that do die of it do seldom or never recover . . . I wish you joy o' the worm." And then :

> " Give me my robe, put on my crown ; I have
> Immortal longings in me."

You will find it in Scott, whose broad sane vision saw that tragedy and comedy are sisters, and that, like Antæus, neither can live without the touch of her mother, the earth.

III

I come now to the most serious charge of all. There are two counts in it, though they are linked together,

for they imply the absence of the same quality. The
first count is that Scott's delineation of character is
purely exterior and that he has no deep insight into
human souls. Hazlitt suggests it when he finds him
lacking in " what the heart whispers to itself in secret " ;
Carlyle states it flatly : " Your Shakespeare fashions
his characters from the heart outwards : your Scott
fashions them from the skin inwards, never getting
near the heart of them ; " Walter Bagehot puts it
precisely after his fashion, when he finds Scott weak in
his treatment of love and of religion. The second count
is that he lacked high seriousness, a profound vision
of life ; that he is without the moments which

> " tease us out of thought,
> As doth eternity."

" We have mind, manners, animation," says Bagehot,
" but it is the stir of this world. We miss the con-
secrating power." And Carlyle shakes the disapproving
head of a fellow Scot, who would fain revere but can
only admire. " Not profitable for doctrine, for reproof,
for edification, for building up or elevating in any shape !
The sick heart will find no healing here, the darkly
struggling heart no guidance ; the Heroic that is in
all men no divine awakening voice."

It is a grave charge, so grave that if it were sub-
stantiated it would exclude Scott from the inner circle
of greatness and relegate him to the populous borderland
of mere skilful entertainers, for the " stellar and undiminishable something " would be lacking. Before
we examine it let us try to set down what were Scott's
limitations. Bagehot, I think, is right in the main in
his strictures, though I dissent from his general con-

clusion. Scott's world was a very large and rich one, larger and richer perhaps than that of any other novelist, but it had its boundaries. It was a world in which things worked out normally by some law of averages, where goodness was on the whole rewarded and evil punished, a friendly universe not at war with human aspirations. It was above all a healthy world, founded on common sense and honest sentiment. It was not grievously perturbed with thought. Hence we do not find in it figures of profound intellectual or moral subtlety. I will go further and say that I do not believe that Scott could have portrayed that type; he could picture a Hotspur or a Henry V., but not a Hamlet. Such an historical figure, for example, as Montrose, could not have been drawn in detail on his canvas ; for what Bagehot has called the " labours of the searching and introspective intellect," were, I think, altogether beyond his scope. Nor has he given us, nor could he have given us, any deep studies in the religious consciousness. These matters did not interest him ; he had a robust and simple faith of his own, but by one who lived, in Emerson's phrase, " at large leisure in noble mornings " the struggles of the twilight of the soul were scarcely to be understood.

Again, I am ready to admit that he is no great exponent of the female temperament and mind—in his own class, that is to say, for the criticism is certainly not true of his peasants. For women he had an old-fashioned reverence, and, as some one has said, regarded them very much as a toast to be drunk after King and Constitution. But with the *nuances* of feminine character he was little concerned, and toward high passion between gentlefolk he showed always a certain timidity and repugnance. He was incapable of delving into the psychology of sex, for a reason which I think does him credit. He felt it ill-bred to pry into matters which a gentleman does not talk about in public. I do not suggest the severe doctrine that no man can write intimately of sex without forfeiting his title to gentility, but I do say that for Scott's type of gentleman to do so would have been impossible without a dereliction of standards. But, indeed, the question scarcely arises, for even had he tried he would almost certainly have failed. I agree with Bagehot's pontifical sentences. " The same blunt sagacity of imagination which fitted him to excel in the rough description of obvious life, rather unfitted him for delineating the less substantial essence of the female character. The nice *minutiæ* of society, by means of which female novelists have been so successful in delineating their own sex, were rather too small for his robust and powerful mind." Woman—cultivated, gently-born woman—remained for him a toast.

What do these admissions amount to ? That his knowledge and imaginative understanding of life had its limits, a charge which is true of every writer that ever lived, even of Shakespeare ; that with certain rare types of character, in which Shakespeare excelled, he must have failed ; that he regarded gentlewomen with perhaps too respectful an eye. Not certainly that the interest of the novels depends only on costume, and that the characters are drawn from the skin inwards and have no souls. Within the wide range of his understanding Scott drew character with a firmness, a subtlety, a propriety, which are not easy to match outside Shakespeare. The proof is to be found in the reading of the novels, and I should weary you if I were to make a list of the living, three-dimensional figures, who are as completely realized in their minds as they are vividly depicted in their bodies—from people that hold the stage for long like Bailie Nicol Jarvie and Jeanie Deans and Dandie Dinmont and Edie Ochiltree, to those who merely enter and go, like Mrs. Howden in *The Heart of Midlothian*, or mine host Mackitchinson in *The Antiquary*, or Bessie Maclure sitting by the cross-roads to warn the Covenanters in *Old Mortality*. But since we are on the point of psychological subtlety let me give three less familiar instances. One is Robin Oig in " The Two Drovers," in whom the whole code of the perverse but logical Highland ethics is brilliantly summarized. Another is Chrystal Croftangry in the second series of *Chronicles of the Canongate*, a moving figure of regret and disillusioned philosophy. The third has been noted by Dr. Verrall, and can be verified by a careful reading of " Wandering Willie's Tale." That is a story where the explanation seems to be supernatural, and the narrator plainly believes this. But Scott knew so profoundly the average man and his incapacity for exact evidence, that he made Wandering Willie in telling the story give two different versions of the crucial incident—first, one which is consistent with a prosaic explanation, and a second in flat contradiction and full of excited detail, which transports the whole affair into the realm of the occult. It is a masterpiece of insight into character, and also surely one of the most astonishing examples of the *tour de force* in literature—to write a tale of *diablerie* which is overwhelming in its impression, and at the same time incidentally and most artfully to provide its refutation.

It is possible that the charge against Scott's character-drawing made by hasty critics is due to his avoidance of two habits, which have given certain novelists a specious appearance of profundity, but which I cannot but regard as vices. One is the trick of dissecting a character before the reader's eyes and filling pages with laboured analysis. Scott held it his business to make men and women reveal themselves in speech and action, to play the showman as little as possible, to present a finished product and not to print the jottings of the laboratory. The other is the spurious drama which is achieved by a frequent recourse to the pathological. Leaving the supernatural aside for the moment, Scott is honourably averse to gaining effects by the use of mere ugliness and abnormality. He was perfectly conscious of the half-world of the soul and glances at it now and then to indicate its presence, but he held that there were better things to do than to wallow in its bogs. The truth is, the pathological is too easy. Take the case of religious mania, which Scott sketches in a figure like Ephraim MacBriar. You will find James Hogg treating it at length in his *Private Memoirs and Confessions of a Justified Sinner*, with a subtlety worthy of the most modern realist and with a distinction of style to which unhappily few modern realists attain. But are we therefore to assume that Hogg had gifts of psychological penetration denied to Sir Walter? It was the same with other forms of ugliness. There is a wonderful little scene in *The Antiquary*, where Mrs. Mailsetter and her gossips meet and Mrs. Heukbane recalls the gallantries of her youth.—" Ah! lasses, an ye had kend his brither as I did—mony a time he wad slip in to see me wi' a brace o' wild-deuks in his pouch, when my first gudeman was awa at the Falkirk tryst." In that scene you have the essence of all the sordid amours of a little Scots village, and Scott just notes their existence, and then goes his way to better things. For him the kitchen-midden was the kitchen-midden, a necessary and even a useful institution, but not one to be planted under the dining-room windows.

There remains the last and gravest count, which is principally Carlyle's—that the novels lack the high translunary things of literature, that they are adapted only for the type of reader called in America, I believe, the " tired business man," what Carlyle terms " the task of harmlessly amusing indolent languid men " ; that, again in Carlyle's words, " opinions, emotions, principles, doubts, beliefs, beyond what the intelligent country gentleman can carry along with him, are not to be found ; " that " they do not found themselves on deep interests, but on comparatively trivial ones ; not on the perennial, perhaps not even on the lasting." Some of this criticism, if you are in agreement with what I have already said, you will be prepared to reject at once. Clearly Scott carries us far beyond the country gentleman's intellectual equipment, and clearly he does much more than amuse. I suspect that Carlyle at the back of his mind hankered after something which we have no right to ask from an imaginative writer, something for which we must go to the professed philosophers or certain poets—a definite, formulated creed of life. He was a serious man, come of a serious stock and belonging to a very serious generation, and the tradition of Scottish Calvinism was in his blood. He wanted a message, a creed. Now there are good writers—but very few great writers—whose work is patently didactic, and about whom little handbooks can be written called " The Teaching of Mr. A—— " or " The Philosophy of Mr. B——." I do not underrate the value of the moralist in letters. But it is not easy to pin the greatest imaginative writers down to one moral, or even to a code of morals. What is the teaching of Homer ? What is the lesson of Shakespeare ? It would be hard to say, for there are a thousand lessons. Genius such as theirs reveals men and women to themselves, and with a divine compassion expounds all the frailties and strivings of humanity. It would wrong their magnificence to force them into the bonds of any creed.

But Carlyle has still to be reckoned with. We have a right to demand from the greatest not only a brilliant picture of life but an interpretation, something, as he says, profitable for doctrine and edification, an awakening voice to the heroic that is in all men. " The sick heart will find no healing " in Scott, says Carlyle, but it is to be noted that Hazlitt took an opposite view. " How many sad hearts," he exclaims, " have been soothed in pain and solitude ! " I confess myself of Hazlitt's opinion. It seems to me that Scott at his best accomplishes that enlargement and purification of life which is the test of great literature ; he makes the world at once more solemn and more sunlit. The first he accomplishes by his sure instinct for the tragic, which is the failure of something not ignoble through inherent weakness or through a change of circumstance to which it cannot adapt itself. The Master of Ravenswood, whose quality is expended idly in a waste of pride ; Fergus MacIvor carrying his high tradition to a felon's death ; Redgauntlet watching the Cause, which had been entwined with the arrogance of his decaying house, shattered on the Solway beach—these are figures of a moving greatness. They are mirrors in which to read the transience of human glory and the fragility of human hopes. Always in his bustling world Scott is aware of the shadow of mortality. In his orderly scheme of rewards and penalties the Fates are permitted now and then to snap their illogical shears. It is a gay world, but at the last it is a solemn world, and few can so cunningly darken the stage and make the figures seem no longer men and women, but puppets moving under the eyes of God and Eternity.

I have left till now the question of Scott's use of the supernatural. Admittedly it is not always happy, and I am not prepared to defend the White Lady of Avenel, or to be enthusiastic about the Bodach Glas. But there are moments when he uses it as Shakespeare uses it, to trouble the mind with a sense of powers beyond our understanding, as if the monitors of another world whispered in our ear. He was a master of the eccentric and the uncanny, just because his outlook was so sane and central, for only a mind solidly buttressed with fact can bring mystery out of cloud-land into our common life. An instance is that grim scene at the tavern-board in Hell in "Wandering Willie's Tale"; another and a greater is to be found in the chapters of *The Bride of Lammermoor*, when Ailsie Gourlay predicts the Master's fate in the weird rhyme about the Kelpie's Flow, and when the witch-wives talk in the churchyard.

" He's a frank man, and a free-handed man, the Master . . . and a comely personage—broad in the shoulders and narrow around the lungies—he wad mak a bonny corpse— I wad like to hae the streaking and winding o' him."

" It is written on his brow, Annie Winnie . . . that hand of woman, or of man either, will never straught him—dead-deal will never be laid on his back—make you your market of that, for I hae it frae a sure hand."

" Will it be his lot to die on the battle-ground then, Ailsie Gourlay ? Will he die by the sword or the ball, as his forbears hae dune before him, mony ane o' them ? "

" Ask nae mair questions about it—he'll no be graced sae far," replied the sage.

" I ken ye are wiser than ither folk, Ailsie Gourlay—but wha tell'd ye this ? "

" Fashna your thumb about that, Annie Winnie," answered the sibyl ; " I hae it frae a hand sure enough."

" But ye said ye never saw the foul thief," reiterated her inquisitive companion.

" I hae it frae as sure a hand," said Ailsie, " and frae them that spaed his fortune before the sark gaed ower his head."

" Hark ! I hear his horse's feet riding aff," said the other ; " they dinna sound as if good luck was wi' them."

" Mak haste, sirs," cried the paralytic hag from the cottage, " and let us do what is needfu', and say what is fitting ; for, if the dead corpse binna straughted, it will girn and thraw, and that will fear the best o' us."

Observe the art of that phrase " frae a sure hand " ; observe the cumulative impression of the broken dialogue with its ghoulish details ; observe, above all, the tremendous effect of the sound of the horse's feet breaking in. It is a scene which for unearthly tension is not far behind the knocking at the door in *Macbeth*.

But if he makes the world more solemn he also makes it sunnier. That is the moral consequence of comedy, and in comedy in the widest sense Scott is most clearly the master. It was this side of his work that made Byron declare in that famous correspondence between the two that among the living he found no one of whom

Scott could with reason be jealous, or, all things considered, among the dead. The novels enlarge our vision, light up dark corners, break down foolish barriers, and make life a happier and more spacious thing. If they do not preach any single philosophy, they, in Shelley's words, " repeal large codes of fraud and woe." They restore faith in humanity by revealing its forgotten graces and depths.

Is there nothing here for comfort and edification ? Is there no more than the utterance of the intelligent country gentleman ? One instance of this enlargement I will give you, and then I have done. No professed prophet of democracy ever achieved so much for the plain man as this Tory Border laird. Others might make the peasant a pathetic figure, or a humorous, or a lovable, but Scott made him sublime, without departing one hair's-breadth from the strictest faithfulness in portraying him. It is not a queen or a great lady who lays down the profoundest laws of conduct ; it is Jeanie Deans.

" Alas ! it is not when we sleep soft and wake merrily ourselves, that we think on other people's sufferings. Our hearts are waxed light within us then, and we are for righting our ain wrangs and fighting our ain battles. But when the hour of trouble comes to the mind or to the body —as seldom may it visit your leddyship—and when the hour of death comes, that comes to high and low—long and late may it be yours—oh, my leddy, then it isna what we hae dune for oursells, but what we hae dune for others, that we think on most pleasantly. And the thought that ye hae intervened to spare the puir thing's life will be sweeter in that hour, come when it may, than if a word of your mouth could hang the haill Porteous mob at the tail of ae tow."

It is not the kings and captains who most eloquently preach love of country, but Edie Ochiltree, the beggar, who has no belongings but a blue gown and a wallet.

" *Me* no muckle to fight for, sir ? isna there the country to fight for, and the burnsides that I gang daundering beside, and the hearths o' the gudewives that gie me my bit bread, and the bits o' weans that come toddling to play wi' me when I come about a landward town ? Deil ! . . . an I had as gude pith as I hae gude-will and a gude cause, I should gie some o' them a day's kemping."

And it is the same Edie who in the great scene of the storm speaks words which, while wholly and exquisitely in character, are also part of the world's poetry.

" That's not worth the counting," said the old man. " I hae lived to be weary o' life ; and here or yonder—at the back o' a dyke, in a wreath o' snaw, or in the wame o' a wave, what signifies how the auld gaberlunzie dies ? "

" Good man," said Sir Arthur, " can you think of nothing ? —of no help ?—I'll make you rich—I'll give you a farm— I'll——"

" Our riches will be soon equal," said the beggar, looking out upon the strife of the waters—" they are sae already ; for I hae nae land, and you would give your fair bounds and barony for a square yard of rock that would be dry for twal hours."

We are familiar enough with laudations of lowly virtue, but they are apt to be a little patronizing in tone; the writers are inclined to enter the " huts where poor men lie " with the condescension of a district visitor. It is Scott, the Tory country gentleman, the worldling, whom some would have us discard as superficial, that lifts them into the clear air of the heroic.

II

THE OLD AND THE NEW IN LITERATURE

II

THE OLD AND THE NEW IN
LITERATURE

THE OLD AND THE NEW IN LITERATURE[1]

IN the ancient foundation of Queen's College in Oxford every Christmas Day a dinner is held, at which choristers sing antique carols, and a boar's head, crowned with laurel and rosemary, is brought in by a stately procession. The ceremony commemorates, it is said, the adventures of a scholar of the College who, walking one afternoon in a glade of Shotover Forest, reading a work of Aristotle, was suddenly attacked by a boar. The scholar was a man of action ; he thrust his book down the boar's throat, crying " Græcum est," and the beast curled up and died. What is the moral of the tale ? Perhaps that a boar might have digested a translation, but could not swallow the original text— in which case it is an encouragement to read a work in the language in which it was written. Perhaps it teaches the value of books as defensive weapons, and is therefore an advertisement for booksellers. But on the whole I am inclined to think that it points to the compelling power of the classics. The latest contemporary work of, say, St. Thomas Aquinas or Duns Scotus would not have been so effective. It was because the book was Aristotle and in Greek that the

[1] A paper read to the Royal Literary Society, January 26, 1925.

scholar triumphed. Wherefore, if we are attacked by a boar, in animal or human guise, let us thrust a classic down his throat and he will cease from troubling.

It is an expedient which has been adopted since the beginning of the history of letters. The Athenian conservatives confounded the young radicals with Homer, Aristophanes flung Æschylus at the head of Euripides, the Roman Tory silenced the literary youth of his day with Ennius. The strife of old and new, classic and modern, has been going on merrily since the cave-man discovered a new way of making pictures on bone, and was snubbed by the elders of his tribe, who pointed to certain ancient daubs on the cave wall as the last word in art. It is a mistake to say, as I have heard it said, that the strife can only be waged in an era which lacks a strong creative impulse, for we find it in the Elizabethan age. Gabriel Harvey was preaching, not without acceptance, his thin classicism, when Spenser was inventing new melodies, and Shakespeare was creating new worlds. The conflict reached its height perhaps about the close of the seventeenth and the beginning of the eighteenth centuries, when the comparative merits of Ancients and Moderns turned the educated world into one vast debating society. The French Academy, you remember, led off, when Charles Perrault in 1687 cast a doubt on the plenary inspiration of the Ancients. The English Universities followed with an extravagant defence, and the issue was joined in the domains of art and science as well as of literature. A " battle of the books " in which Sir William Temple and Richard Bentley and Jonathan Swift were protagonists was no mean quarrel, and if we take sides to-day in the same causes we are following august precedents.

I propose this afternoon to try to state the issues in contemporary terms, for I think you will agree with me that these issues are still alive. But let me preface my remarks by saying that it is the best kind of quarrel, since it can never be settled. Thank God, we shall always have both conservatives and radicals among us, for they represent eternally the two sides of the human head. Both defend a truth which is not all the truth. Their dogmas are what philosophers call " antinomies," opposites but not necessarily contradictories. The Moderns in the Bentley-Temple controversy fought, as the late Sir Walter Raleigh has said, for " the ideals of progress and of science, the right of a nation to its own literature, the enfranchisement of art from the eternal reproduction of old models, and of science from the dogmatic pedantry of the schools." The Ancients opposed the cheap self-gratulation of the new age, argued in favour of the existence of eternal principles in art, foreshadowed the historical standpoint, and combated an atomic individualism and a petulant anarchy. In such a war we may hope for an ultimate harmony and peace, but the victory of either side would be disastrous, for each is in the right.

Let us be clear about one point at the start. Neither creed has its beginnings with the artist himself. The poet, the creator, if he be worth the name, follows the instincts of his own genius. It is only when he grows self-conscious, when he begins to theorize about his art and becomes a critic, that the quarrel starts. It is when he transforms his perfectly sound tastes into what may be very dubious judgments. I should like to see an anthology compiled of critical dicta, the work of wise men, which time has made ridiculous. Thomas Hobbes, who had a mind of remarkable range and vigour, thought that Sir John Davenant's *Gondibert*, which we do not now greatly admire, " would last as long as the *Æneid* or the *Iliad*." Byron thought Samuel Rogers a good poet and Mr. Hayley's *Triumphs of Temper* an enduring work. Lord Jeffrey, after disparaging some of the noblest things in Scott and Wordsworth, praised Felicia Hemans in language which would be extravagant if applied to Sappho. The *Quarterly Review* considered Milman's unreadable epic *The Fall of Jerusalem* certain " of whatever immortality the English language can bestow." These, be it noted, are instances, not of insensitiveness to a new and strange voice, which is natural enough in human nature—an ear attuned to Pope would take some time to get accustomed to Blake—but of preposterous praise given to contemporaries. They are examples, which might be indefinitely multiplied, of the fallibility of mortal judgment, and they are due to a bias, which may now be conservative and now revolutionary—a distortion caused by temperament or circumstance. Hobbes praised *Gondibert* because there was a touch of the new rationalism in it ; Jeffrey, who was a conservative at heart, liked Mrs. Hemans because he liked the familiar sentimental conventions.

But behind all these accidental biases there seems to me to be a broad distinction between minds, which gives reality and dignity to the eternal dispute. There is the mind which loves law and order, and which exults in the continuity of things, and there is the mind which craves adventure and change and likes to think of the

world as each morning a new birth.   It is the distinction
(shall we say ?) not so much between age and youth, as
between the conformist temper and the non-conformist ;
between the static and the dynamic ; between Apollo
and Dionysos ; between ordered power and disordered
ecstasy ; between the pæan and the dithyramb ; or in
the words of the Book of Isaiah, between those who
say " In returning and in rest shall we be saved : in
quietness and in confidence shall be our strength," and
those whose cry is " We will flee upon horses, we will
ride upon the swift."   Define these two moods by their
virtues, and it is the opposition between learning,
discipline, tradition, service, the slow labour of art,
and freedom and originality ; define them by their
vices, and it is reaction, ossification, convention, set
against revolution, slovenliness, wilfulness, impatience.
It is cool blood against hot blood, sobriety against
enthusiasm.   As a matter of fact, of course, the opposition is never complete ; for the most fiery voluntary
is not independent of tradition, and the most stubborn
conservatism has its odd romantic moments ; but we
can fairly place the two schools by their predominant
qualities.   Not schools, indeed—the word is a misnomer ; let us rather say moods and attitudes and
inclinations of mind.

First, let me present to you my young friend Theophilus as a type of intellectual youth, and a very good
type he is.   He is not one of those pallid, whiskered
people in strange garments who live in æsthetic suburbs.
Theophilus is no product of black coffee and indifferent
cigarettes.   He smokes a pipe and is an amateur of
Rugby football.   He left school to join the army in

1917, had a roughish time in France, and returned to civilian life with a number of passionate enthusiasms for things which he understood, and a multitude of not less passionate contempts for things of which he had no knowledge at all.   Youth, as he saw it, had been cruelly victimized, and it was now the business of youth to vindicate its rights.   He makes his living as a journalist, and a very honest and competent journalist he has become ; but in his leisure he has written several novels and books of verse which have won him attention, and have been on their appearance respectfully and elaborately reviewed in the intellectual weeklies by young men and women of his own way of thinking.   Let me add that he is an earnest, if somewhat critical, member of the Independent Labour Party.   He had a sound education, and has assiduously enlarged it.   During the war he became an excellent French scholar, and the language of M. Marcel Proust presents no difficulties to him as it does to me.   He has more than a smattering of science, has dabbled in metaphysics, and has read widely in English and foreign literatures.   Indeed in our own literature he has tastes which one might almost call antiquarian, and is perpetually discovering some obscure seventeenth century divine or eighteenth century versifier whose merits he preaches to his friends. He is particularly eloquent about one William Stump, an eighteenth century Warwickshire ploughman, whose solitary piece of verse he puts in the highest class.   With much of his preference for our older writers I agree, but Theophilus is also an ecstatic admirer of the work of our own time.   As he sees it, we are living in an age of adventure, and embarking on all manner of hopeful voyages.   The verse, the prose, the criticism, the speculation, the fiction of our youth are all to him good in themselves and full of an infinite promise. He is no decrier of the past, indeed he loves to wander in its by-paths, but he will have none of what he calls its " dead hand." Each generation, he holds, has to make its own canons and forms of art, and to accept those of our fathers and grandfathers is merely to hobble our feet in the race. " We may take some bad tosses," he once told me, " but at any rate we are moving, and it is better to bark our shins than to be dead."

I have a great admiration and liking for Theophilus, and the other day, when I lunched with him in Soho, I put to him some of my difficulties. We talked first, I remember, of poetry. I said that I found it hard to get my ear accustomed to certain modern licences in rhythm—that, in fact, I found them cacophonous. I added that I could not find the clarity and simplicity I liked, that poetry had become a palimpsest of chaotic reflections and impressions, and that I missed form and architecture. He smiled indulgently.

" That's merely because your ear has grown dull. Anybody who had got accustomed to the Popian couplet would have felt the same thing about Blake or Shelley. We are making new tunes, and in fifty years the world will have grown accustomed to these too, and will have to make others."

" But I don't call them tunes," I objected.

" No more would the Popian have called Shelley's tunes. He would have called them the discords of Chaos."

I was silenced, so I changed my ground. " You choke up your verse with details. You don't select enough. You jumble the essential and the trivial in one rag-bag."

He was inclined to admit some truth in this, but he had his defence. " It's our richness," he said, " like the Elizabethans. We love Nature and we want to give the effect of ' God's plenty.' The old way of writing about her was to have some dozen conventional phrases—' bosky glades,' ' verdant groves,' ' silver floods '—that sort of thing. Then Tennyson came along, and made the phrases very recondite and beautiful, and put some real observation into them, but they were still conventional. He didn't see Nature as she is, but as a set of blank verse lines. . . . Our fellows get right down to her and look at her for themselves. It is no case now of doling out a few dozen literary epithets, but of a patient and intimate observation of all her moods."

" That's very fine," I said, " but it doesn't always come off. I'm not a poet, only a humble field-naturalist. But I read a poem the other day about a moor in autumn, full of your patient and intimate observation, and in six lines I found three bad mistakes about the habits of birds. One might have thought the writer had never been outside Bloomsbury."

" Oh, they make mistakes, no doubt," he replied airily, " but the spirit is right, and it's a new thing in our literature, except for——" and he quoted two poets long since dead of whom I had never heard.

After that we began to talk about fiction. He cross-examined me about my tastes with a twinkle in his eye, for he firmly believes that I have no interest in stories which are not concerned with pirates. Rather to his surprise he found that I had read quite a number of novels of which he specially approved, and was ready to admit their merits. With much skill he drew

from me my halting criticisms. Then he thoughtfully
filled his pipe, and fixed me, like the Ancient Mariner,
with his glittering eye.

" The novel," he began impressively, " is the modern
epic, the modern ballad, the popular form in which the
life of our age naturally expresses itself. That form has
been widening its bounds ever since Defoe. It enlarged
itself from the novel of polite manners to embrace the
life of the past, with Scott ; with Dickens it took hold
of all strata of society ; Meredith gave it psychological
subtlety ; Victor Hugo brought epic poetry into it ;
Tolstoi gave it a social philosophy ; the later Russians
carried it into the dark places of the human soul. It
is steadily advancing in subtlety and scope, and why on
earth should we set limits to it ? It claims complete
freedom, because it deals with all there is of life and
death.

" Now for your objections. You say that Mr. So-
and-So and Miss This-and-That write badly. Well,
you can't expect the glib, pat Stevensonian style.
They are not carving nut-shells or painting fans, but
trying to reproduce the rough-and-tumble of life. I
am sick of this cant of style. Anyhow, they write as
well as your precious Scott or Dickens." (" No, they
don't," I interjected, but he took no notice of my
interruption.)

" Then you say that the form is crude. You only
mean that there is not the neat beginning, middle, and
end to which the older novelists accustomed you. Why
should we not make new forms for ourselves ? We are
dealing with a far greater complex of life, and must
burst the trammels of earlier conventions. We saturate
ourselves with life, and instead of fitting it into the

Procrustean bed of a literary form, we let life produce its own form, its own unity. Your criticism might have been urged by Lady Fanny Flummery against Thackeray, and by Mrs. Henry Wood against Tolstoi, and by Miss Braddon against Thomas Hardy. It is the perpetual conflict of the conventionalist against the new creation.

" Again you say that a novel must have a story, and depends for its value upon its moments of high drama. I agree. But the story may be of the processes of the mind, the action and the drama may lie wholly in the spiritual sphere. You say that the diary of the thoughts and emotions of a chemist's assistant in Balham is not a subject for fiction. I utterly disagree. It may afford the profoundest drama. You are obsessed, my dear fellow, with the old sword-and-cloak romance. To you action is something violent and melodramatic, a fight or an escape ; but you may get drama which is spiritually more significant out of crossing a room or writing a letter. You forget that to-day we know far more about the human personality. We don't think of it as a smooth, well-defined thing, but as a perpetual conflict of conscious and subconscious, so that there may be elements of ape and tiger in your amiable young woman which would scare a Wild West desperado. Your hero or heroine need never leave the streets of a suburb to have adventures stranger than those of any figure in Dumas. There may be conflicts in the soul of a provincial schoolmaster with more dramatic value for art than the taking of Jerusalem. . . . What you and fellows like you hanker after is not the artistic but the theatrical—you want a dapper *coup de théâtre*, an effective curtain. Well, all I have got to say is that that is not life, nor any sort of reality.

" You complain, too, of the excessive predominance of sex in our novels. Why not ? It is the most important thing in life, and we can't get near the truth without it. Freud has taught us that our whole unconscious self has a sexual basis. We have none of the old glutinous sentimentality about the relations of men and women. We look at them with a healthily scientific eye, but the immense significance of sex cannot be shirked. We are following the normal path ; it is you, who would shut your eyes to it, that are the abnormal."

I confess I was much impressed by these last remarks, for I know Theophilus to be the least morbid or susceptible of my friends, and, as I have said, to be more interested in Rugby football than in female society. His creed was clearly the outcome of reflection and not of natural bias.

As we walked together towards Fleet Street, he gave me in a few general sentences his philosophy of letters.

" Life," he said, " is our raw material—all there is of life. There is no subject which is not worthy and significant. We decline to rule out any province from art, merely because our predecessors neglected it. A man must let life soak into him, and let life itself dictate the artistic form. I am all for the older books, but you said rightly the other day that my interest in them was mainly antiquarian. I refuse to let them influence my work or determine my methods. Our duty is to the living breathing world around us, and not to the dead. We must serve our age as our grandfathers no doubt tried to serve theirs. What was it that Walter Pater said—that the soul of man should be a transparency through which the lights of the world will shine ? That's my creed, and I want to keep the transparency clear, neither dulled by the fog of the past, nor with the flowers of sentiment painted on it, like a plush mirror in a lodging-house. We want the truth, because only the truth will make us free."

The sight of the clock at the Law Courts made him bid me a hurried farewell, and he departed to write an article for his paper on the political deficiencies of Mr. Baldwin.

I was greatly interested in what Theophilus had said, and I pondered over it for the better part of a week. Then it occurred to me that I could best hear the other side from my friend Septimus. Septimus is a gentleman somewhere between fifty and sixty years of age, who, having been left a competence by his father, has devoted his life to the formation of a fine library, and to county business in his native Gloucestershire. At Oxford he was a distinguished classical scholar, and a Fellow of All Souls' College, but since he left the University he has interested himself rather in historical research and the by-ways of our own literature. He has published little beyond an edition of Gray, and a monograph on the classical elements in English nursery rhymes—he derived *Nuts in May*, I think, from Martial's " Jam tristis nucibus puer relictis "—but he has delighted his friends with various private publications in the nature of *jeux d'esprit*—I remember especially his proof that Shakespeare was mainly responsible for the Authorized Version of the Bible, and that the Roman Wall was built, not by the Romans to keep the Picts out, but by the Picts to keep the Romans in. From Septimus I confidently expected to get the corrective to Theophilus, if corrective was needed, for, though a voracious and omnivorous reader, he has that stout

conservative temper of mind which is found chiefly
among those who in politics have been lifelong Liberals.

I found him in the smoking-room on the top floor
of the Athenæum, in vigorous enjoyment of tea and
crumpets. When he had stayed his hunger, I put
before him the views of Theophilus, as well as I remembered them. He is an admirable listener, and heard
me out patiently while I repeated the arguments of
my gifted young friend. Sometimes he chuckled, sometimes he dissented, and frequently, to my surprise, he
nodded his head in approval.

" That sounds a good class of lad," he observed
when I had finished. " He takes the trouble to know
his own mind. He's all right."

" But you don't agree with him ? " I asked with some
anxiety.

" Of course I don't agree with him. But then, in
ten years' time he won't agree with himself. At any
rate he's alive, and that's the great matter.

" Your friend," he continued, " is dead right about
one thing. Each age has to decide its own forms in
art for itself. If it merely accepts the traditional ones
it becomes a gramophone, drearily grinding out old
records. It is the same with philosophies and religious
creeds. A man may call himself a Platonist or a
Hegelian, but he is a humbug unless he re-thinks these
philosophies for himself, and makes them his own, and
gives them the accent of his age. The first virtue in
everything is sincerity."

" Then you agree with Theophilus ? " I put in.

" Up to a point. But where we should differ, I fancy,
is in our definition of form. Art demands shape and
selection and infinite labour. Scrap all the old modes,

if you like, and invent new ones—but the new ones must still be *forms, structures*, not waywardness and slackness. Mere casual wilful eccentricity is just as bad as conventionalism—worse, indeed, for it speedily becomes itself a convention, only uglier and more shapeless than the old. There is nothing more terrible than the conventionality of the insincere unconventional. Take the instance you quoted—the poetry of Nature. We have got a sort of field-naturalist's attitude into our verse, and we aim at close and intimate observation. That is all to the good, but if we shirk the duty, and give bogus observation and a merely literary intimacy, it is far worse than the old niminy-piminy pastoral business, for we profess far more, and our humbug is the more shameless.

" But on the whole," he added, " I have not much fault to find with the work of our modern poets. The chief lack is a strong poetical inspiration—but that will come no doubt—that will come. The war was very bad for the poor fellows. It was too severe an experience, and they haven't quite found an adjustment. The stuff of poetry, as we are all agreed, is ' emotion recollected in tranquillity.' They had the emotion, but they haven't yet found the tranquillity. We may look for the beneficent effects of the war, I fancy, in about ten years' time. . . . Indeed, my complaint is that these young people are too much preoccupied with form. They have more form than inspiration. Their declared revolt against traditionalism shows it. When a man is full of original stuff, he soaks in tradition as naturally as he breathes, and glories in it. Look at Burns. There, if you like, was a new voice, and yet it was the product of five hundred years of Scottish song-making which found in him its culmination."

I was beginning to think that Septimus was much of a piece with Theophilus, and that one whom I believed to be a *laudator temporis acti* was in reality an ultra-modern. But presently he reassured me.

"On the other hand," he said, "I have very little sympathy with your friend's views on the novel. That, I confess, seems to me to be in a parlous case, in spite of an inordinate number of clever writers. I agree with him that the novel should be always enlarging its boundaries, and I would exempt no part of life from its legitimate province. But there my agreement stops."

Septimus got to his feet and warmed his back at the fire, for the hearth-rug is the natural pulpit of the conservative Englishman.

"There is an infernal lot of nonsense," he said, "talked about Life. Life and art can never be the same thing. Art is Life interpreted and made significant, the beauty and the drama and the meaning of our confused existence elicited by selection, the essential relieved from the surplusage of the trivial. Therefore a novel must have shape and purpose, and the shape and purpose must be given it by the creative mind. You may have an infinity of detail, or you may have very little, but it must all be significant. I read the other day an American novel—*Babbit*, I think, was its name—the best I have read for years. At first I thought it was simply a welter of details about a hideous kind of life and most unpleasant people, and then slowly I saw it shaping and composing itself, until the vulgar little hero became a universal and eternal thing—yes, and mightily attractive, just because he was so honestly interpreted. But "—and here Septimus's voice became doleful— " I have struggled through novels which were simply a desert of accurate trivialities, not the less trivial because they were ugly. Photographs, if you like, but not art ; information, but not the truth. Ghastly unreality I call it. There is more reality and more art in the shilling ' shocker.' "

Septimus was now fairly mounted upon his high horse. " That stuff is raw material, and it is mere impudence to present it as if it were anything else. I don't want to be shown the incoherent thoughts and emotions of some middle-aged virgin unless these things *get me somewhere*. They have no value in themselves. They are not life—they are literature, only bad literature, for they represent the abstraction and isolation of one aspect of the complex we call life. Or rather they are science, and rather bad science—the kind of thing that psychological laboratories produce, and have the decency not to label art. You must have somewhere drama and beauty, and that stuff has never a spark of it. It is like dining off a bran-mash.

" But I go a great deal further. In one sense the field of fiction is as wide as the world, but in practice a good many provinces may be ruled out. The merely pathological, for instance. For true drama, we must have action, striving, and not only suffering. The final result should be beauty, and that means some kind of triumph, not merely drab acquiescence. That is why most of the Russians, who are now the fashion, seem to me to be eternally in the second class. You will find it all in Aristotle."

Septimus looked round the shelves for a copy of

the *Poetics*, and not finding one, seized upon a volume of Matthew Arnold.

" Here," he cried, " is the same thing in other words," and he read :

" What are the situations from the representation of which, though accurate, no poetical enjoyment can be derived ? They are those in which the suffering finds no vent in action ; in which a continuous state of mental distress is prolonged, unrelieved by incident, hope, or resistance ; in which there is everything to be endured, nothing to be done. In such situations there is inevitably something morbid, in the description of them something monotonous. When they occur in actual life, they are painful, not tragic ; the representation of them in poetry is painful also."

He laid down the book. " That is God's truth. It is from Arnold's 1853 Preface, and it is as true of the novel as of poetry. Drab, dismal pathology is not true to life—if any man had the unfeatured existence of some characters in modern fiction he would have cut his throat long ago—and it is desperately untrue to art. For a writer to declare that his dinginess is art, is just as if a sculptor of a fat provincial mayor claimed to be the equal of Michelangelo because he had been faithful to his model. The mayor's statue is not true to life because, as a statue, it has no relation to what is significant in humanity.

" Then," continued Septimus, " I utterly dissent from all this twaddle about sex. If your friend says that the subconscious self is mainly concerned with sex, I reply that that is a theory for which not an atom of true scientific proof has ever been forthcoming. It is a return to mediæval superstition. Anyhow I am sick of this psycho-analysis chatter. What is new in it is mostly rubbish, and what is true is as old as the hills. The real reason why sex plays such a part in fiction is commercial—it is the circulating libraries, where most of the customers are women. The modern novelist who specializes in sex is not being bold and original ; he is following a bad commercial convention of his craft which arose because the old novel has to be made to appeal to idle and sentimental ladies. It has nothing to do with art, and less with life."

I observed that Septimus was a crusted bachelor, and therefore scarcely entitled to speak on such high matters. At that he exploded.

" All the more reason why I should speak. I have no bias, but I have seen a good deal of life and read a good deal of literature. Does any one seriously pretend that the love of a man and woman is the only thing of first-class importance ? What about the relations of man and woman to their God, to their fellows, to their country ? Some donkeys talk as if the only real tragedy was a disastrous love affair. Bosh ! There's as much tragic material in the relations of parents and children, or the relations of friendship, or some great impersonal cause like statesmanship or war. The only love tragedy in the *Iliad* is the story of Anteia and Bellerophon, and it occupies exactly six lines out of fifteen thousand. You remember Dr. Johnson on one of Pope's poems ? He said that ' poetry is not often worse employed than in dignifying the amorous fury of a raving girl.' I agree—raving girl or raving hobbledehoy. Do you realize how few of the very greatest of Shakespeare's plays deal with love in the ordinary sense ? Dr. Johnson said the reason was that ' love has no great influence on the sum of life.' I think that perhaps is to go too far, but love is only one among the major influences, and of late years it has been ridiculously over-rated. Why does your young friend, while clamouring for the extension of the province of the novel, want in practice to confine it to that dreary farmyard ? The thing is Oriental, a bad derivation from the East, and I fancy that the root of the trouble is that we have too many bright young Hebrews, male and female, trying their hand at the novel to-day."

I was rather shocked at this way of talking, and, as I had to leave to catch my train, I was forced to cut short the flow of Septimus's eloquence. But I remember his last words : " It is foolish to worry about revolt in anything—literature or politics. We human beings are what many generations have made us, and even if we want to we cannot divest ourselves of the past and march naked into a new world. It is quite right that youth should be hostile to tradition and hot for new things, but if a fellow has any real stuff in him, he will come to see that the only freedom is that which comes from the willing and reasoned acceptance of discipline, and the only true originality that which springs from the re-birth of historic tradition in a man's soul."

Then, just as I was leaving, he said a thing which gave me ground for reflection on my journey home. " There is nothing wrong with the *practice* of youth," he said. " It is bound to experiment and splash about till it finds itself, and the more vigorously it splashes, the better I like it. The trouble only begins when it embarks on *theories*. These are bound to be crude and partial. *Si jeunesse savait, si vieillesse pouvait.* Power and energy can be attributes of youth, not wisdom. Its deeds are right, but its creeds are usually wrong, and its literary criticism is apt to be damned nonsense." He shouted something after me as I left the room, which I think was a quotation from Aristotle.

I have tried to make clear to you the points of view of my two estimable friends. On thinking over their words, I began to suspect that the whole dispute might be largely a bogus one. On the major matters there seemed to be a surprising agreement. They recognized the same fundamentals, but from slightly different angles of vision. The full truth might lie in neither case, and both in their way might be right. As I reflected in my confused way, I wondered if there might not be two legitimate attitudes, the one proper for youth and the creative artist, and the other for maturity, the scholar and the critic ?

I am inclined to think myself that if a man has not been a revolutionary at some time in his life he will never come to much. A certain arrogance and revolt at one stage are proof of a vigorous personality, which has first to assert itself against the world before it can accept and remodel the world so as to make it its own. At that stage a man should be very sensitive to the atmosphere of his time, and should rate it extravagantly high, simply because it is his own. It is the medium in which he must live and work, and if he shuts himself off from it he will become a fossil. If he is a writer or painter or musician, he ought to think that he lives in a new dawn of the world, for that will give him courage and confidence. It is right that he should over-rate the work of his own day, because it speaks to him with a living and intimate voice. When Hobbes said that

Gondibert was better than the *Odyssey*, he did not really mean that Davenant was greater than Homer, but that *Gondibert* had an appeal to him and his contemporaries, something new and hopeful, which he did not find in the Greek. When an undergraduate tells me that some writer whose books seem to me like the howling of a demented wolf is a greater novelist than Meredith, he means—unless he is merely repeating like a parrot somebody else's opinion—that this writer is trying to do with the novel something which nobody has quite tried before, and in which he (the undergraduate) is deeply interested. I am all for a man living the life of his contemporaries, even if these contemporaries are rather silly; it is a great deal better to be silly than to be dead.

Therefore, on thinking over the talk of my two gifted friends, I have come diffidently to the conclusion that for a man who wants to make things and do things, whether he be an artist or a man of affairs, the attitude of Theophilus is the right one from which to start. It has the motive power, the gusto, the impetus, which is the foundation of achievement. But if it halts to expound itself and formulate principles it will be apt to make a mess of it. *Si jeunesse savait, si vieillesse pouvait*—youth eternally has the power but not the wisdom. Youth makes a bad critic, for it simply has not the knowledge. Therefore I confess I am a little bored with some of the solemn interpretations of youthful work written by youth in the serious weeklies. Criticism is primarily judgment, and judgment is a matter of perspective, and perspective is a matter of knowledge. Let youth create and build, for, if it is honest with itself, as it toils, it will acquire the wisdom which does not come from hasty generalization.

And this wisdom will be in substance the wisdom of the ancients. Each successive generation will contribute to this wisdom, will modify and enlarge it, but the enduring stock remains. That is where the reconciliation lies between old and new, age and youth. In the mature canon of Delphi there is harmony between Apollo and Dionysos. Life is a process in which we slowly and painfully discover the quality of our fathers. We must discover it for ourselves, and not take it docilely from their lips, but discover it, if we are honest, we certainly shall. There is uncommonly little that is new under the sun in the greater matters of life. We may alter our material environment beyond recognition, but we make no change in the human heart. The eternal dramas are the same ; young love is the same, whether it be Nausicaa in Phæacia, or Juliet in Verona, or Lucy Desborough in Surrey ; courage against odds does not change from Hector in Troy to Bussy d'Amboise in Paris ; a wild journey of rescue has the same thrill if the rescuer be a horseman clattering along the French roads or a pilot in an aeroplane ; and in the inner warfare of the soul, Phædra is not less subtle than a creation of M. Marcel Proust. The ideals and the canons of art remain the same, infinitely elastic yet inexorably binding, from Homer to Mr. Thomas Hardy ; and generous youth, which begins with revolt, ends with acquiescence, simply because anarchy is not a creed in which a man can abide. Stevenson has put this truth in a famous passage :

" So in youth, like Moses from the mountain, we have sights of that House Beautiful of art which we shall never enter. They are dreams and unsubstantial ; visions of style that repose upon no base of human meaning ; the last heartthrobs of that excited amateur that must die in all of us before the artist can be born. But they come to us in such a rainbow of glory that all subsequent achievement appears dull and earthly in comparison. We were all artists; almost all in the age of illusion, cultivating an imaginary genius, and walking to the strains of some deceiving Ariel; small wonder, indeed, if we were happy ! But art, of whatever nature, is a kind mistress ; and though these dreams of youth fall by their own baselessness, others succeed, graver and more substantial ; the symptoms change, the amiable malady endures ; and still, at an equal distance, the House Beautiful shines upon the hill-top."

" Graver and more substantial." It is the just and natural course of life, and I am inclined to amuse myself with a picture of my friend Theophilus some ten years hence eating crumpets in the upper smoking-room of the Athenæum, and talking in much the same strain as the Septimus of to-day.

There are of course melancholy cases of arrested development. In each generation there are instances of coteries which never change, youth which never grows up, and which carries its crudities noisily into middle life. Those *petites chapelles* generally make some clamour in the world, for they are adepts at advertisement and propaganda. I remember that, when I was very young and just beginning to be interested in literature, there was a school much in vogue which I did not love. Its members made a fetish of style and a great parade of looking clearly and boldly at life, deriving their creed, I think, from a few misunderstood sentences of Walter Pater. In ethics they expounded an unscholarly paganism, they made little excursions in flamboyant naughtiness, and their style was a painful search for the inapposite word. I remember that their vogue irritated me profoundly, till I came across similar schools, who, except for a mention in the histories of letters, are now utterly forgotten. Well, the æsthetes have shared the fate of the Della Cruscans and the Spasmodics, and so with the other coteries that have succeeded them. They make a little noise and vanish ; *securus judicat orbis terrarum.* For honest youth let us have every tolerance, but on such senile and decaying youth we need not waste our charity. Yet the grasshoppers are apt to become a burden, and if they are insistent and provocative, there is no other recourse but to the great canon of the past. We are entitled, if we meet this kind of bore, to follow the example of the mediæval scholar of Queen's in Shotover Forest, and, exclaiming " Græcum est," to thrust Aristotle down his throat. If the book does not slay, there is at any rate a good chance that it may silence.

III

THE GREAT CAPTAINS

THE GREAT CAPTAINS [1]

TO-DAY we are very weary of war, and there is no one of us but hopes that in the future, by some happy conversion of heart and an adjustment of the mechanism of Government, the danger of it may be lessened and may ultimately disappear from the world. But our interest in war will not cease with its abolition. Even if that interest be only historical it must continue, for since the beginning of recorded time war has been the preoccupation of the leaders of mankind, and we mortals must have a perpetual curiosity about all great human effort. Again and again the course of things has been altered by the soldier, and if we set ourselves to make a catalogue of the greatest men of all ages, the odds are that even the most pacific among us will have several soldiers in the shortest list.

What is that which we call military genius ? What is it that constitutes the great captain ? I ask you to make the inquiry with me to-night, for I think it is a matter of some interest. Even if the need for this form of genius should no longer exist, it is worth while to understand that with which we are dispensing. For one thing, such genius has been immensely potent. It has changed the fate of peoples and the face of the world. For another, it is one of the rarest of human endowments.

[1] An address delivered to the Edinburgh Philosophical Institution, January 19, 1920.

There have been fewer captains of the first rank than
there have been poets, philosophers, or statesmen. I
will give you another reason why it is worth our study.
It is not different in kind from other forms of genius.
There has never been a very great soldier who was only
a soldier. The foremost captains have been statesmen
actually or potentially ; they have been poets—without
the gift of singing. In the rarefied air at the very
summit of human achievement I am inclined to think
that all genius is one. It is the accident of environment
and opportunity that gifts of that high order are applied
to the conquest of armies or the shaping of states rather
than to the devising of philosophies or the creation of
masterpieces in art. The special interest of the soldier's
achievement is that it is accomplished in a medium of
exceptional stress and strain. The poet and the thinker
work at ease with words and thoughts ; the soldier's
material is the intractable stuff of living humanity.
The statesman, no doubt, has also for his material
human beings, but he has leisure and the opportunity
of retrieving mistakes. The soldier alone leads a life
of perpetual crisis. He is fighting always against time,
and a false step can rarely be retraced. From this it
follows that in the great captain genius cannot be
divorced from character. A fine artist may be a trivial
fellow apart from his art, but in the profession of arms
a major talent involves some, at any rate, of the major
virtues.

I

Well, now for our inquiry. In all talent there are
two aspects—that which is produced by training, and
that which comes by nature. We may call them the

explicable and the inexplicable ; the acquired and the given ; the scientific and the artistic. War is both science and art—a truth too often forgotten. On one side it is a huge technical business to which a man must serve his apprenticeship, as a writer learns the use of words and a banker the laws of currency.

Now the history of war has been the history of the growth of technique and, therefore, of complexity. To-day there are no short cuts to military renown ; there is too much to be learned before the apprentice becomes a master. It was different in earlier times. Then Alexander could conquer Western Asia at the age of twenty-five ; Charles XII. of Sweden brought Poland to his feet and threatened the existence of Russia while a young gentleman of nineteen ; Montrose went straight from college to command troops without any previous military training, and he had won all his astonishing victories before he was thirty-five. Again, in earlier days a man could leave civilian pursuits when well on in middle life and become a successful soldier. Cæsar took the field as an elderly party politician, and in six years made himself the first captain of the age and one of the greatest of all time. Cromwell is perhaps the most remarkable case. He did no soldiering till he was forty-three. He was a pacific English country gentleman, much concerned with civil problems and the state of his soul. But in a few years he had revolutionized the art of war as traditionally practised, and made himself one of the foremost cavalry leaders in our record.

Nowadays these things are not possible. The complexity of war began with the improvement of missile weapons and the increase in the size of armies. In these respects there is a world of difference between the

English Civil War and Marlborough's campaigns sixty years later. All through the eighteenth century, in the wars of Marshal Saxe and Frederick the Great, the complexity grew, and Napoleon, when he appeared, fell heir to a body of technical knowledge infinitely larger than anything Marlborough required. With him, too, dawned the age of gigantic armies—no longer small bodies of professional soldiers, but the *levée-en-masse* of nations. Yet I think it is impossible to study Napoleon's campaigns and not to realize how elementary was much of the technique of his day. The system of supply and transport was amateurish, and troops for the most part were compelled to live on the country they marched through. Staff work, which is the key of modern warfare, was still in its rudiments. Berthier has a great and deserved reputation as Napoleon's chief staff officer, but Berthier made appalling mistakes in almost every campaign, and one cannot but feel that Napoleon's great conceptions were often realized more by luck than good guiding. For example, the orders for crossing the Danube from the island of Lobau to Wagram sent Davoust and Oudinot to the wrong bridges. In the march from the Channel to Ulm the orders involved an entanglement between the corps of Davoust and Soult. Berthier told Murat and Davoust on several occasions to concentrate in two different places at once. Bernadotte's instructions, which he obeyed, kept him away from Jena and Auerstadt; so would have Ney's, only that remarkable person chose to disobey them.

But Napoleon, being a genius of the first order, was always reaching out towards new methods, and even when he was unable to perfect a weapon he left a specification of it for his successors to follow. I should be inclined to take the Duke of Wellington as the last of the older type of captains, the man who conceived of war on a limited scale and under these limited conditions had completely mastered its processes. During the nineteenth century revolution succeeded revolution. In the American Civil War the combatants, in their long and desperate struggle, stumbled upon many of the devices with which we are now familiar. Moltke created staff work in the modern sense. The wars of 1866 and 1870 introduced the needle-gun and the mitrailleuse. The Russo-Japanese War showed the world armies of a magnitude hitherto undreamed of. The invention of the internal-combustion engine gave us motor transport and aeroplanes. Field telephones and wireless revolutionized the system of communications among troops. The cannon passed through a series of bewildering metamorphoses till it reached the French .75 field gun and the mighty siege howitzer. No single weapon of war but has a hundredfold increased its range and precision. The old minor tactics, the old methods of transport and intelligence, are now as completely out of date as the stage coach and the China clipper.

This means that the technical equipment necessary to a great general has been enormously enlarged. He must face a long apprenticeship before he can learn his trade. The size of modern armies makes the task of feeding, moving, and directing them far more complex. The variety and precision of weapons make every tactical problem more intricate. Staff work has become a science instead of an improvisation. And yet— the new professional equipment is curiously similar in essentials to the old. The scale is different ; the kind is the same. The great captain of to-day must have high powers of organization, for he has millions to command where his predecessors had thousands ; but modern inventions, which have made these millions possible, have provided facilities for leading them. The great captain, again, must have an orderly memory in which all vital matters are pigeon-holed for future use. He must have ingenuity, a trained readiness to appreciate and use new methods which the occasion may provide. He must have a trained eye for land-scape, and a trained consciousness of what a fold of hill or a stream running at a certain angle means to himself and the enemy. All this training is more elaborate than before, but the root of the problem is the same. When Hannibal crossed the Alps he showed the same quality as an organizer of transport which Maude showed in his advance on Baghdad, or Haig when, in 1918, he rolled his great armies to the French frontiers. The scale and the complexity have increased ; the gift is unchanged.

There is one side of the soldier's equipment which is identical in every age—the knowledge of the eternal principles of strategy as exemplified in former wars. Tactics alter with each generation ; strategy in its essentials has not changed since some genius among primitive men first discovered that it was better to outflank an opponent than to assault him in front, and won a kingdom by his ingenuity. The principles of strategy are determined by the changeless categories of space and time and that unknown x which is the spirit of the fighting man. They can be learned only from the study of campaigns, and that is why Napoleon was so eager a student of the doings of his predecessors. No great captain can afford to be unlearned in military history, and it is significant that the foremost living soldier is perhaps the foremost living scholar on the subject. Readers of Foch's two masterpieces will remember how he emphasizes the imperishable character of strategical principles, and works them out from past examples in the terms of modern war. Strategy can be learned ; that is why it is part of the orthodox professional equipment ; but it demands a high order of mind in the learner. Now it is just here that, to my mind, the German system of training—very wonderful in its way—broke down. They trained their officers to perfection in matters of organization, in all that we call staff work ; they trained their men and N.C.O.'s in an admirable corporate discipline which did not crush initiative. They appreciated the value of every modern invention for the purposes of war. But their system fell short in the greatest matter of all—in strategy. They studied military history with immense industry, but they seemed to lack the true acumen. They made false deductions. They neglected campaigns like the American Civil War, which were highly suggestive for modern practice, and they centred their interest on campaigns like the war of 1870, which were already out of date. This fault was most apparent in their reading of the Napoleonic methods. They were consumed with admiration for Napoleon, but they misread him gravely, and drew wooden and mechanical deductions from a system which had all the freedom and elasticity of life itself. They interpreted the great Frenchman with something of the pedantry with which they have interpreted Shakespeare ; whereas Foch had so brought his

mind into tune with that mighty intellect that he
absorbed his methods like a collaborator rather than
a pupil.

II

So much for that side of the art of war which can be
acquired, which presupposes only industry and reasonable intelligence. It is a necessary attainment of the
soldier, but by itself it will never make more than a
subordinate. It is the other side which determines the
rank of a captain in history. All well-constructed
foundations are pretty much the same, and without
a good foundation no building can stand ; but it is not
the foundation that decides whether a church will be
an ugly edifice of bastard Gothic or a thing of light
and air and mystery. This second side implies a
special gift of nature, and, unlike the first, it is not
capable of prosaic definition. It may be analysed,
but it can never be explained. For there enters into
it that infinite and inexplicable thing which we call
genius. It is of the intellect, but not entirely of the
intellect—at least not of the intellect as we commonly
understand it. There is an unreasoned element in it,
the rational becomes the instinctive, intuition at high
moments takes the place of calculation. In a word,
it is science merging in art, and you will no more
wrest its full secret by searching than you will find
the heart of the rose by laboratory analysis, or discover the spell of a great poem by expounding its
syntax.

I need not weary you with a catalogue of the instances
in history where military genius seems to partake of the
miraculous. The greatest are familiar to you—Han-

nibal's campaign in Italy; Cæsar at Alesia; Marlborough at Blenheim, and still more in his marvellous West Flanders campaign of 1710; Napoleon at Austerlitz; Lee in Virginia in 1862, and in his last struggles in the Wilderness. I will take one modern example from a man of whom I shall have something to say later, Ferdinand Foch, and I will take it from the battle which first brought him to general fame, the First Battle of the Marne. You remember the position. On the 9th day of September 1914, the critical day, Manoury's flank attack with the Sixth French Army seemed to have exhausted its impetus. Kluck had wheeled round to meet him, and his left and Bülow's right were also holding Franchet D'Esperey. Now there was a position, a practical position, which at that juncture the Germans could have taken up and which in my belief they could have held as easily as the Heights of the Aisne. That position would have made Paris subject to the kind of bombardment which Dunkirk suffered throughout the war. On the morning of 9th September there was every probability that the Germans would either stand, or retire in good order to that position. Foch lay with his Ninth Army at the apex of the western salient opposite Bülow's left and Hausen's right. He had suffered severely in the previous fighting. Locally he had been forced to the defensive, and all that morning it seemed as if he could not maintain his ground. The ordinary general would have contented himself at the most with a stubborn defence. But Foch, with the eyes of genius, read what could have scarcely been revealed by logic, the fact that the enemy had overreached himself, and though still advancing was losing his balance. So with the last strength remaining to him he resolved to strike, and was in the act of striking when the German retirement began. You remember his famous report to Joffre: "My centre is giving; my left wing is in retreat; the situation is excellent. I am attacking." That was not bravado; it was a calm and considered decision which could not be defended by any logical argument.

We cannot explain these things, but we may reduce them to certain elements. These elements are, I fear, in turn inexplicable, but it is always something to understand more precisely in what our ignorance consists. It seems to me that there are three qualities specially implied in this kind of genius, three powers which raise their possessor to the small inner hierarchy of leadership.

The first is difficult to set down in a few words. We may call it visualizing power or synoptic power, but these are ugly phrases. I mean the power of seeing a battle-front as a whole. A war is a contest between the total strength of two sides, not the strength in one section, not the strength in the field alone, but the sum total of qualities and assets by which nations are strong. Now there is nothing so common as the sectional view in war. A general selects one battleground as the crucial one, but unless he is a very wise man he may be wrong, and the victory which he seeks immaterial to the main issue. This is especially true in modern war, where the total assets of a nation are pledged to a degree unknown in the past, and where the calculations as to where lies the true centre of gravity must necessarily be highly intricate. Indeed, I think they are too intricate for human *calculation*; to divine the key-point something more is needed than methodical reasoning.

Let us look at Germany's performance in the late war. Ludendorff's *Memoirs* give a wonderful picture of a man of great ability, assisted by a most competent staff, labouring to decide in which part of the globe lay the key to victory. The great initial attack in the West had failed, and the grandiose plan made by Schlieffen had to be scrapped. The first thing was to stem the Russian advance in the East ; this was done ; and then Ludendorff, who was already the brain of the business, resolved to concentrate on putting Russia out of action. The great attack of May 1915 was the result. It gave Germany Warsaw and some hundreds of thousands of miles of Russian land, but it did not put Russia out of action. Then the thoughts of the High Command flew to the West, and the Battle of Verdun followed—a second strategic failure. Next came the long Battle of the Somme, during which Germany's discomfort in the West grew acute, and at the same time she had the Rumanian invasion on her hands. In the latter quarter, by a really fine effort, she removed the peril, and fell back on the defensive in France. Then followed her decision to have unrestricted submarine warfare, which brought in America against her ; then the Russian Revolution, an enormous piece of luck which enabled her to wage war on a single front. So Ludendorff made his last great decision—to put in everything he had on the West and to snatch victory while yet there was time. He failed, and with him Germany. Now every single step in this process was the result of the most elaborate calculation and careful reasoning. On narrow data it is hard to say that any of Ludendorff's decisions was wrong. But he could not look at the campaign as a whole. He did not see the insanity of bringing in an unwilling America against him ; he did not see that the Brest–Litovsk Treaty, so far from settling the Russian business, started a far bigger problem which reacted terribly upon civilian *moral* in Germany itself. He consistently misread the political situation among his enemies. We can therefore say that in the major strategy of the campaign Germany, after her first plan had failed, showed no power of comprehending the true facts of the case. She swung from one foot to the other, talked loudly about her war map, and followed an opportunist strategy along the line of least resistance. It gave her many temporary and local triumphs, but it brought her in the end to disaster. She could win battles, but not a war.

And the Allies ! At first they were certainly no better. There is this excuse for them, that, being an alliance of independent democratic peoples, it was almost impossible for them to work at the start on a consistent plan. So we see the thoughts of their leaders swaying backward and forward, now to Gallipoli, now to the Balkans, now to Italy, as the theatre where victory might be won. It was mainly owing to Germany's blunders that in 1918 the centre of gravity was finally fixed on the Western front. But that narrowing of the problem would have done them little good had the command on the Western front remained as it was in 1917. In that year the British and the French armies fought a number of desperate campaigns more or less unco-ordinated. You may say that they had a common purpose—the attrition of the enemy ; but attrition in the third year of a war cannot be a serious policy ; it is the confession of the absence of a policy. If they were wearing Germany down, they were wearing themselves out of existence, and competing in a futile race towards bankruptcy. When at the end of March 1918 Foch was appointed Commander-in-Chief, the situation changed. His problem was limited ; there was only the Western front to consider ; but for the first time in the war it was considered as a whole. Every step he took, first on the defensive, then in a brilliant offensive, was calculated to a single end, and the Armistice of 11th November saved Germany from an encirclement more complete than Sedan.

The second quality in the mysterious art of the great captains is easier to define. It is the power of reading the heart of the enemy. It is less easy to practise ; indeed, it is one of the rarest talents in our mortal catalogue. Founded upon a thousand pieces of evidence, it yet cannot be merely a deduction from evidence. In the last resort it is an intuition, an instinct. A general is confronted with another general and staff, as to whose mind he is almost wholly in the dark. He gets stray bits of intelligence on which he can build theories, but even the best intelligence of this sort is imperfect and rarely amounts to a logical proof. He knows that his rival is studying him closely, and that it is a race between them for the extra margin of superior knowledge. He is anxious, and anxiety is not a good basis for clear vision. You remember the famous compliment which Sherman paid to Grant : " I'll tell you where he beats me, and where he beats the world. He don't care a damn for what the enemy does out of his sight, but it scares me like hell." The great soldier must have the power of throwing off the restless anxiety of the competitor, and judging his opponent's mind calmly and objectively, and in the last resort flinging forward his own mind in a kind of inspired guess and divining that for which in the nature of things there can be no full evidence. All surprise in war is based on such intuitions. I will give you one example which shows the quality at its highest. In the spring and summer of 1862 Lee and Jackson had armies much inferior to the North, but they knew their own mind. They read the puzzled and nervous officials at Washington like a book. Accordingly, while McClellan with 150,000 men was moving against Richmond, and Banks with 40,000 men was protecting his right rear, Jackson with 3,000 men attacked Shields at Kernstown. He was of course beaten off, but he returned to the assault, and for three months led the Federal generals a wild dance in the Shenandoah Valley. It happened exactly as Lee foresaw. Lincoln grew anxious, Shields was not allowed to co-operate with McClellan, McDowell's corps was detached from McClellan to support him. The result was that the attack upon Richmond ended in a fiasco ; and presently the North was chased out of Viriginia. In that campaign 190,000 men were paralysed and defeated by 16,000. That is the advantage of being able to read your enemy's soul.

The third quality I find hard to describe. Perhaps I can best state it as the power to simplify, the capacity to make a simple syllogism, which, once it is made, seems easy and inevitable, but which, before it is made, is in the power only of genius. No great step in history, whether in war or in statesmanship, seems to us otherwise than inevitable in the retrospect. The ordinary man flatters himself that he could have done it too, it seems so easy. There is a famous saying of Nietzsche's to the effect that the good is always easy; "everything divine runs with light feet." It is like great poetry. Take some of the world's immortal lines. Take Shakespeare's

> "We are such stuff
> As dreams are made on, and our little life
> Is rounded with a sleep."

There is nothing remarkable in the thought. It has been a platitude since the days of the Book of Job. There is nothing recondite about the language. It is composed of short simple words which we use every day. Wherein then lies the secret? Ah, that we cannot tell. The alchemy of genius has compounded these simple ingredients into something immortal. Even so is it with the great military plans. Remember that at the time they are conceived the general is faced with a multitude of confused details and a dozen different possibilities. He has to simplify under the most baffling conditions, and no mere logical reasoning can give him the right simplification. Napoleon used to be in a state of nervous unrest for days till the details sorted themselves out in his mind into a plan, and he saw the future campaign, as he said, in a blinding white light. Something of this miraculous process is always present. There may be the most careful and meticulous weighing of all possible data, but at the end there is always the flash of white light, which is inspiration.

To illustrate what I mean let me briefly sketch Foch's strategical plan during the last phase of the war. Let us take the position as it must have presented itself to

his mind in the spring of 1918 after he had assumed
supreme command. His first business was to check
the enemy's advance ; he assumed that this could be
done, and his main preoccupation was with the offensive
when he was in a position to undertake it. He knew
that some time during the summer the numbers under his
command would exceed those of the enemy, but that
was not enough. Superior numbers in the past four
years had failed to break through a defence. The whole
of the war had been a struggle to discover the best means
for an attack to overcome the extraordinary defensive
power which modern weapons give to an army anything
like equal in numbers. At Neuve Chapelle we tried
blasting our way through with artillery on a narrow
front, and merely created a salient. At Loos we tried
it on a broad front, but we underrated the defence in
depth of the enemy, and found that our troops of assault
were exhausted and could not be supported by artillery
long before they had broken through into open country.
In the Battle of the Somme we revised our plans, aiming
at limited objectives, supporting each new stage with
fresh troops and a new bombardment. That method
was like the procession of the tortoise ; it was slow, but
it was bound to arrive in time, provided the enemy
received no new great accession of numbers. But the
defection of Russia made the Somme methods impossible,
for a slow attrition was futile against an enemy which
had received a big new accession of man-power.

Germany now made a really bold and creditable
effort to be the pioneer. All former offensives had after
a shorter or longer time come to a halt for the same
reason—wearied troops were met by fresh reserves.
The battle became stereotyped, and even after further

success was impossible there was a tendency in the attacker to continue hammering at an unbreakable front, because he had set the stage for action in that one area and could not easily shift his batteries and communications elsewhere. In a word, all the offensives lacked mobility. Germany's first business, therefore, was to make the battle mobile and bring in the element of surprise.

She did it, as you know, by the new tactics which were first used at Riga and Caporetto, and afterwards with devastating effect in the attack on our line at St. Quentin in March 1918. These tactics have been described so often that I will not recapitulate them here. The essential points were the superior mobility of the attack and the element of surprise. The German plan brought them to the very gate of Amiens, but it did not give them victory, for they were not faithful to its principles. They allowed an action which was based essentially on surprise to drift into a stationary battle. They permitted themselves to become *accrochés*, and therefore, sooner or later, they were faced by Allied reserves and brought to a standstill.

This was the situation when Foch was called upon to make his plan as the Allied Commander-in-Chief. The world at the time was full of false doctrine. There were many who counselled a defensive campaign till America was fully ready, and the surrendering of large tracts of France to the enemy. Foch refused, for he saw very well that if the Germans were not beaten by superior brain-power they would not be beaten by mere mass. He looked at the German plan, appreciated its merits, detected its flaw, and then made a simple syllogism.

What was this syllogism ? The Germans had made the battle highly mobile at the start, but they had not kept it mobile. He must improve upon this ; he must bring in the element of surprise as they had done, and he must keep bringing it in and never relapse again into a stereotyped action. He remembered Byng's surprising success at Cambrai with the Tanks, and he saw in them a weapon to his hand. I well remember a talk I had with Sir Douglas Haig at a very dark hour during the Battle of Arras in 1917, when he spoke to me of the new light Tanks which he desired and which he believed to be the true weapon to break down trench warfare and lead to the open battle. Foch in this as in other matters saw eye to eye with the British Commander-in-Chief. With the Tanks he secured a surprise, and he could secure it more easily than the enemy, for with them he could pave the way for the infantry better than by any artillery preparation, and they did not need any elaborate staging.

But he was not content with an initial surprise. He carried the argument further. The battle must begin mobile and must remain mobile. Therefore, after striking a blow, he would stay his hand as soon as serious resistance developed. He would not permit himself to become *accroché*, as the British had been on the Somme, at Arras, and at Third Ypres, and as Ludendorff had been before Amiens and on the Lys.

Then came the next step. Having stayed his hand, he would attack instantly in another place. His Tanks permitted him to mount a new offensive rapidly and frequently ; they gave him a method to obviate the clumsiness of the modern military machine. His policy must be a perpetual *arpeggio* along the whole front, which would wear down the enemy's line and diminish by swift stages his reserves.

There was one last step in the logical process. Foch was like a fencer pinking his enemy again and again, baffling him, wearying him, and drawing much blood. There must be no attempt to give a premature *coup de grâce*. Following Napoleon's maxim, which had also once been the maxim of the German staff, he made it his business to keep the battle " nourished " till the moment came for the final stage. He would not press in any section for an ambitious advance or endeavour to force a decision. The action must develop organically like a process of nature.

Consider what happened. From the 21st of March 1918 to the 18th of July he stood patiently on the defensive ; from 18th July to 8th August he won back the initiative, freed his main communications, and hopelessly dislocated Ludendorff's plan of attack. From 8th August to 26th September he made it his task to crumble the enemy's front, to destroy the last remnants of his reserve, to force him beyond all his prepared defences, and to make ready for the final stroke. From 26th September onward we have the last stage, until on the 11th November the enemy surrendered.

Looking back it all seems brilliantly simple. Foch's reasoning seems elementary. Surely there could be no alternative conceivable. Foch's way was the right way, the only way, the obvious way. But in the summer of 1918, when the Allied forces were struggling on the Aisne and the Marne, there was no such simplicity in the problem. Everything which seems to us now to be patent and axiomatic was a confused tangle of guess-work. There were a dozen policies mooted, most of

them highly complex and many of them extraordinarily
ingenious.   There were distinguished soldiers who looked
upon Foch's plan in its first stages as an insane gamble.
There were few indeed either among soldiers or civilians
in any country, who, when Haig made his great attack
of 27th September against the Siegfried Line—there
were few who saw in that stroke anything but a mighty
hazard taken at random, few who realized that it followed
mathematically from the main plan.   As I have said,
every great conception in life is simple, but its simplicity
is not revealed at the moment of its inception save to
minds of the rarest quality.   To them only is it given
to see the immortal verse implicit in the prosaic parts of
speech and the perfect statue in the shapeless marble.

III

So far I have dealt with the equipment of the great
captain from the point of view of the intellect—the
power of reasoning, and that more subtle thing, the
power of subconscious reasoning which we call instinct.
But with this second power we approach another side—
the side of character, for the faculty of intuition shades
inevitably into the sphere of ethics.   Its possession is
something more than a mental endowment ; for it presupposes a character built upon massive lines.   *Some*
moral qualities every successful soldier possesses ; he
has courage and patience and resolution.   But he may
have a most powerful and trenchant intellect and yet
remain morally wanting, selfish, brutal, with low and
earthy ambitions.   Many famous conquerors have been
of such a type.   But to reach the inner circle of greatness he must have the artistic gifts, and these presuppose

a high moral development. To this rule I know few exceptions. You remember that Joseph Bonaparte was once asked what he thought about his famous brother, and he replied that in his opinion future ages would look upon Napoleon not so much as a great man as a good man. We are accustomed to laugh at this as an example of fraternal ineptitude, but the judgment has an element of truth. Napoleon was one of the greatest of all soldiers, and in so far as he was very great he was also, in the largest sense of the word, good. When he was ignoble he ceased to be great, and failed ; when he was swinging from victory to victory, pruning the rottenness from Europe, and patiently devising the reconstruction of France, he forgot his personal ambitions in something worthier.

In the last resort you cannot separate mind from character—least of all in the soldier. For the soldier, as we have seen, has for his material that intractable thing, the human spirit. He builds his fabric out of the endurance and suffering of other men. Whatever his defects, he cannot last for a day unless he possess in a high degree certain fundamental virtues. They are not the fugitive and cloistered virtues, but the virtues which are happily most common and are indubitably most valuable in the " difficult but not desperate " life of man. To succeed he must be a leader, and leadership means that he has a personality which dominates and inspires masses of men who rarely see him. The personality which can thus be diffused must be a rich and potent thing, a sterling thing which can endure through good and evil report and lift others into a confidence beyond their sufferings. Loyalty and devotion will never be accorded to a small man or a

selfish man or an inhumane man. I need not labour
the point. No one who during the war was brought
into contact with such men as Foch or Gouraud or Haig
will deny that their fineness of spirit was at least as
notable as their powers of mind. Wordsworth's character of the Happy Warrior has been misunderstood.
It is not a noble dream ; it is a manual of worldly
prudence, a practical handbook of the maxims which
lead to success in the business of war.

We can make a catalogue of the moral qualities of
the greatest captains but we cannot exhaust them
First there will be courage, not merely the physical kind
which is happily not uncommon, but the rarer thing,
the moral courage which Washington showed in the dark
days at Valley Forge, and which we call fortitude—the
power of enduring when hope is gone, the power of
taking upon one's self a crushing responsibility and
daring all, when weaker souls would play for safety.
There must be the capacity for self-sacrifice, the willing-
ness to let worldly interests and even reputation and
honour perish, if only the task be accomplished. The
man who is concerned with his own prestige will never
move mountains. There must be patience, supreme
patience under misunderstandings and set-backs, and
the muddles and interferences of others, and the soldier
of a democracy especially needs this. There must be
resilience under defeat, a tough vitality and a manly
optimism, which looks at the facts in all their bleakness
and yet dares to be confident. There must be the sense
of the eternal continuity of a great cause, so that failure
and even death will not seem the end, and a man sees
himself as only a part in a predestined purpose. It may
not be for him to breach the fortress, but the breach will

come. I would add another quality which will not be lacking in the foremost leaders of men in war—I mean human sympathy. We see it in Julius Cæsar's strange magnanimity, in Lee's tenderness and chivalry, in that something in Napoleon at his best which bound the souls of his veterans to him, and which was far more than his record of unbroken triumph. The greatest captains have laid their spell not only on the mind and spirit, but on the heart of their armies.

I told you at the start that military genius was not different in kind from other sorts of genius. In the same way the military virtues are not different from other virtues. Indeed, these virtues, as I have sketched them, seem to me merely the civic virtues in their highest form. The equipment of the great soldier is the equipment which the world must always desire in those who are to lead it to a further stage in its journey. That is why we dare not make a clean cut, and write down wars and all that made for success in them as relics of a barbarous age, like the cave-man's skill in chipping flint arrow-heads. Wars have shown human nature purged in elemental contests, and human talent exercising itself in the most difficult and exacting of labours. If they are to cease—and pray God they may —then let us transfer the genius of mind and character which they brought forth into civil affairs, or humanity will be vastly the poorer. Until the citizen acquires something of the soldier's discipline and endurance and power of sinking himself in a common purpose we shall not achieve the progress of which we dream ; and until the statesman has the courage, the singleness of aim, and the insight of the great captain, we shall not find the leaders we need. If the soldier of the old days is to pass, let us cherish his bequest. Like Mr. Valiant-for-Truth he leaves his sword to those who suceced him in pilgrimage, and his courage and skill to those who can get it. It is our business to find that courage and skill —if we can, and to reverence his sword, for it is the sword of the Spirit.

IV

THE MUSE OF HISTORY

THE MUSE OF HISTORY[1]

CLIO, according to the best accounts, was, like her sisters, sprung from a proud parentage, being the daughter of Zeus and Mnemosyne, and therefore the offspring of a union between the homely memory of mankind and the Heavenly Fire. She was also, if we are to believe the poets, the mother of Orpheus, so that song and witchery were among her gifts to the world. But nowadays this long-descended lady is in some danger of falling into straits unworthy of her ancestry. There are those among us who would make her only a schoolmarm, a humble drudge in the house of learning ; and there are others who would paint her face and set her capering on a stage for the amusement of the groundlings. Let these few pages be the plea of a humble votary on behalf of a goddess whose divinity is sometimes forgotten.

The most casual reader is aware, in turning over publishers' announcements and library lists, of a large literature which purports to be historical. There are memoirs of dead ladies who were more fair than virtuous, and of ancient lords whose actions do not blossom in the dust ; of old courts and *cénacles* which have still a faint flavour of scandal ; and of anybody and everybody who had unhappy love affairs. Diligent hacks

[1] An address to the Workers' Educational Association ; reprinted from *Blackwood's Magazine*, January 1914.

have compiled from the more obvious authorities a sort of narrative, which, illustrated by bad half-tone plates, is retailed to the public in two volumes at two guineas, or in a single volume at half that price, if the materials be scanty or the writer unskilled in padding. We are familiar enough with the memoir of to-day, in which a gentleman who has once shaken hands with a monarch describes his sensations under some title like " The Real King ——," or a poor old tattered reputation tricks out again in broad daylight its withered fineries. But that is harmless enough, for it makes no pretensions. The mischief begins when the public is given the same thing a little further removed in date and told that it is history, for thereby a prurient appetite is created which cannot relish the true fruits of Clio's garden.

One extreme produces another. History has become too much a thing of the gutter, because those who should know better would make it altogether a thing of the schools. The archivist has been running wild of late, and in the high places of the craft we are told that the one damning vice of history is popularity. Half a dozen years in the fourteenth century are accounted the work of a man's lifetime, and periods are allotted and determined with the rigidity of Calvinistic dogmas. Far be it from me to decry exact scholarship and laboured research. They are the foundation of all good history, but their results are the raw material, not the finished product. Indeed, if one had to choose, I think the mistake of the pedant is greater than the mistake of the hasty litterateur, for the latter, at any rate, attempts to use his material, to tell a tale, and to link the record of the past, however vulgar his method, with the arts and the humanities.

By history I mean the attempt to write in detail the story of a substantial fragment of the past, so that its life is re-created for us, its moods and forms of thought reconstructed, and its figures strongly represented against a background painted in authentic colours. Hence for my argument I exclude memoirs and biographies, which are side-shows in the historical theatre. The historian's task differs from the biographer's, for while the latter produces a miniature, or at best a kit-kat, the former works with a large canvas and a multitude of figures. In history quantities as well as qualities are demanded. As in a novel of Scott or a play of Shakespeare, a great piece of life must be taken, the threads of it distinguished, the motives and causes diagnosed, and the movement of it represented with something of the drama of the original. Some will concern themselves chiefly with the evidence, for unlike fiction history must produce its credentials ; some will prefer to dwell on the evolution of ideas and the birth of movements and the contribution of the period to the world's stock of thought ; while others will see only the bright colours and the sounding deeds. Each half-view will claim to be the whole, and will label history accordingly as a science, as a philosophy, or as an art. But the truth is, that no more than a drama or a novel can history afford to be only one of these things. It must have science in its structure, and philosophy in its spirit, and art in its presentation.

The historian who rashly proclaims himself a scientist can have only a nodding acquaintance with the character of the physical sciences. Where is the clockwork uniformity which science postulates in its effects and causes ? Where are the historical laws of universal validity ? The " teaching " of history is as various and contradictory as the theories about the Pentateuch. M. Bergson has shown us that half the blunders of philosophy are due to the application of the methods and ideals of physical science to spheres of thought where they are strictly inapplicable. In the kaleidoscope of the past we cannot sort out effects and causes with any precision, nor can we weigh evidence in the scrupulous scales which science demands. Even when causes are reasonably plain, their classification eludes us ; we cannot tell which is the *causa causans*, which are proximate or efficient or final. We must be content with generalizations which are only generalizations and not laws, with broad effects and massed colours, like a landscape seen from a far hill-top. The vice of the scientific historian is that he underrates the complexity of human nature. He would turn mankind into automata, motives into a few elementary emotions, and the infinitely varied web of life into a simple geometrical pattern. Order and simplicity are great things, but they must be natural to the subject and not due to the colour-blindness of the historian. Of this fault Buckle is perhaps the worst example, and Sainte-Beuve's comment on Guizot's writing is the final analysis of the intellectual habit.

" [They] form a chain from which you cannot remove a link. His aim is to rule and organize the past as well as the present. I am one of those who doubt if it is given to man to embrace the causes of his history with this completeness and certitude. He finds it almost beyond his strength to understand the present. History seen from a distance undergoes a singular metamorphosis. It produces the illusion—the most dangerous of all—that it is rational.

The follies, the ambitions, the thousand strange accidents which compose it, all these disappear. Every accident becomes a necessity. Guizot's history is far too logical to be true." [1]

Would-be scientific history is not only untrue—because it aims at the wrong kind of truth—but it is apt to be woefully dull. Its writers are so concerned with their method that they neglect their matter, and give us drabs and subfuscs instead of the colours of life. It forgets that blood once flowed in the veins of the old protagonists ; that men fought and schemed to win queens and thrones, and not to point a moral for a scholar some centuries later. " It has a compactness," Carlyle wrote of Mignet's *Précis*, " a vigour as of riveted rods of iron, the symmetry, if not of a living tree, yet of a well-manufactured gridiron." The scientific method may give us order, but that order is angular, not shapely ; and, being an artificial imported thing, in no wise indigenous to the facts, it will obscure and distort rather than clarify.

A more venial fault of the scientist is that he sometimes grows so interested in the search for facts that he forgets all about order, proportion, method, and everything else. It is venial because it is in defiance of his theory ; he slips into it from the tendency of human nature to become absorbed in any sporting quest. Facts, for their own sweet sake, however trivial, become the passion of the inquirer, and the shaping spirit of history takes wing and departs. It would be easy to point to many historical works which are simply coagulated masses of raw material, the

[1] The translation is from Mr. G. P. Gooch's admirable work, *History and Historians of the Nineteenth Century*.

tabulated results of the archivist or the excavator. They are spade-work, not architecture ; immensely valuable when used, but till then meaningless. It is ungracious to decry such painstaking toil ; but even industry may be harmful if it imagines that the house is built when the quarryman has done his job.

The trouble about science in history is that it is so little scientific. It either simplifies unduly, or in its passion for facts it forgets that truth is a reconstruction and that facts incorrectly focussed may be merely untrue. At the same time the fashion has its valuable side, if only because it inculcates a greater conscientiousness in the collection of data. It drives out the smatterer, and if it does nothing else it provides a foundation for abler men to build on. Some share of the scientific temper is indispensable to the historian. He must go soberly about the business of finding evidence, he must distinguish first-hand from second-hand, and in his quest of truth use some at any rate of the methods of the laboratory. The analogy with the physicist is perhaps misleading, and the better parallel is that of the lawyer, who can test his data by the eternal laws of evidence and stands in no foolish awe of the expert witness. Unless an historian be prepared to dig his own foundations and find his own material, or, when this has been done for him, to scrutinize jealously the results, he may erect a pretty building, but it will not be numbered among Clio's temples. It may have many charms, but it will not merit the name of history, for history in the fullest sense is the pursuit of truth.

Philosophy and history are old allies, but they have separate kingdoms, though they are in the habit of

contracting reciprocal loans. A score of popular epi-
grams—" History is philosophy teaching by examples ; "
" *Die Weltgeschichte ist das Weltgericht* "—testify to the
connection. Philosophy, it is true, has sometimes in its
high *priori* vein risen to views which made nonsense of
its neighbour, as when Hegel, contemplating the stately
process of the Absolute Will, found its final expression—
up to date—in the Germany before 1840, and thereby
gave occasion for one of Renan's happiest efforts of wit.
The professional metaphysician has rarely made a good
historian—David Hume is not a case to the contrary,
for his metaphysics were of a sober and critical cast.
The awful gambols of the *Welt-Geist* would make havoc
of any narrative, and we should not know our forefathers
when translated into the terminology of Dialectic. But
the historian must have some kind of philosophy of life
to be a lantern in the intricate ways of the past. He
must have an eye for movements of thought as well as
of armies, and trace the genealogy of ideas not less dili-
gently than the pedigrees of ruling houses. He must
also have certain moral canons, for he has not only to
chronicle but to judge.

Human nature being what it is, in ninety-nine cases
out of a hundred his philosophy will be imperfect and
frequently degenerate into bias. This is perhaps just
as well in the interests of his readers, for the passionless
detachment of a Ranke grows wearisome after a time,
and we long for one lusty prejudice. Provided the bias
is open and not too violent it does little harm, for we
can allow for it and correct it. It is far worse when
with an air of divine impartiality we are given history
where the bias subtly influences the presentation of
facts and does not merely weight the judgment on them.

Sir Archibald Alison wrote history to prove that Providence was on the side of the Tories, while Macaulay would have it that the Celestial Armies fought dutifully on behalf of the Whigs. To Froude the Protestant Reformation was a cause so noble that it dignified even its faultiest professors ; to Mr. Belloc it is the beginning of the long decline from freedom to slavery. To Michelet the Revolution was the dawn of light and reason, to Taine a black darkness of folly. Treitschke wrote his great history as the prophet of Prussian nationalism, Mommsen told the story of Rome as a devotee of that Cæsarism which was to him at once the greatest of imperialisms and the truest of democracies. It is hard to condemn such prepossessions, for they give enduring vitality. We can correct Mommsen's view of the Senatorian case, we can forgive him his treatment of Cicero ; but we could not do without his unmatched portrait of Julius.

One condition only must be laid down—the thesis in the historian's mind must be more or less rational. History written with a bias towards preposterous dogma becomes farce. The caution is needed, for this way lies a spurious originality only too seductive to certain minds. If the point of view is fantastic, the whole grouping of events will be novel. The history of the world as illustrating the domination of red-haired men would be the kind of inquiry that would lead to startling results. The truth is, that the past is easy to pervert, and must be approached with sincerity and reverence. Some sort of case can be made out for the wildest view, just as the embarrassed politician will find historical warrant for his craziest theories. The crowd applauds such gymnastics, but the lover of history averts his

face. It is so easy and so useless. Happily, there is
one corrective. If you read history as the triumph of
red-haired men, some one else with equal justice will
read it as a triumph of the black-haired, and the two
follies will balance each other. Some years ago Mr.
Houston Stewart Chamberlain's book, *The Foundations
of the Nineteenth Century*, had a great vogue in Germany
and a certain popularity here. It found in the history
of the Christian era an eternal strife between Jew and
Teuton, and adopted the pleasing habit of dubbing as
Teutonic everything and everybody that the author
admired. The corrective presently appeared in Werner
Sombart's *Die Juden und das Wirtschaftsleben*, where
a variety of heroes—from Christopher Columbus to
John Law of Lauriston—were claimed for the race of
Abraham.

History is neither science nor philosophy, though it
enlists both in its service ; but it is indisputably an art.
As a reconstruction of the past, it demands precisely
the qualities that we look for in a novel or a play.
It is primarily a story, and must have the swiftness and
cohesion of good narrative. It must have drama, so
that the sequence of events is shown as issuing in some
great moment, and, contrariwise, the great moment
appears not as an isolated crisis, but as linked to a
long chain of causes and inspired by the characters of
the protagonists. These protagonists must be made to
live again with something of the vigour of reality, and
psychology must lend its aid to make them credible
human beings. The past must be no design in snow
and ink, after the fashion of the minor moralist, but
a picture with all the shades and half-tones of life.

There is need, too, of a background, for we must see
the drama of the past with its correct appurtenances of
manners, customs, costume, and landscape if we would
see it in its truth. In all this, perhaps, drama is the
keynote. Thucydides, the most perfect historian that
ever lived, so ordered his great narrative that with
little trouble it could take the form of a play. History
is more than a pageant, as some would have us believe,
for events do not follow each other merely as successors
in time. It may not possess the perfect causal links
of the physical sciences, but it has its own inevitableness.
A crisis or a movement is not an unrelated fact, and a
calamity must affect us as something which, granted
the antecedents, was as certain as that night follows day.

The most scientific of historians, however he may
disclaim it, is apt to feel this need for drama, and he
often seeks to achieve it by illegitimate means. Surprise is essentially dramatic, and if an accepted view
can be upset then the world will be thrilled. If you
can paint Henry VIII. as a model husband, or Helio-
gabalus as a great religious reformer, or Nero as a far-
seeing statesman who sacrificed his private love of virtue
to the interests of the Empire, or Cæsar Borgia as a mild
and scrupulous ruler, or Lucrezia as a saint misunderstood, or Messalina as a pattern housewife, you will
certainly get drama of a kind. Or you may get it by
upsetting the good and great—by portraying Marcus
Aurelius as a libertine, or Luther as a hypocrite, or
Napoleon as a bungler. Or you may find it by taking
some obscure figure and exalting him into a man of
destiny, as Ferrero has done with Mummius. Or,
lastly, you may adopt the plan of providing some explanation of an historic change remote from accepted

beliefs, like Ferrero's version of Antony's motives,
or the theory that the decline of ancient Greece was
due to the advent of malaria. There may be truth of
a sort in each of these views, but it is a dangerous practice. To run counter to the world's judgments needs
great sincerity and a scrupulous good faith on the part
of the historian, and we must examine most jealously
his passport. Such drama is like impressionist effects
in painting ; it is too easy to be convincing, and when
carried to any length it degrades the seriousness of the art.

If we are to keep history from the charlatan it is
important to determine very clearly each of the artistic
qualities which are necessary for its perfection. Drama
may be overdone. Froude, in his essay on "The Science
of History," seems inclined to make it the be-all and
end-all of historical writing, which it is not. The aim
of history is to tell the truth, so far as it can be ascer-
tained, about the past life of humanity, and it is
dramatic only because human life is dramatic. If
drama be made the sole object, it will be sought at all
seasons, and will soon be perverted into melodrama.
The temptation to make a good story will run away
with the historian, and we shall have climaxes and
surprises which are artificial and therefore inartistic.
Froude himself is a sinner in this respect, but he errs
less than Macaulay. It is not that the latter is unfair,
for he can see faults in his friends and merits in his
enemies ; but his antithetical habit made him constantly prone to exaggerate for the sake of a dramatic
contrast, and this exaggeration is found not only in
his character-drawing, which lacks subtlety and breadth,
but in his narrative, where he is almost always working
for an effective "curtain." It is all very fascinating

and exciting, but it has rarely the dramatic force which a more conscientious artist attains. Mommsen, for example, never apparently strives after drama, but when the great moment arrives naturally, as in Cæsar's crossing of the Rubicon, he rises easily to its height. " It was not merely the man of genius versed in the knowledge and skilled in the control of men's hearts, whose brilliant eloquence shone forth and glowed in this crisis of his own and the world's destiny "—it is impossible to read the passage without a thrill ; and when he concludes with " The die was cast," we are convinced that the future of mankind was indeed in the balance. False drama is sometimes achieved, too, by historians who are not of the popular school. Taine is an example—Taine, who believed that history was a soluble problem, a science analogous to physiology : who, when he had once found his formula, thought that its application was as simple as the rule of three. The formula mastered him, and compelled him to resort to violent shifts to prove its efficacy. No one can deny the dramatic power of his portrait of Napoleon, but it is as perverse and unhistorical as the tearful pages of Lamartine.

Of the other artistic qualities, " background " and style are the most vital. The picture must be complete, with landscape and atmosphere, if we are truly to comprehend the past. But here there is a great need of the artist's sense of proportion, or the background will overwhelm instead of setting off the figures. The temptation is strong for a learned man to pour forth antiquarian details, but if such details are not to be an encumbrance they must be rigorously selected. There is probably no greater master in this domain than Macaulay, for, while he equips his stage with all its rightful furniture, the actors are never allowed to stumble over the " properties." Carlyle is inclined to over-decorate, like some recent productions of Shakespeare ; Mr. Gardiner to fall into the other fault of an Elizabethan bareness. It is customary to find Gardiner's one weakness in his style, but that is simple and workmanlike, and capable at times of true eloquence. But his backgrounds are thin and drab, and though we know intimately the figures he presents, we think of them rather as souls than as bodies.

Style in the verbal sense is indispensable if only to make the narrative easy and compact. In sheer mastery of words Thucydides still ranks first in the literature of the world ; Gibbon stands high ; and among the moderns Froude is unsurpassed. Style such as these men possessed has both colour and light in it. Macaulay and Carlyle are a little weighted by their mannerisms, and Michelet, who had far more balance and scrupulosity of mind than he is usually credited with, is at the mercy of his effervescing rhetoric. Style, indeed, is a somewhat double-edged gift, which too often cuts the hand of the user. If the historian be a hot partisan, then his writing will have fire and speed, whatever its other vices ; whereas, if he be detached and passionless like Ranke, his use of words will be apt to be flat and chilly. To get the best results as literature it is unfortunately true that the narrative must generally fail a little as history. That is why a flavour of partisanship seems almost essential in the historian, for a perfect bloodless urbanity will almost inevitably desiccate the style. Provided the bias be reasonable and not too violent, it is perhaps to be welcomed. Let the historian present his facts with the impartiality of a judge, and there is no harm in his stating his view with the fervour of an advocate, for then the reader has the material for forming his own opinion and is not bound to agree with the advocate.

I have spoken, hitherto, of history which deals with the complete life of a people or a continent during a space of time. But history does not cease to be an art when it is concerned less with the human comedy than with institutions. Here indeed the drama is not of the passions but of the intellect, and there is no room for ordinary emotion. But the artistic graces of precision, an adequate design, a wise proportion, and an attractive style are as necessary as ever. Fustel de Coulanges, though he held a theory of history as arid as Professor Bury's, yet could not forget the artistic sense of his race, and his work, like some rare wine, has a dry and tonic charm. The intellect is delighted by the exactness and grace of his demonstrations. Stubbs's *Constitutional History* is a masterpiece of art as well as of scholarship, and for all the bleakness of his subject he keeps the reader's interest alive. An even better example is F. W. Maitland, for he had not only the dry lucidity and exact proportions which belong to the province, but wit, vivacity, and imagination, so that without abating the rigour of the game he managed to link formal institutions to our common life. His books are more than masterpieces of technique ; they are the reflection of a wise and fascinating soul. " The history of institutions," Stubbs once wrote, " cannot be mastered, can scarcely be approached, without an effort. It has a point of view and a language of its own. It reads the exploits and character of man by a different light from that shed by the false glow of arms. It holds out small temptations to the mind that requires to be tempted to the study of truth." Nevertheless it is part of Clio's domain, and Clio is a Muse ; and there will always be those who will prefer its clear distances and pale colours to the more garish and bustling world of ordinary history.

The good historian, whatever his period, must have in his composition something of the scientist, much of the philosopher, and more of the artist. Perhaps the elements have never yet been perfectly compounded ; perhaps, indeed, they are of the nature of incompatibles and can never mix, the scientific impulse striving against the artistic to the end of the chapter. Who among men have come nearest to the perfect harmony ? Gibbon, undoubtedly, among the moderns, for in spite of the limitations of his sympathy he understood as no other man has understood the organic continuity of history, and the surge and roll of his great narrative has qualities of art which have not been surpassed. Next to him perhaps stands Mommsen, less of the philosopher, more of the scientist, a little less of the artist, who, according to Mr. Gooch, " alone has achieved the complete assimilation and reproduction of a classic civilization." In our own day S. R. Gardiner would, in my view, stand highest. He selected one of the most intricate and controversial epochs in our history, where passion and prejudice had run riot, and for forty years he laboured to set the truth patiently before the world. His industry was unwearied, and he who gleans after Gardiner will find little to show for his pains. He has his clear canons of political and moral worth, but he has no bias ; he is as just to Charles as to Pym, and no modern writer has been less dominated by the glamour of Cromwell. His psychological insight was infallible, and he has rescued figures like Strafford and Montrose for the pantheon of national heroes. In the fullest sense he is a philosophical historian, for he not only chronicles but explains. Nor does he lack the gift of drama, and his sober narrative is haunted often with a sense of brooding fate, all the more impressive because he resorts to none of the stock arts of the dramatic writer. His style is simple, homely, and effective, but it exactly clothes his thought, and I cannot admit the charge of ungainliness which has sometimes been brought against it. His fault, it seems to me, is rather that he is careless of background. He does not stop to fill in the details of his picture, so that his masterful figures, painted with all the hues and vigour of life, seem at times to be only of two dimensions, and to be warring in an unfeatured desert.

History is a work in which the talents of the English race have shown at their happiest. We are a history-loving people, desirous of keeping open our communications with the past, and basing our institutions on historical rather than logical grounds ; hence it is only right that we should have produced in the last century some of the masterpieces of the craft. Clio has reason to be proud of her English votaries. But, lest we fall from our high estate, it is well to be on our watch against the heresies which would limit history to the collecting of raw material on the one hand or to popular sciolism on the other, and would deny it the rank of an art. Clio is still a Muse, with the fire of Zeus in her veins. She is still the mother of Orpheus, and can stir our blood like poetry and song. *Vera incessu patuit Dea.*

V

A NOTE ON EDMUND BURKE

A NOTE ON EDMUND BURKE [1]

I

BURKE'S career is unique in the history both of English literature and of English politics. He was never in a Cabinet, and the highest office he held was the modest one of Paymaster-General. He developed early, publishing his *Vindication of Natural Society* at the age of twenty-six, but he did not enter Parliament till he was thirty-five, a late age in those days for one who hoped for a political career. He was admitted to be the most eloquent speaker of his time, but he was certainly not the most effective, and his speeches were prone to empty the House. All his life he stood a little apart from his contemporaries, and his detachment gave him a unique distinction, so that he became a kind of impersonal magazine of eternal truths. He had none of the usual political aims, and in a generation of place-hunters scarcely deigned to think of the rewards of office. This detachment gave him immense force as an elevated and infallible mentor, but it made him impossible as a party leader or even as an ordinary politician. His mind and temperament were not quite human. It was as if all his emotions

[1] An address delivered to the Glasgow Democratic Unionist Association ; reprinted, *mutatis mutandis*, from the *Fortnightly Review*, November 1913.

had been raised to a cosmic scale and the whole world viewed *sub specie æternitatis*. He hated abstractions, and appealed to present realities ; but the realities were always magnitudes—a constitution, a war, a nation's destiny—never the state of Mr. A's purse or the variability of Lord B's political conscience.

Long ago Burke lost all party character. Even before his death he was regarded as an armoury from which both sides could draw their shafts. Erskine, who differed widely from him on the subject of Irish policy, could declare that he viewed Burke as " upon an eminence too high to be approached." Canning owed to him nearly all that philosophical equipment which was at once his strength and his weakness. Disraeli is, at his best, simply Burke with a more modern accent, and his extravagances, like his speech at Oxford in 1864, are often curiously like the extravagances of his master. But, indeed, the thought of Burke is so woven into all English creeds that it is hard to say where his influence begins and ends. Gladstone, whose standpoint was ethical rather than historical, and who in many ways is Burke's antithesis, has a hundred passages of which the spirit and even the phrasing are due to this immense and enduring inspiration.

Burke was not, it should be remembered, a political philosopher, in the sense in which Plato and Aristotle, Hobbes and Locke, Hegel and T. H. Green deserve the name. His aim was not to inquire into the genesis and first principles of human society, or even of civilization, though incidentally he has left many acute suggestions on these matters. His business was to deal with what he found existing—Britain, the British Empire, the British Constitution ; to discover what were for them the laws of success and failure ; and to apply these laws to the problems which confronted his country in his lifetime. In reality he was a philosophic historian—the first of the school—who was able to draw a practical moral.

The philosophy of Burke is, therefore, only at odd moments universal truth, valid for all times and circumstances. Most of it is valid only under conditions which Burke very clearly indicates. He distrusted universals and absolutes, anything which had not a comfortable local and temporal setting. The notion of a pure democracy was regarded by him with little favour, as we may read in his *Appeal from the New to the Old Whigs.* He hated anything plebiscitary in government, anything which tended to break down the sacred walls of party, property, and the Constitution. There was only one English democrat in the eighteenth century, the elder Pitt. Burke in temperament was mainly Whig, detesting absolutism on the one side and popular anarchy on the other. He was a Whig in his aversion to any breaking down of the class system. To him a discreet monarchy, a peerage of public-spirited landowners, and a carefully selected Commons were the pre-conditions of civilized government—at least for Englishmen. But of the new Whigs of the Charles James Fox and Sheridan school he had a profound distrust. They seemed to him doctrinaires trying to settle the difficult problems of human conduct by a shallow reason. Also he founded modern Toryism by his insistence upon the historical method of treating state policy and by his distinction between reform and innovation. " A state," he wrote, " without the means of change is without the means of its conservation."

(2,709)   8

All human institutions, he argued, must have flaws ; but he refused to tamper with them if on the whole they worked well.   On Irish and Indian questions, and on questions of public economy he was an ardent reformer ; but on matters touching the Constitution he saw no reason for change merely because the system was indefensible on grounds of pure reason.   " The old building stands well enough, though part Gothic, part Grecian, and part Chinese, until an attempt is made to square it into uniformity.   Then, indeed, it may come down upon our heads altogether in much uniformity of ruin, and great will be the fall thereof."

In the details of his political teaching Burke was not always consistent.   In 1770 liberty seemed to him to be the vital conception ; in 1790 he was more enamoured of discipline and order.   In his early works he is, in phraseology at least, more democratic.   He declared that the House of Lords was a form of popular representation, while later he talked about its original and indefeasible rights.   It is possible to harmonize these discrepancies, for they are often different facets of one truth ; but undoubtedly, under the influence of the French Revolution, his mind took on a more conservative colour.   It is his later teaching which is his real contribution to the world's thought, for now he is addressing, not an English party, but the whole thinking world.   His earlier precepts, admirable as they may be, are too often limited in their application, and to get at their value we must be very clear about his presuppositions.   But his later doctrines are less an exposition of a party creed than of an eternal attitude of the human mind.   Liberty without content is a barren dogma ; it must be a " manly, moral, and regulated liberty." It is order and discipline that bind the state together. Civilization is no gift of Nature to man; it is man's creation, and if the cohesive powers of Law be weakened little will remain for Right. In politics we must look at facts and their historical relations, not at vague rules of reason or the speculations of theorists. Whatever is, has the presumption of right in its favour; and, before we alter it, let us be careful that we are altering in accordance with the organic conception of the state. Such, in a few sentences, is the gist of Burke's philosophy; but never was a doctrine dressed in more imperial robes. He is the most eloquent of English prose writers, for not only has each sentence its perfect rhythm, but the great argument rolls in a noble cadence to its climax. His wealth of fancy, his learning, his command of splendid and apposite images are inexhaustible. He is the " fullest " of writers, not only in thought and knowledge, but in mastery of golden and melodious words. As was said of Cæsar, he has the " facultas dicendi imperatoria."

II

I propose to-night to consider with you one of Burke's earlier precepts, which, as I have said, are often limited in their application. It is worth while to examine more closely his doctrine of Parliamentary representation, for it is not only typical of the massive good sense and clarity of his mind, but it shows how free he was from the baser kind of dogmatism, how anxious to make an ideal policy harmonize with gross facts. And the inquiry may shed some light upon our own contemporary problems.

I suppose that no two phrases are more common in

the press and on the platform than "Democracy"
and "Representative Government." They are used in
many senses. You may find the first applied to that
which the people desire but which may not be good
for them ; you may find it used again in exactly the
opposite sense, as that which is good for the people but
which they may not desire. It is a little puzzling for
plain men. But, roughly speaking, we may say that
there is one meaning running through most of its
various uses. Democracy is supposed to be the rule
of the majority of the citizens of a country, each citizen
counting as one and no more. Representative Government, too, is a wide word, at least as it is used in politics
to-day. During the pre-war discussions on the Parliament Act we used to be told by one side that that
measure was necessary to complete and safeguard
Representative Government, and by the other side
that it would put an end to Representative Government altogether. Clearly the disputants must have
used the words in different senses. Let us examine
very briefly, with the help of Burke, what Representative
Government means historically, and what is its position
to-day in a democracy, which, whether for good or ill,
is far more advanced—far " purer," as the phrase goes
—than in the days of our grandfathers.

In our grandfathers' days people lived beyond doubt
under a system of Representative Government. I will
take my definition of that system from Burke. It is
from his speech to the electors of Bristol after the poll
in November 1774:

" It ought to be the happiness and glory of a representative to live in the strictest union, the closest correspondence,
and the most unreserved communication with his con-

stituents. Their wishes ought to have great weight with
him ; their opinion high respect ; their business unremitted
attention. It is his duty to sacrifice his repose, his pleasures,
his satisfactions, to theirs ; and above all, ever, and in all
cases, to prefer their interests to his own. But his unbiassed opinion, his mature judgment, his enlightened
conscience, he ought not to sacrifice to you, to any man,
or to any set of men living. These he does not derive
from your pleasure; no, nor from the law and the Constitution. They are a trust from Providence, for the abuse
of which he is deeply answerable. Your representative
owes you, not his industry only, but his judgment ; and
he betrays, instead of serving you, if he sacrifices it to your
opinion. . . . If Government were a matter of will upon
any side, yours, without question, ought to be superior.
But Government and legislation are matters of reason and
judgment, and not of inclination ; and what sort of reason
is that, in which the determination precedes the discussion ;
in which one set of men deliberate and another decide ;
and where those who form the conclusion are perhaps
three hundred miles distant from those who hear the
arguments ? . . . Authoritative instructions, mandates
issued, which the member is bound blindly and implicitly
to obey, to vote, and to argue for, though contrary to the
clearest conviction of his judgment and conscience,—these
are things utterly unknown to the laws of this land, and
arise from a fundamental mistake of the whole order and
tenor of our constitution."

A representative, in Burke's view, is a member of
a party which places before the nation a certain system
of national policy. He is elected partly because he is
a member of that party and an advocate of that system,
but largely for his own sake. For what his constituents
buy with their votes is not only his party loyalty—
Burke ranked that high, though not too high—but very
specially his own judgment and conscience. They
choose him to do their political thinking for them under

the belief that he is better qualified than themselves. He is not their delegate with a mandate, nor their ambassador to act on their instructions, nor their advocate to speak from a brief, but their *representative*— a free man bound to act and deliberate freely to the best of his powers, subject, of course, to the approval of his constituents at the next election.

That is a very noble and rational doctrine ; none nobler or more rational has ever, in my opinion, been evolved in the history of free governments.   Before we proceed to examine its applicability to the conditions of to-day we may note two facts about it.   In the first place, it is closely linked to another doctrine, the doctrine of the legal sovereignty of Parliament.   I should define this as the right of Parliament to do anything it pleases in legislation, subject to the ultimate right of the people to undo it.   We have grown so accustomed to this doctrine that we think of it as extending, in spite of the misdeeds of kings and nobles, far back into the childhood of British history.   But the truth is, it is a very young doctrine.   When Burke spoke the words I have quoted it was not very much more than a century old. In feudal England people talked of a law fundamental, a law of the land, which no king or council could tamper with.   Magna Charta was a solemn embodiment of one portion of this law fundamental.   In 1604 the Speaker of the House of Commons divided the laws into (*a*) the Common Law, not mutable, (*b*) the Positive Law, to be altered by the occasions of the times, and (*c*) Customs and Usages which have time's approbation ; and we find Cromwell repeatedly making the distinction.   Sir Edward Coke maintained that the function of King and Parliament was not *jus dare*—to make new law—but *jus dicere*

—to declare existing law. I could multiply instances, but these will suffice. The Long Parliament first invented the theory of legislative sovereignty, and the statesmen of the Restoration acquiesced in it. Thenceforth there was no law fundamental in Britain, but any Parliament could legislate to any extent and on any subject of its own free will. It was a remarkable discovery, and a violent, and in many respects a valuable innovation ; for though it lost us the American colonies it gave us modern Britain. Now legislative sovereignty involves the doctrine of representation. A sovereign Parliament, once it has been elected, must own no other sovereign. A member of it owes his chief duty to the august body of which he is a part.

The second fact to be noticed is that Burke's doctrine is not democratic in the sense in which we commonly use the word. He was no believer in government by mere numbers, in what Archbishop Magee called " the plenary inspiration of the odd man." In a quarrel between the people and their rulers he thought there was generally a presumption of right on the side of the people, because a people does not quarrel for fun. A people has needs and discontents and wants, but not views ; or, if it has, its views are negligible. He thought it the business of a representative to fit a policy to the needs, but not to take it ready-made from those who suffered. The popular voice he considered a more or less unintelligible *patois*, bearing no sort of relation to the voice of God. That may be in the truest sense democratic doctrine—far be it from me to deny it ; but it is not the sense in which we use the word to-day.

If we want the pure milk of this doctrine let us turn to Windham, who was Burke's closest friend and most faithful disciple. One of his Norwich constituents wrote to him on the question of the peace with France, announcing that he differed from his member, and might have to withdraw his support. To this Windham replied in an epistle which the unfortunate gentleman must have long remembered. " If you think," he wrote, " that I am a man generally unfit for the situation which I occupy ; that I am disposed to betray its duties to purposes of my own advantage ; that I am apt to be led away from my duty by party connections ; that I do not deal fairly and openly with my constituents, but profess opinions that I do not believe, and dissemble those that I do :—if any of these things have determined your judgment, there is no disputing the propriety of the change that is represented to have taken place. But if, thinking of me in all respects as you have heretofore done, you mean to vote against me . . . merely because I am of opinion, in common with nine-tenths of the thinking part of the community, that the present peace is big with the most alarming dangers to the very existence of the Empire ; while you, on the other hand, who have hardly considered the question so much as I have, are induced to think well of it, being led perhaps to the opinion more by some immediate, local, and personal advantages, which you may hope may result from it, than by any other consideration,—then I must think that you act upon principles less liberal, less enlightened, and less just than I should have ascribed to you." [1] There speaks the representative in all the pride of his independence.

Burke, as I have said, was not a successful politician ;

---

[1] *Windham Papers II.*, 179.

but he was a great thinker and he had a horror of dogma.
He would have been the last man to put his views on
Representative Government too high. Like all other
maxims of politics he considered them true under
certain definite national conditions. It is worth our
while to look at these conditions, and to inquire if they
hold good to-day. Nowhere in his writings does Burke
lay them down categorically ; but we find him constantly
arguing from certain presumptions, and we may take
these to be the pre-suppositions of his Representative
Government when we find them clearly and organically
related to it.

1. The first condition is the existence of the two-party
system. This needs a few words of explanation. Burke
seems to have held that politicians should be brigaded
into two parties for the sake of legislative and administrative efficiency. Men fight and work best in a band
under a chief and a banner. The Government who have
to do the work and the Opposition who have to criticize
it are alike more effective when disciplined and organized.
He had no love for what he called a " desultory and
disconnected part " in public life. But these two
parties are not the forces of Ormuzd and Ahriman, of
light and darkness. They differ chiefly in the accident
of personnel. If they differ in theory it is in the matter
of emphasis rather than of belief. They are agreed
upon the fundamentals ; they believe alike in class and
property and the traditional polity of Britain. He
constantly foresaw a man changing from one party to
another honestly and conscientiously, and he never
would have admitted the honesty of such a practice had
the parties differed in fundamentals.

Now apply this view to the question of the representa-

tive. If parties are organized mainly for efficiency, if
they do not differ greatly except in emphasis, if party
loyalty is only general loyalty to companions in a fight,
then obviously a representative is a free man. The
doctrine holds good ; he is free to decide and act according to his conscience and his judgment, which is what his
constituents elected him for. But assume a different state
of affairs. A pledge-bound party or a party with a rigid
programme and a sleepless caucus leaves little freedom
to the representative. He is there to do the bidding
of his chiefs, and trot docilely into the appropriate lobby.
In voting for him the electors do not choose a man who
will judge, but a man who will obey ; they vote, not for
a representative, but for a partisan. Carry your imagination a little further and conceive a full-blown group
system, such as we see to-day on the Continent, where
politics tend to produce a number of small and large
sodalities sworn to uphold certain ideas or personages. There a man sticks to his group, but he may
at any moment change his party, for any moment
may see his group brigaded in a new alliance. What
does the elector choose in such a case when he records
his vote ? Not a will and judgment free to act, for
experience shows that the discipline of a party is but
milk-and-water to the discipline of a group. Not a
representative of a party, for he does not know into
what undreamed-of coalition his member may be swept.
It may be said that he chooses the exponent of a creed,
but if he believes that he must have a rare confidence
in human nature, for groups are singularly forgetful
of creeds and singularly mindful of tactics. The right
answer, I think, is that he does not choose a representative in Burke's sense at all. For that fine flower we

need two parties, brigaded for business reasons, and differing not in principle but in emphasis.

2. A second condition is the maintenance of the three estates of Parliament—King, Lords, and Commons—with virtually co-ordinate powers. There is no need to search for proof of this in Burke ; it pervades nearly every passage he wrote. He believed in the legislative supremacy of Parliament, but it was the whole Parliament, not a part of it ; and he would have shrunk with horror from any talk of the legislative supremacy of the Lower House. Like most of his countrymen in his day and since, he had a bias against change. He would have his representative free to act and decide, because he knew that there was no chance of any violent revolution being carried unless the country were ripe for it. The constitution of his day was a thing of checks and balances, and this machinery was in working order and not for show. The King governed as well as reigned ; the House of Lords competed both in popular prestige and political talents with the Commons ; the three estates had substantive and practically co-ordinate powers. Therefore the people might trust their representative, for the honest man could not go far wrong. Were it otherwise, then representation must go by the board. On this Burke had no manner of doubt. I take one sentence from the *Thoughts on the Present Discontents* :

" I see no other way but the interposition of the body of the people itself, whenever it shall appear, by some flagrant and notorious act, by some capital innovation, that these representatives are going to overleap the fences of the law and establish an arbitrary power."

3. The third condition is the maintenance of the House of Commons as a true deliberative assembly.

Of what use is it to entrust a representative with the
duty of deciding for you, if he is given no chance to
exercise this duty ? Parliament must be a place where
opinion is made, where a question is fully argued, and
where good reason may turn votes. But—let me quote
again from the passage I cited before from the Bristol
speech—" What sort of reason is that, in which the
determination precedes the discussion ; in which one
set of men deliberate and another decide ? " Obviously,
it is no place for a representative. The poor soul is
there to do what his constituents sent him to do ; he
wants to form his opinion to the best of his ability and
act upon it—to assist his party, it may be, to maintain
a good cause ; but he is told that the thing is settled.
This or that must be done ; if debate there must be,
it will have a foregone conclusion. I do not say that
this system is wrong ; no doubt it is a much more
expeditious way of dispatching business ; but clearly
it makes nonsense of Burke's notion of a representative.
Under it, we ask again, what do the people vote for ?
Not for a man to act freely according to his reason and
conscience. Not for a programme and a man to support
it, for half the questions on which a member must vote
have never been before the electors. As far as one can
see, they vote primarily for a Ministry to which they
entrust unlimited powers. The private member is a
henchman in its household, and it, the Ministry, is the
true representative.

III

We may now consider the question whether these
three conditions exist in Britain to-day. As I have told
you, I am a great admirer of Burke's doctrine ; I never

met another I liked so well. But in Cromwell's famous
words, " It is needful at all times to look at Things,"
and it is no good pretending that we have Representative
Government if the thing be impossible. Looking about
with an open mind I find it difficult to discover much
trace of Burke's conditions. We have certainly not
got the two-party system in his sense. There are at
least three parties, together with various odds and ends ;
and, remember, they are not parties such as Burke
wanted, brigaded together for the more efficient conduct
of government, and agreeing more or less on fundamentals. They differ profoundly on fundamentals, and
the reason of their existence is that they differ. Take
even the two parties which have most resemblance to
each other, the Unionists and the Liberals. They
appear to have much in common, but I cannot help
thinking that if an honest Liberal and an honest Unionist
who had given any thought to the matter could be
induced to set down the principles and preferences
which lay at the bottom of their creeds, the difference
would be found to be vital. Again, I am afraid that
not one of these parties is pledged to uphold in their
integrity the things which Burke thought the foundations
of English policy. Then as to the maintenance of the
three estates of Parliament with co-ordinate powers—
well, it is many a day since that doctrine died. Yet till
yesterday we were left with two authoritative estates ;
but now one is for the moment *in articulo mortis*, and so
insensitive have we become to constitutional revolutions
that the average man seems very little concerned about
it. We are governed by a predominant Lower House,
and the nation is so heartily sick of the question that
not all the eloquence of reforming peers can turn its

apathy into fright. Lastly, is the House of Commons
any longer a serious deliberative assembly in Burke's
sense ? I do not share the contempt of our legislature
which is fashionable in many quarters—the view of
the gentleman who recently declared in the press that
there were only two opinions about Parliament : the
opinion of those inside that it was the last word in
human wisdom, and the opinion of everybody else that
it was a damned monkey-house. To me it seems that
the House of Commons represents now, as it has always
done, a very high level of intelligence and public spirit.
But for serious and independent discussion—No. For
one thing, there is not the time, and for another, permission would not be granted. The House has become
an automatic machine which registers the edicts of a
transient majority. " What sort of reason is that in
which the determination precedes the discussion; in
which one set of men deliberate and another decide ? "

The question remains whether, in spite of Burke's
view, these conditions are really necessary for Representative Government. Well, "representative" is a
blessed word of wide meaning, but in Burke's sense I
think they are. How can a man be given *carte blanche*
to use his reason when he is at the same time forbidden
to use it ? How can an electorate confidently appoint
an automaton when that automaton in combination
with other automata has such absolute powers ? If you
elect a free man whom you trust, you give him a wide
discretion ; but if you elect a puppet, in common
prudence you want to pull the strings yourself. I agree
with Burke. In his words, " I see no other way but
the interposition of the body of the people itself."

It is hard to come to any other conclusion than that

we are assisting at the obsequies of Representative
Government in the old good sense. The thing has been
long a-dying, and the last hour is at hand. On sentimental grounds I lament its fate, but no human institution can maintain its vigour for ever, and I think I can
offer you a few modest consolations.

The first is that Representative Government depended
largely upon the old two-party system, and it is impossible to expect that system to continue intact in
our modern world. In a chaos of parties Representative
Government becomes not only unfruitful, but highly
dangerous. It is perpetually exposed to the chance of
coalitions formed, not for administrative efficiency, but
for the purposes of fancy legislation. A, B, C, D, and
E are five parties, each with a particular legislative fad,
and no one of them is strong enough to achieve its
desires unassisted. A bargain, therefore, is struck on
the classic principle of " You scratch me, and I'll
scratch you," under which each group, for the sake of
attaining its own end, agrees to co-operate in achieving
the ends of the others. If the people have no means of
interposing their veto on such a bargain, the result
may be that measures to which the vast majority of the
nation are opposed may be carried by means of this
legislative " combine." An even greater evil is that
since a coalition is a difficult thing to handle, the most
austere of ministries may be tempted to keep the
different sects in good temper by legislative sops which
are intrinsically undesirable, and, so far as the nation at
large is concerned, wholly undesired.

A second consolation is that we are only doing what
all the world has done already. The doctrine of parliamentary sovereignty has long been dead everywhere

but in Britain. As we have seen, it was born about
1641, and began to die some time about the period of
the First Reform Bill. The truth is, that it does not
go well with democracy. It never really existed on
the Continent, and it has never flourished in America.
Democracy has a great gift of trusting its leaders, but
it does not trust representative assemblies, which are
only itself, so to speak, in a pocket form. It prefers
the large-paper edition. I suppose there is no subject
in the world on which more nonsense is talked than
democracy, and it is difficult to understand the circular
argument so common to-day—that a measure is good
because it is democratic, and democratic because it is
good. But if we take the simple definition that democracy is the rule of Everyman, and the more democratic
a state is the more directly Everyman recognizes his
political responsibilities, we shall agree, I think, that the
doctrine of Representation is insufficiently democratic.

For consider. For a man to be a good representative,
and for a place to be adequately represented, there is
no need that all should vote, there is no need that even
many should vote. A member elected by half a dozen
elderly gentlemen over a bowl of punch may be a very
good representative. It depends entirely on the character of the member. If a man represents the kind of
way of looking at things that is shared by the ordinary
citizen in his division, then it matters very little whether
he is voted for or not. If the representative is an
independent being with a right of acting on his own discretion, then whether he represents me or not depends
entirely upon his own nature. He may act and reason
as I should do myself, or he may not ; and it makes
him no better representative of me that I should have

the right of voting for him. The late Duke of Devon-
shire, for example, was highly representative in temperament of most people in England ; Mr. Gladstone,
though he was several times Prime Minister, yet so far
as his temperament was concerned represented very
few besides himself. On Burke's theory, the franchise
really counts for very little. That was why he was
always against electoral reform. To us, looking back
to-day, the opposition to the First Reform Bill seems
very difficult to understand, and it is almost impossible
for us to put ourselves in the place of the men who
so passionately opposed it. Yet that opposition was
perfectly reasonable and logical, and Burke's " representative " doctrine was at the root of it. If a man
is a free representative, the one thing you demand
is that he should have the representative character ;
whether everybody has a chance of voting for him or not
is altogether beside the point. If he has not the right
character, manhood suffrage will not make him more
representative.[1]

But there are several difficulties about this excellent
doctrine on the practical side. One is that unless you
give the ordinary citizen a chance of sharing in an
election, he is apt not to realize his citizenship. Another
is that it provides no way of making sure that you get
the proper man. A popular election certainly provides

[1] This was the view of the Duke of Wellington : " As to Reform,
if you wanted thirty good men in the House of Commons, you were as
likely to obtain them from rotten boroughs as through the suffrages
of a big manufacturing town. What did it matter how they became members of Parliament so long as they were fit to sit in it "
(Fortescue's *Wellington*, p. 237) ; and of the young Disraeli : " In
a hasty and frivolous effort to get rid of representation without election,
it will be as well if eventually we do not discover that we have only
obtained election without representation " (*Vindication of the English
Constitution*, 1835).

no infallible way, but it gives on the whole a better chance, and the essence of democratic government is that it ensures a practical compromise, a second-best, half-way between unattainable perfection and flat inferiority. So in practice we have to descend to a lower level, and say that the representative man is the man whom the majority of the people choose. We give almost everybody a voice in the election, trusting to luck to turn up a good card.

That is the recognized democratic usage, and it is only a short step from that to consulting the people, not on men only, but on measures; and a still shorter to consulting them on measures at a time when you are not asking their judgment on men. To Burke, the man, the representative, mattered enormously, but to democracy he matters comparatively little, unless he is a party leader. The essence of a popular constitution is that one or two individuals should have supreme influence, but that the average politician should be only a minor wheel in a great machine. Unlike his predecessor, he does not think for the people; he is only the conduit pipe to convey the people's will. And so in time we get to some sort of referendum—we have had it for several generations. The principle has long been established in Britain; for what is the rejection of a measure by the House of Lords but a kind of referendum, what was the plea for shorter Parliaments but the claim of the people to decide *directly*, not only on men, but on measures? Like Burke, I am not greatly enamoured of what is called plebiscitary government, but if we are going to be democrats we must face the consequences. If you have members elected with freedom to debate and act in a free House of

Commons, you have the representative system ; if you elect automata with a mandate, you have democracy ; but if you elect automata to act docilely under the executive and trouble yourself no further about their doings you have an oligarchy—a form of government which has never in the history of the world been either stable or beneficent.

It is inevitable, then, this change, and it has its compensations. I will not be suspected of any desire to flatter democracy when I say that it has merits, even surpassing merits. Everyman is a pretty sagacious fellow. He is not the neurotic being, living in a whirl of elementary emotions, that some would have us picture him. He is, as a rule, much wiser, much more steadfast than his official interpreters. He has no jealousy of the State, but on the other hand he has no morbid craving for its attentions. He is not a doctrinaire, and he is eminently practical. If you present him with fantastic paternal schemes, he will be apt to reply as the Highlander replied to a certain Commission, which offered him a holding if he was prepared to keep some thirty official commandments—he declined on the ground that he could get the whole Kingdom of Heaven for keeping ten. At the same time, he is no anarchist, he is an obedient soul, and he has a strong respect for all reasonable laws. In his heart of hearts he is profoundly unrevolutionary. If I have any complaint to make against our present political conditions, it is that the plain man has not the influence he deserves. We have the sectional cleverness of the fringes, but where is the solid good sense of the centre ? I am not without hope that a more advanced democracy may restore him. I would rather be governed by Burke's kind of representative ; but if I cannot have him I am quite willing to trust myself to the plain man, the man who in every class of life does the world's work, and who should, if right goes for anything, hold the world's government. Burke's was an aristocratic régime, and to a large extent we in Britain are still living under aristocratic forms, but without the substance of an aristocracy. It is a situation which cannot continue, and since we have accepted the principles of democracy the sooner we devise an adequate machinery the better.

There must, of course, be checks and balances. No human government can do without them, least of all democracy, which is peculiarly subject to violent and transient moods, and in its own interests needs a period of reflection between impulse and deed. A Second Chamber, with the proper powers of a Second Chamber, is as vital a part of its machinery as the ultimate popular appeal. But I do not believe in too rigorous a system of artificial restraints. We cannot at this time of day restore the old doctrine of the " law fundamental," even in its more modern form of a written constitution. The " law fundamental," indeed, remains as an unwritten, but authoritative, restraint upon the popular will. The people nominally can do anything, but there are certain things—unjust confiscations of property, tyrannical interferences with conscience—which they cannot do and retain their claim to civilization. In the last resort we must trust to the good will and fundamental decency of the plain man. If a nation is to be free, it must be free to make mistakes ; and the national conscience and the national good sense, provided we give them fair play, are stronger barriers against folly than any paper safeguards.

VI

LORD BALFOUR AND ENGLISH THOUGHT

LORD BALFOUR AND ENGLISH THOUGHT [1]

VERSATILITY is a dangerous endowment for an English statesman. The ordinary man likes to think that his masters, as the phrase goes, " attend to business," and regards the liberal arts as things to be generously eulogized at public functions, but not to be practised without a certain loss of prestige. Learned serjeants " shook their heads at Murray as a wit," and honest Tories thought none the better of Disraeli for writing novels. If a statesman's political effectiveness is thereby weakened, so also does his political notoriety prevent him from getting fair play in his unpartisan interests. Critics who may follow him into the grove of the Muses seek, as a rule, only blackthorns to beat or laurels to garland the politician. So he may be said to suffer both ways, being an Israelite in Gath and a Philistine in Jerusalem. But if the career be sufficiently prolonged and illustrious the fashion changes, and what was once counted to a man for weakness becomes an added glory.

Lord Balfour has outlived the prejudice of his detachment. He is recognized as possessing an intellectual equipment not surpassed, and probably not equalled,

[1] Reprinted, *mutatis mutandis*, from the *Times Literary Supplement*, May 7, 1914.

among contemporary statesmen. In the 'eighties worthy
people were a little disturbed by the *Defence of Philosophic Doubt*; he has since discoursed on a similar
subject to the delight of crowded audiences and to the
admiration of every one who reads the newspapers.
What is interesting in his case is that there are not two
Lord Balfours. Early in life he discovered what
attracted him, selected a standpoint, and developed
the complex of tastes and views which we call a temperament. The æsthetic creed of the essay on Handel
is the same as that of the Romanes address. The
argument of *Philosophic Doubt* is more or less that of
the Gifford Lectures. And further, the gifts which
made him an incomparable Parliamentarian are the
gifts which appear in all that he writes and says on
matters never mentioned in the House of Commons.
The temperament remains the same, though the medium
alters ; an uncommon temperament, curiously self-
contained and complete, and free from loose ends and
misty corners. It is sharply outlined against its background ; and this is what we mean when we talk about
distinction.

I

Lord Balfour's mind has few contemporary affinities,
but it suggests many kinships in the past, especially
in the eighteenth century. This is not to say that he is
as one born out of due season ; for your true Georgian
was exquisitely in tune with his age, and Lord Balfour
is alive to every *nuance* of the modern world. But in
his interest he preserves a certain aloofness, always
moving a step or two back to get a better view. He is
conscious of the present ; but he is also and at all times

overwhelmingly conscious of the past. He has the eighteenth century sense of living in a world which was not made yesterday, and will certainly not be remade to-morrow ; he sees the long descent of the most novel problems ; he is tolerant because he does not ask too much of humanity ; but, like Malvolio, he thinks nobly of the soul, and has a modest confidence in the human reason if it keeps to rational limits. He believes with De L'Isle Adam that "sans illusion tout périt," but he must first be convinced of the honesty and the social value of illusion; and he is merciless to insincerity and pretence. He has the eighteenth century belief in society, and is always reminding us that we are not isolated creatures but members of an intricate community. Hence, like Burke, he will not destroy what many generations have built merely because some of the plaster work is shaky. To him the desert hermit and the iconoclast are equally repugnant, for the one is not a social being, and the other is the foe of society. In a word, he is the critical Conservative, as were the best Georgians. We have his own confession :

" It so happens that I dislike the seventeenth century and like the eighteenth. I do not pretend to justify my taste. Perhaps it is that there is a kind of unity and finish about the eighteenth century wanting to its predecessor. Perhaps I am prejudiced against the latter by my dislike of its religious wars, which were more than half political, and its political wars, which were more than half religious."

No more does he like the high noon of the Victorian era :

" I justify it [the dislike] to myself by saying that it reminds me too much of Landseer's pictures and the revival of Gothic ; that I feel no sentiment of allegiance towards any of the intellectual dynasties which then held sway ; that neither the thin lucidity of Mill nor the windy prophesyings of Carlyle, neither Comte nor yet Newman, were ever able to arouse in me the enthusiasm of a disciple ; that I turn with pleasure from the Corn Law squabble to the Great War."

We find the preference in his style, in his fondness for the neat antithesis and the ironic interjected sentence ; in his love for Handel ; in his fastidiousness, akin to the younger Pitt's ; in his equal dislike of crude heresy and withered orthodoxy. His mind is the exact opposite of the " half-baked," which sees things in lurid flashes and unrelated visions. To his broad, lucid outlook, form, line, and proportion seem infinitely more important than colour. The temperament is revealed, again, in his distrust of high-sounding generalities and pretentious dogmas. Naturally he makes war against the half-dozen maxims to which the philosophic Radicals reduced the art of statecraft. He believes in the plain man, but is doubtful about the thing called popularity. " No science," he says, " can become popular with impunity." False rhetoric is his pet aversion, and of such is the common ecstasy of politicians :

" They never need find difficulty [he says in his essay on " Cobden "] in placing their conduct in an interesting light, whatever view the public may happen to take of it. Are they the popular favourites ? Then are they the representatives, the tribunes, of the people, and speak almost with the voice of inspiration. Does the people burn them in effigy ? It is a sign and measure of the extent to which they are ahead of the public opinion of their time."

And so we have the tremendous letter on Dr. Clifford's pamphlet, in which the apocalyptic style is pilloried with, for Lord Balfour, surprising acerbity. " The ear gets wearied with their unrelenting scream ; the palate jaded with their perpetual stimulants."

Such a temperament means that there can be no very strong inspiration, no infectious gusto of belief. Lord Balfour is prone to a gentle pessimism. He sees no golden age in the future, and he has grave doubts of the existence of any in the past. Hope and dream, he seems to say, but if you are wise do not look for too much ; the world is a bridge to pass over, not to build upon. Here is a passage which, except for a phrase or two, might have been written by Burke in one of his cosmic moralizings :

" Literary immortality is an unsubstantial fiction devised by literary artists for their own especial consolation. It means at the best an existence prolonged through an infinitesimal fraction of that infinitesimal fraction of the world's history during which man has played his part upon it.   And during this fraction of a fraction, what, or rather how many things, does it mean ?   A work of genius begins by appealing to the hearts of men, moving their fancy, warming their imagination, entering into their inmost life. In that period immortality is still young ; and life really means living.   But this condition of things has never yet endured.   What at first was the delight of nations declines by slow but inevitable gradations into the luxury, or the business, or even the vanity, of a few.   What once spoke in accents understood by all is now painfully spelt out by a small band of scholars.   What was once read for pleasure is now read for curiosity.   It becomes ' an interesting illustration of the tastes of a bygone age,' a ' remarkable proof of such and such a theory of æsthetics.'   ' It still repays perusal by those who have sufficient historic sym-

pathy to look at it from the proper point of view,' and so
on. The love of those who love it best is largely alloyed
with an interest which is half antiquarian and half scientific.
It is no longer Tithonus in his radiant youth, gazed at with
the passion-lit eyes of Luna, but Tithonus in extremest
age, reported on as a most remarkable and curious case
by a committee of the Royal College of Physicians."

From such a standpoint we expect tolerance and
moderation, but the moderation is of an austere kind.
It is not the facile sort which halves extremes, as if
one were to look for safety in sailing up a river channel
by keeping equi-distant from both shores. It is of the
school of Halifax the Trimmer, the moderation which is
based on clear thinking, or—to continue our metaphor—
which means the use of a good chart of the estuary.
And here we reach one of Lord Balfour's really strong
persuasions. He believes in and reverences the reason.
It may not be a perfect guide, but it is all we have,
and he will not consent to forgo its use. " It is true,"
he writes, " that without enthusiasm nothing would be
done. But it is also true that without knowledge nothing would be done well." By reason he does not mean
any narrow logic. It would be not unfair to call it
common sense. He is content to admit provinces of
life which are unrationalized ; indeed, his whole aim
is to impress upon us the need for looking honestly on
facts and not fitting them into the rigid bed of a theory.
To think that a few dogmas will exhaust the universe
is not reason, but unreason.

" Imagine [he says in his rectorial address on " Progress "]
nicely adjusting our loyalty and patriotism to the standard
of a calculated utility. Imagine us severally suspending
our adhesion to the Ten Commandments until we have

leisure and opportunity to decide between the rival and inconsistent philosophies which contend for the object of establishing them ! These things we may indeed imagine if we please. Fortunately, we shall never see them. Society is founded . . . not upon criticism but upon feelings and beliefs, and upon the customs and codes by which feelings and beliefs are, as it were, fixed and rendered stable."

Reason is common sense, a wise appreciation of the working rules of human society, the free play of the intellect, indeed, but an intellect which can understand the intractable subject-matter it works with.

His second strong persuasion is of the value of our common human instincts, of the ordinary consciousness of the plain man. It used to be the fashion to regard Lord Balfour as an aristocratic dilettante, dwelling retired with a rarefied metaphysic. But the whole trend of his writings is towards the exaltation of the simple, practical soul. If we were to seek one word to describe his quality, it would be " humanism," eighteenth century humanism, with no very roseate dreams about humanity, but a profound consciousness of its homely worth and homely wisdom. His enthusiasm, such as it is, is for what is practicable, for the business of carrying on the work of the world, and his hero is the man who is willing to take a hand.

II

His philosophy, as we should expect, has none of the far-stretching raptures of the metaphysician. Not for him the great all-inclusive world-philosophies, which satisfy that hunger and vague longing which, as he has told us, the music of his favourite Handel does *not* satisfy. He seeks a more concrete and more homely speculative faith, something a little less chilling to common human blood than the thin air of the Hegelian Infinite. His standpoint throughout is curiously business-like. Science, he argues, rests upon many unprovable postulates, which we accept, not for their logic, but because of their " values." Why not grant the same privilege to speculations which look beyond the material world ? He offers us no system, but only a suggestion towards a provisional explanation—an explanation, be it noted, not so much of things themselves as of our modes of thought.

Here as always Lord Balfour is a humanist. When he first became interested in these questions, the pre-vailing school was the naturalism of Mill and Spencer; and in his first book he vigorously attacked its un-warrantable assumptions and the many gaps in its logical equipment. The fashion changed, German idealism became the vogue ; and though it found Lord Balfour more sympathetic, it did not find him a con-vert. Now the wheel has moved again, and the popular creed, in the hands of the various schools of realists and Bergsonians, is something not unlike what Lord Balfour has always been saying. In his essay on " Berkeley " he tells us that it is essential for the philosopher to possess " the instinct which tells him where, along the line of contemporary speculation, that point is to be found from which the next advance may best be made." He has shown this instinct in a remarkable degree, and his channel of thought, which forty years ago was a backwater, is now perhaps the main stream. He is content with the ordinary consciousness, the ordinary hopes and beliefs of mankind. When very clever

people try to demolish the plain man's creed, he takes
up cudgels in its defence. Why? Because these beliefs work, he replies; because they give hope and
comfort and joy, and until you have something better
to take their place they must stand. It is no answer to
say that they are not always logically demonstrable.
No more are the beliefs of science, not perhaps so much;
and he proceeds to find appalling gaps in the logic of
the proud naturalists. To-day the men of science con-
cur, and it is the greatest of them, like the late Henri
Poincaré, who are most willing to point out the gaps.
Faith is to be defended, because science is also largely
an act of faith; religious belief, because its critics, on
their own postulates, are constantly believing.

Such a position is sceptical, but it is sceptical chiefly
of conventional scepticism. It is critical, but always
with a conservative purpose. Lord Balfour approaches
the world of simple faiths with a profound reverence.
He will not heedlessly disturb them. As Mr. Wilfrid
Ward (I think) once said, he is on the side of the angels,
for where fools rush in he fears to tread. He is always
a man of action in thought, with a keen eye to practical
values. This is not to say that he is in any way of
the Pragmatists' school. He is too critical of logical
hiatuses and a ragged metaphysic; and the alluring
fancies of M. Bergson, with whom he has many affinities,
find in him a friendly but a trenchant critic. No school
can claim him with justice; he remains a detached
mind, clearly perceiving practical utilities, admitting
many a breakdown in proof, but declining to accept
iconoclasm until the iconoclasts make out a better case.
He has that rare combination, a real earnestness and a
thorough-going scepticism.

Three doubters, it is said, do not equal one believer ;
but Lord Balfour is no ordinary doubter. He is both
believer and doubter, and his doubts are exercised
chiefly against the foes of belief. Speculatively, it is
true, such a position has many difficulties. Its importance is chiefly negative, it does not establish any
reasoned foundation of belief, and inclines to be conservative rather than constructive. Its merit lies in
the fact that it clears the air and defines and delimits
with much acumen the exact nature of a problem which
it leaves for later and more fortunate philosophers to
solve. All this is done in a philosophic style, which in
its own way is very nearly perfect. Lucidity never
fails him, and his subtlety is the result of a line of thought
so completely realized in his own mind that it is apt to
deceive the reader by its simplicity. We shall not find
in him the poetry of the great system-makers, the
sudden high visions of Plato and Spinoza and Hegel.
He is never *exalté* ; his metaphors are never grandiose :
he builds no cloudy cities. But for the lover of exact
thinking there is a rare beauty in his orderly argument
and the perfect aptness of his illustrations, and there is
a tonic vigour in his strong sceptical sincerity.

III

His purely literary merits are to be found principally
in his style. Questions of æsthetics interest him deeply,
and in his " Handel," and especially in his Romanes
lecture, he has done something to orientate the ordinary
critical standpoints. But his style is so distinctive and
possesses virtues so uncommon in these high-coloured
days that it is worth a little consideration. Formally

it is far from perfect. He can commit on occasion almost every grammatical fault except the split infinitive, and his misuse of " and which " almost rivals Thackeray's. His manner is what our forefathers would have called " well-bred " ; that is, it has generally a conversational pitch, and hardens at intervals into a delicate eighteenth century formalism, and above all it is exactly adequate to its substance. Its great quality is its logic, which interpenetrates the sequence of sentences, the choice of illustrations, the selection of epithets. Hence while his writing is often chilly, and sometimes a little thin, it is always restful and satisfying. It is unsatisfactory only to those who ask a satisfaction that is foreign to his purpose.

" Argument is all I have to offer," he tells us in his *Philosophic Doubt*, but there can be a real æsthetic beauty in mere argument in the hands of a master. This is best seen by his use of illustrations, which are at once graceful and mathematically exact :

> " Do they follow, I mean, on reason *qua* reason, or are they like a schoolboy's tears over a proposition in Euclid, consequences of reasoning, but not conclusions from it ? "

> " The right of any individual to judge for himself is like the right of any man who possesses a balance at the bankers to require its immediate payment in sovereigns. The right may be undoubted, but it can only be safely enjoyed on condition that too many persons do not take it into their heads to exercise it together."

Generally the illustrations are more or less tinged with irony :

> " The science [of sociology] has been planned out by some very able philosophers, much as a prospective watering-place is planned out by a speculative builder."

10

" The cultivation of emotions at high tension towards humanity, deliberately dissociated from the cultivation of religious feeling towards God, has never yet been practised on a large scale. We have so far had only laboratory experiments. There has been no attempt to manufacture in bulk."

Observe the *esprit malin* of these scientific and commercial phrases.

" There are those, again, who reject in its ordinary shape the idea of Divine superintendence, but who conceive that they can escape from philosophic reproach by beating out the idea yet a little thinner, and admitting that there does exist somewhere a ' power which makes for righteousness.' "

The ironic interjected sentence is a favourite mannerism.

" Though not, so far as appears, a very profound political economist himself, he [Cobden] was of opinion that political economy was more difficult of apprehension than any of the ' exact sciences.' Which of the exact sciences he had mastered (unless phrenology be one) Mr. Morley does not, so far as I recollect, inform us."

Sometimes, in his more controversial work, the irony ceases to be delicate and becomes vigorous satire. The masterpiece of this form is the famous letter on Dr. Clifford's pamphlet. Why, he asks, should conscience forbid the payment of rates towards denominational schools and yet permit the payment of taxes ?

" Is there not a certain over-subtlety of distinction in this ruling, which, if I may say so without offence either to Dr. Clifford or the Jesuits, is almost Jesuitical ? Can we seriously believe in the pre-established correspondence between the frontier which eternally separates right from wrong, and the transient line which technically distinguishes local from national taxation ? "

There is the rapier ; here is the broadsword :

" It [the Bible] is apparently to be treated as a collection of elegant extracts and edifying maxims. The sixth Commandment may be taught, for, taken by itself, it is simply a moral pronouncement. The first Commandment, on the other hand, must be treated only as ' literature ' ; for manifestly it has a theological implication. Of the two precepts which contain ' all the Law and the Prophets,' the second may be taught, but not the first. The Lord's Prayer may be used as an introduction to Burns, but not as the outpouring of the spirit of man to his Maker. According to Dr. Clifford, Parliament would be going beyond its functions in teaching, at the cost of public funds, that man *has* a Maker."

For the more coloured graces of style we need scarcely look. But there are moments when, in Plato's phrase, the quest of truth does not lack the warmth of desire, and the writing takes on a sober sheen, and even kindles into something like eloquence. Such a passage is to be found at the close of " The Religion of Humanity " :

" The ' religion of humanity ' seems specially fitted to meet the tastes of that comparatively small and prosperous class, who are unwilling to leave the dry bones of Agnosticism wholly unclothed with any living tissue of religious emotion, and who are at the same time fortunate enough to be able to persuade themselves that they are contributing, or may contribute, by their individual efforts to the attainment of some great ideal for mankind. But what has it to say to the more obscure multitude who are absorbed, and well-nigh overwhelmed, in the constant struggle with daily needs and narrow cares ; who have but little leisure or inclination to consider the precise rôle they are called on to play in the great drama of ' humanity,' and who might in any case be puzzled to discover its interest or its importance ? Can it assure them that there is no human being so insignificant as not to be of infinite worth in the eyes of Him who created the Heavens, or so feeble but that his actions may have consequences of infinite moment long after this material system shall have crumbled into nothingness ? Does it offer consolation to those who are in grief, hope to those who are bereaved, strength to the weak, forgiveness to the sinful, rest to those who are weary and heavy laden ? If not, then, whatever be its merits, it is no rival to Christianity. It cannot penetrate and vivify the inmost life of ordinary humanity. There is in it no nourishment for ordinary human souls, no comfort for ordinary human sorrow, no help for ordinary human weakness. Not less than the crudest irreligion does it leave us men divorced from all communion with God, face to face with the unthinking energies of nature which gave us birth, and into which, if supernatural religion indeed be a dream, we must after a few fruitless struggles be again dissolved."

There is reason for the view that Lord Balfour at his best writes the purest prose of our generation, the prose most in consonance with the special qualities of our speech. A different style is in fashion to-day. The startling word, the haunting phrase, the impassioned epithet are more generally acclaimed. But it may be argued that in the best prose there should be a certain formalism, that clarity should be crystalline rather than watery, and that, in the prose of argument at any rate, perfect aptness and coherence are qualities more valuable and certainly rarer than flowers and tears. To those who share this view there will always be a peculiar attraction in the dry purity of Lord Balfour's writing.

VII

TWO ORDEALS OF DEMOCRACY

TWO ORDEALS OF DEMOCRACY [1]

I COUNT it a high privilege to be with you here to-day. You are permitting me to share in the commemoration of your dead, and by so doing you are treating a stranger as a kinsman. A memorial such as yours must be more than a mere record of a gallant adventure and a costly sacrifice. It is there before the eyes of the generations as a perpetual reminder of a path which to some degree every young man can travel, the path of duty and courage and devotion ; and it is a reminder, too, that history is a continuous thing— that past, present, and future are in a true sense indivisible, that we enter upon a heritage bequeathed by others, and that in our turn we hand on a potent legacy to those who follow after.

I am honoured, deeply honoured, by your invitation, and I can best show my sense of that honour by claiming the right of an intimate friend and speaking to you not of my own country, but of yours. The Great War, which we are here to commemorate, made us for a time one household. I propose to exercise my privilege as a member of that household by giving you an Englishman's reading of one page, perhaps the greatest page, of your national life. My object is to illustrate the continuity of history. I want you to realize how, half

[1] An address delivered on the Alumni War Memorial Foundation at Milton Academy, Massachusetts, October 16, 1924.

a century before the Great War, you in America faced
most of its problems and brilliantly solved them.   There
was a time after your Civil War when America seemed
to do her best to forget it.   Old warriors met in clubs
and corners to fight their battles over again, but for
many years there was little popular interest in the
matter.   Am I wrong in partially attributing the change
in this attitude to the publication by an Englishman,
Colonel Henderson, of his classic life of Stonewall
Jackson ?   To us in Britain, and especially to British
soldiers, the subject never lost its attraction, and it was
well for us that, when German staff officers regarded it
as a mere squabble of amateurs, and devoted their
attention to their own barren campaign of 1870, our
Staff College for two generations made a careful study
of the battles of North and South.   I cannot claim that
during your ordeal my country always behaved either
with sympathy or with discretion, but I can claim that
we were always alive to its tremendous importance.   I
have an uncle still living, an old general of eighty-two,
who, as a very young officer in our Life Guards, managed by some nefarious means to escape from his duties
and to ride with Sheridan.

It is a habit of a great invention to supersede its predecessors, and only the antiquary concerns himself now
with the first embryonic steam-engine or the clumsy
early flying-machines.   In the same way, the war
which ended six years ago may be said to have super-
seded, so far as military interest goes, the campaigns
of the nineteenth and the early twentieth centuries.
But there is one exception.   It cannot supersede your
own Civil War, for in that four years' struggle, as I see
it, all the main strategic and tactical developments of

the Great War were foreshadowed. Its scale may have been small, but we must not confuse scale with kind, and its quality was transcendent. Moreover, it was a conflict of great men, leaders of the heroic stamp. Again, it was a clash of honest ideals—half-truths, or otherwise there would have been no clash, but ideals, each in itself reasonable, and each forming the highest allegiance for those who had been brought up under a particular kind of tradition. Again, because each side stood for no mean cause, it was one of the cleanest and most chivalrous, as well as one of the most heroic, campaigns ever fought. Finally, for the lover of romance and the student of human nature I do not know where you will find a richer harvest. It was singularly free from military formalism, and its story is a succession of strange and moving pictures :—Jeb Stuart and his men flitting like ghosts through the forests with their hats garlanded with flowers ; the charge at Chattanooga silhouetted against the harvest moon ; Leonidas Polk, the last of the warrior bishops, baptizing on the eve of battle his fellow generals in a mess tent out of a tin dish by the light of a tallow candle ; the eve of Chancellorsville, when in the quiet twilight the rush of birds and deer from the woods first told the Northern army that Jackson was on their rear.

I

He would be a bold man who would set down glibly in a sentence or two the cause of the Great War. The proximate causes are clear enough—the nervousness of Austria, the ambition of Germany—but for the true and ultimate causes you must dig deep into the history

of the last century. It was the same with your Civil
War, as it has been the same with all wars. The
proximate cause was slavery, but the roots of strife
lay deeper. The truth is that in America before 1862
there were two societies not yet integrated. Both
North and South would have subscribed to the general
principles of what we call a " democratic " creed :
representative government, the rule of the majority,
and so forth. Both accepted the Constitution of the
United States, but in reading that Constitution they
put the emphasis differently. To the South the vital
thing, the thing with which all its affections and sentiments were intertwined, was the State. The North,
on the other hand, had for its main conception the
larger civic organism, the Nation. Hence, if a difference of opinion arose between a State or a group of
States and the rest, the Southerner would think naturally of secession ; under secession the sacrosanctity
of the State, the civic unit about which he cared,
remained intact. To the Northerner the secession of a
State or States seemed treason to that larger unit,
the Nation, to which his loyalty was owed. There,
roughly, you get a very real difference of outlook, due
to a variety of historic and social causes. But it was
a difference of emphasis rather than of principle, and I
think it might fairly be said that each represented a
half-truth. There is no real inconsistency between a
sovereign Nation and a self-contained and locally
autonomous State. In 1862 the wisest Southerners, if
pressed, would have agreed on the importance of the
national conception, and the wisest Northerners on the
necessity of preserving a vigorous individual State life.

But now came in the question of slavery, with which

were involved all kinds of economic interests which cloud a man's reason. The wisest Southerners disliked the system and looked forward to its gradual disappearance, and the wisest Northerners had no desire to abolish slavery there and then and fling the South into bankruptcy. But since the matter touched the livelihood of many, passions were excited, and on both sides intolerance increased, so that presently what was merely a question of policy became a dogma, and this dogma grew more arrogant as the argument progressed. So very soon we find the sovereignty of the State being exalted in the South as the first object of the citizens' loyalty. From this the right to secede logically followed, and on that the issue was joined.

We can see the stages in the growth of the dispute in the career of Lincoln. Long before he was President he had been a vigorous opponent of slavery, but he was very unlike the extremer abolitionists, and on the question of slavery alone he would not have entered into the war. He fought first and last for the integrity of the Nation. You remember his famous letter to Horace Greeley in which he wrote : " I would save the Union. I would save it the shortest way under the Constitution. . . . If I could save the Union without freeing any slaves, I would do it ; and if I could save it by freeing all the slaves, I would do it ; and if I could save it by freeing some and leaving others alone, I would do that." But Lincoln also saw that slavery would force on war by exacerbating men's feelings, and might drive them to transform a difference of emphasis into a difference of principle.

When, on February 11, 1861, he left his home for Washington to become President of the United States, after borrowing money—for he was very poor—to pay the expenses of his early months at the White House, he had one of the most difficult decisions to make that ever fell to the lot of mortal man. He had to decide at once, for Fort Sumter was besieged. If he reinforced or provisioned it, war with the South would follow ; if he left it alone he surrendered tamely a piece of national property of which he was the trustee, and assented on behalf of the American nation to the dictatorship of a section. Let us examine these difficulties, for only thus can we get the measure of the greatness of the man.

He was a President elected by a minority vote. It is certain that there was no majority in his favour in the United States, and it is by no means certain that there was a clear majority for him even in his own party. He was a country lawyer with little experience of men and cities, self-educated, uncouth in manner and appearance, utterly unfamiliar with the details of government. No one of the members of his Cabinet but considered himself far his superior in ability, and most lost no opportunity of making this plain to him in public and private. He was the most pacific of men, tender-hearted to a fault, and from the Indian campaign of his youth he had learned a deep horror of war. The war which he was contemplating was the most terrible of all struggles—a strife between kinsmen. For what was he going to fight ? For Democracy ? But the Southerners were democrats and were using his own phrases against him. They declared that they fought for the free development of their own specialized society against outside dictation. It was very easy to turn the ordinary democratic shibboleths in favour of secession. He had no army to speak of, and the best soldiers had cast in their lot with the South. General Scott, the Northern commander, had given it as his opinion that Fort Sumter should be evacuated and " the wayward sisters allowed to go in peace." The Northern abolitionists told him that he could never raise an army. Wendell Phillips declared: " You cannot go through Massachusetts and recruit men to bombard Charleston or New Orleans." Remember Lincoln was no fire-eater. He was exceedingly cautious and diplomatic, as was shown in all his electioneering campaigns and in the way in which he angled for the allegiance of the border States, declaring that " he hoped to have the Almighty on his side, but he must have Kentucky." But no diplomacy availed him now. He had to decide yes or no, and yes meant inevitably war.

What could he hope to win by war ? A hundred years before, Chatham had said : " Conquer a free population of three million souls ? The thing is impossible," and the phrase had become an axiom in politics. If war came he would be confronted with five and a half million people in deadly earnest, with three and a half million slaves behind them to grow food while the men took the field. Could even victory, the most sweeping victory, bring these men back into the national fold ? The difficulties were so deeply felt by his colleagues that we find Seward, his Secretary of State, proposing seriously to relinquish Fort Sumter, to attempt to get slavery out of the question altogether, and to try to fake up a quarrel with Spain and France over Mexico, in order to unite the nation. To such casuistry Lincoln replied that the issue before him was union or disunion and that Fort Sumter lay at the heart of it. But the incident showed how deep was the confusion into which even brave, clear-headed, and public-spirited men had fallen. Lincoln, in deciding, had to stand alone.

He decided for war, and I think that decision one of the most courageous acts in all history. He had no illusions about the coming conflict. He believed that it would be a long war and a bloody war, and he saw no light at the end of it. But, with that noble fatalism which is a source of weakness in fools but of inspiration in the great, he felt that God had mysteriously guided his steps to this desperate brink, and that the leap was ordained of Heaven. In his slow, patient way he reasoned it out and could reach but the one conclusion. He fought for the Nation and the integrity of the historic state, the sacrosanctity of the work of the great men who had built it in the past. He believed that such a fabric is a trust which men weaken to their own undoing. If we look for Lincoln's creed in its simplest form, we shall find it in a private conversation at that time recorded by John Hay. " For my own part," he said, " I consider the central idea prevailing in this struggle is the necessity upon us of proving that popular government is not an absurdity. We must settle this question now, whether, in a free government, the minority have the right to break up the government whenever they choose. If we fail, it will go far to prove the incapability of the people to govern themselves." Lincoln fought to prevent Democracy making a fool of itself, and if that noble but most brittle type of polity is to be preserved to the world, we have not done with the fight. To most of his colleagues it seemed a mere debating issue, an absurdly narrow ground on which to plunge the nation into war ; but I am inclined to think that every great decision in history has been taken on a fine point. The foothold may be narrow, but if it be of granite it will suffice.

I pause, gentlemen, to remind you, if you will permit me, that in the great crises of life every man must stand alone, as much alone as at the moment of death. No friend or wife, no parent or child, can share that austere responsibility. The controversy is within his own soul, or, to put it in the language of theology, it is between himself and his Maker. His only consultant must be the valour of his heart. It is so in the history of war, from the day when Cæsar crossed the little stream called the Rubicon, which the Roman constitution forbade the Pro-Consul of Gaul to pass, to that day in September 1918, when Sir Douglas Haig decided to play the great game, and, in spite of the doubts of his colleagues and the hesitation of his own Government, flung his armies against the Siegfried Line and went through it as through blotting-paper. Generals and statesmen are called upon to make those tremendous decisions, and according to the result they are judged by the tribunal of history. But, as you advance in life, no one of you will escape the same necessity, though your decisions may not affect the fate of empires. You will all be called upon some day to face situations in public or private life where you have to choose between two ways—the right and the wrong, the hard road and the easy, the long game and the short game—and you will have to choose alone. You will find plenty of excellent arguments for the second best, for slackness, for shirking, but if you are wise you will be chary of listening to those soft and facile monitors. For, though peace and

quiet are good things to be earnestly pursued, the best
kind of peace and quiet is that which reigns in a man's
soul.

II

Great enterprises fall into two parts—the preliminary
spiritual conflict, and the task of translating spirit into
matter—or, to put it into the words traditionally
ascribed to Cromwell, first the trust in God and then
the laborious job of keeping your powder dry. We
have seen how Lincoln achieved the first ; let us now
consider how he faced the second. If the war was not
to be fought in vain he must win a complete and final
victory, for no drawn battle would suffice. Now, the
North began with all the advantages but two. She
had a population of twenty-two millions against nine.
She had the great industries, the mineral fields, the
shipbuilding yards. She had all the navy there was.
She had far greater wealth, and was not only far more
self-supporting, but owing to her ships she could import
what she did not produce from overseas. She had all
the rank and file of the regular army and four-fifths of
the officers. The South, on the other hand, had few
industries and few ships. She was mainly agricultural,
a land of big estates worked by negro slaves. She
was poor in the sense that if driven back upon herself
she had within her borders only a limited number of
the necessaries of life and war. But the South had two
advantages which made her triumphant in the first
stages and at one moment nearly gave her the victory.
The first was that her aristocratic squirearchy was
better fitted for a military organization than the Northern democracy. The great majority of her citizens were

country folk who could march and shoot, and she was a nation of horsemen and horse-masters. Obviously, such a people, if armies have to be improvised, have less to learn than men who come from a different kind of environment. The advantage is, of course, terminable ; it is very real at the start, but it lessens as the enemy begins to learn his job. In the second place it was the fortune of the South to have fighting on her side by far the abler generals. Lee and Stonewall Jackson have had few superiors in the art of war. The North produced many competent soldiers—Grant, Thomas, Sherman, Sheridan, Schofield—but no one of them reaches the small and select brotherhood of the greatest captains. On the other hand, if, taking the whole of history, you limit that brotherhood to no more than six names, you must include Lee.

Now, wars are won by superior strength—by weight of numbers, if the numbers are properly trained and supplied. Military history shows no real exception to this maxim. A splendid genius or some extraordinary initial advantage may give to the weaker side an immediate victory, which paralyses and disintegrates the enemy ; but if the enemy refuses to be paralysed, if he insists on fighting on, if he develops a stubborn defensive, if he learns his lessons, and if he has greater resources than his antagonist, in the end he will win. Against material preponderance, if it be wisely handled, the most wonderful generalship will beat ineffectual wings. Hannibal, in the long run, was worn down by the much inferior Scipio. Napoleon fell before the accumulated weight of his opponents. But—and it is a vital proviso—the nation which is strongest in material and human resources must learn how to use them.

Until it learns to use them it will go on being beaten.
The problem of the North was exactly the problem of
the Allies in 1914. She had to assemble her greater
man-power. She had to train it. She had to find a
commander-in-chief who could use it reasonably well.
She had to discover how her greater wealth could be
best applied to cripple her adversary. It took her four
years to understand these things, and when she understood them she won.

Lincoln, as a war minister, had everything to learn.
He had no natural aptitude for the post except an iron
courage, but he had that complete intellectual honesty
which can look clearly at facts, even unwelcome facts.
Let us see how he faced his problem.

I. His first business was to raise the men. He had
about 18,000 regulars, most of them serving on the
Western frontier, and he had four-fifths of the regular
officers. A good many of these officers had had experience in the Mexican War fourteen years before. The
President showed how little he appreciated the nature of
the coming conflict by asking for only 75,000 volunteers,
and these to serve for only three months. Then came the
first engagement at Bull Run, which opened his eyes. He
was empowered by Congress to raise 500,000 volunteers
for three years' service, and a little later the number
was increased to 1,000,000. Recruits came in magnifi-
cently. If we remember the population of the North
I think we must rank the effort as among the most
remarkable ever made by a system of volunteer enlist-
ment. Lincoln began by asking for 600,000, and he
got 700,000. After Fredericksburg he asked for 300,000,
and he got 430,000. Then he asked for another 300,000,
of which each State should provide its quota ; but he

only got 87,000, a little more than a quarter of his demands. Meantime the South for many months had adopted conscription. It was now a year and a half since the first battle, and the campaign had entered on that period of drag which was the time of blackest depression in the North.

Then Lincoln took the decisive step. The North was, I suppose, of all parts of the world at the moment that in which the idea of individual liberty was most deeply implanted. She was a country which had always gloried in being unmilitary, in contrast with the effete monarchies of Europe. The Constitution had been so framed as to be extraordinarily tender to individual rights. The press was unbridled, and the press was very powerful. The land, too, was full of philosophic idealists who preferred dogmas to facts, and were vocal in the papers and on the platforms. Moreover, there was a general election coming on, and since the war had gone badly there was a good chance that Lincoln might be defeated if he in any way added to his unpopularity. There were not wanting men— some of them very able and distinguished men—who declared that it was far better to lose the war than to win it by transgressing one article of the current political faith. There were others, Lincoln's own friends and advisers, who warned him solemnly that no hint of compulsion would ever be tolerated by free-born Americans, and that if he dared to propose the thing he would have an internal revolution to add to his other troubles. Again and again he was told that the true friends of the enemy were the compulsionists, an argument we were very familiar with in England nine years ago. You must remember, too, that Lincoln was in

the fullest sense of the word a democratic statesman,
believing that government must not only be *for* the
people but *by* the people. When he was faced by the
necessity of finding some other way of raising men
than as volunteers, he was faced with the task of jet-
tisoning—I will not say the principles, for principles are
tougher things—but all the sentiments and traditions
of his political life.

But Lincoln was a very great man, and he believed
that it was the business of a statesman to lead the
people—to act, to initiate policy, and not to wait like
a dumb lackey in the ante-chamber of his masters.
He knew that politics were not an abstract dogma, but
a working code based upon facts. He knew also that
in a crisis it is wisest to grasp the nettle. He saw the
magnitude of the crisis, that it was a question of life or
death, whatever journalists and demagogues might say.
So on March 3, 1863, a law was passed to raise armies
by conscription. He answered those who met him
with the famous " thin-edge-of-the-wedge " argument
in words which should be remembered: that "he did
not believe that a man could contract so strong a taste
for emetics during a temporary illness as to insist upon
feeding upon them during the remainder of a healthy
life." At the start there was some resistance, but in
a little the good sense of the country prevailed. It was
one of the two greatest acts of Lincoln's life, and, like
all great acts of courage, it had its reward. Four
months later Gettysburg was fought, Vicksburg surrendered to Grant, and the tide turned. The North
recruited from first to last some three millions out of
a population of twenty millions. The men had been
found, the human resources of the North were fully

mobilized, and two years after the passing of the act came that April day when Lee surrendered to Grant at Appomattox.

II. We come now to the second problem. Mere numbers are not enough unless they are trained and disciplined for war. The North drew by far the greater part of her armies from men who had been engaged in civil life. Let us see how she shaped them.

The armies of both North and South were amateurs, with a small sprinkling of trained officers. I have said that numbers always win, but they must be disciplined numbers. Hordes, however large, will generally be beaten. The North began her campaign with a theory which is very common in popularly governed nations which have had no military experience. She was against all hard-and-fast discipline. The men should serve willingly, because the orders appealed to their intelligence and not because they were given by a commanding officer. The argument ran something like this : " An order understood and willingly obeyed is far better than an order blindly complied with. Officers must therefore carry their men with them, persuade them, humour them, so that all ranks may have the enthusiasm of willing service. Only thus can you have a democratic army."

On this one may remark that the result might be democratic, but it could not possibly be an army. And I do not think it was democratic either, if we understand democracy aright. Democracy as the most living and organic form of government should be also the most elastic, and the most able to adapt itself to the unforeseen facts of a situation. This does not mean that you are to establish a cut-and-dried military

hierarchy and to govern only by fear. If any of you
have ever marched in peace time with French infantry,
such as the Chasseurs Alpins, you probably have been
amazed, as I have been, at what seemed the lack of
discipline. The men chaffed their officers and addressed
them by nicknames, and at night you could see an
officer and a private playing chess together outside
the café door. Yes, but in time of war that was all
changed. The men and officers were still the best of
friends, but there was a rigid discipline, the more rigid
in as much as it came from below. It was the will of
the men themselves, who recognized wherein lay victory and security. I call that army a democratic army.
I call the Allied Armies, as we knew them six years ago,
democratic armies. But the forces of the North during
the first stages of the Civil War were neither democratic
nor an army.

It took a long time to drive out of men's heads the
idea that an order was only to be obeyed when it com-
mended itself to the private soldier's mind. At first
officers were elected by the votes of the rank and file,
and a very mixed lot they were. For one good man
produced in this way there were twenty plausible incompetents. The bonds of discipline were loose, and,
though the world has never seen more patriotic and
intelligent troops, patriotism and intelligence alone
were not enough. The result of the Northern system
was that many vices developed which made them an
easy prey to Lee and Jackson. An undisciplined army
lacks mobility, and so Jackson could do what he pleased
with Pope and Hooker. A lack of discipline means
straggling, and no Northern general could be certain
how much of his force would turn up at a given place

at a given time. Moreover, outpost duties were scamped, and the result was a series of costly surprises. In the battle itself fire discipline was bad, and half the strength was expended in the air. There was the same lack of order all through the army. If a brigadier thought himself slighted, he posted off to Washington to intrigue in Congress, and instead of being tried by court martial and shot as a deserter he was more often than not promoted.

But the North learned her lesson, though the learning was bitter. If you will study that admirable compilation *The Battles and Leaders of the Civil War*, you will see how the best American officers faced the task of securing the highest discipline without impairing enthusiasm or crushing individual intelligence. The time came at last when Lincoln found the right Commander-in-Chief and gave him his undivided trust. Grant was not the man to stand insubordination, and he produced the kind of instrument that was needed. Never has a human instrument been more cruelly tried. The desperate losses in the Wilderness of Virginia would have broken the heart of most armies ; they would have utterly destroyed the original armies of the first months of war. But the weapon had been forged and tempered and it did not break. The North had grasped the nature of her problem. She had not only assembled her manpower but she had trained it, and both numbers and training were essential to victory.

III. We reach the third problem. The North found the men ; after many months she found out the way to train them ; she had also to find the right kind of leadership. Strength, even disciplined strength, is not enough.

Lincoln, as I have said, began the war without any kind of aptitude or experience. His Cabinet was in the same position. It contained three able men—Seward, Chase, and Stanton—and of these the ablest, Stanton, did his best at first to make it impossible for the President to continue in office. Unfortunately, the North had no generals of such commanding and proven ability that they could be blindly trusted. Besides, the President of the United States is the chief executive officer of the country, and Lincoln, whether he wanted it or not, had to assume the direction of the war.

We sometimes talk lightly as if the only thing in war was to find a good general and give him a free hand. But in a modern war, in which the existence of the nation is at stake, the matter is not nearly so simple. To beat the enemy you have not only to win field victories; or, rather, to win the right kind of field victory you must do more than turn out good troops and able generals. You have to use the whole national strength, military, naval, and economic, and therefore, unless the great soldier is also a great statesman like Napoleon, the supreme direction of a campaign must lie in the hands of a civilian Cabinet. That is to say, the Cabinet decides upon the main strategic plan, which involves all kinds of questions of policy, and, having so decided, it chooses the best men it can find to carry out the military and naval parts. Once these commanders have been chosen, they should not be interfered with. Until they have failed, they should be trusted.

Now, to discover and apply a continuous strategic policy you need a Cabinet loyal within itself, and it must be instructed by the best expert advice that can be secured. Lincoln had a Cabinet which, to begin with at least, was indifferently loyal. Its members all wanted to beat the South, but they all thought that they could do the job better than the President. That was bad enough, but in addition there was Congress, which possessed an amazing number of advertising mountebanks who did their best to hamper the Government. You remember Artemus Ward's comment on them. He observed that at the last election he had deliberately voted for Henry Clay. It was true, he said, that Henry was dead, but since all the politicians that he knew were fifteenth-rate he preferred to vote for a first-class corpse. Then there was the press, which was quite uncensored and of which a large part spent its time in futile criticism of generals and statesmen and in insisting upon policies which would have given the enemy a speedy and complete victory. It was always trying to make journalistic reputations for generals and so foist them upon the Government. But, worst of all, there was no expert body to advise the Cabinet. There was no General Staff at Washington. The capable soldiers were all in the field. There had never been any real staff in peace time, and it was impossible to improvise one rapidly in war. Hence Lincoln had to conduct the campaign himself, with little assistance from his colleagues, with no help from Congress,—very much the other way,—with no real military experts at his elbow, and under a perpetual cross-fire of newspaper criticism.

The result might have been foreseen. The first Northern generals were appointed largely because of political and journalistic clamour ; indeed it is difficult to see how they could have been appointed in any other

way, for there were no real formed reputations ; the
good men had still to discover themselves. General
after general failed and was recalled. Transient and
protesting phantoms, they flit over the page of history.
There was one man of real ability, McClellan, whose
difficulties and achievements have not, I think, received
full justice. There were competent soldiers like Meade ;
there were others, unfortunate or incompetent, like
Burnside and Hooker, Pope and Banks. Lee used
to complain in his gentle way that the North always
dismissed its generals just as he was getting to know
and like them. They usually began with flamboyant
proclamations about how they were going to whip the
rebels in a month, and then they were hunted from
pillar to post by Lee and Jackson. Pope, for example,
announced when he took command that his head-
quarters would be in the saddle ; on which some one
observed dryly that that would be a more proper place for
his hindquarters. The chief army of the North, the Army
of the Potomac, was commanded by no less than six
generals, and all but one were dismissed for failure.
But while these honest people were degraded, all kinds
of incompetents who had strong political interest were
retained in their commands. Many of the Northern
generals had one leg in camp and the other in Congress.
It reminds one of those armies of seventeenth century
Scotland which were directed by the General Assembly
and were soundly beaten by Montrose.

Lincoln showed his greatness by living through that
awful period and not losing his courage. Gradually
he brought Congress to heel. Gradually he dominated
his colleagues. Gradually he purged the army of
political influence. Above all, as the war advanced,

he made a zealous search for military capacity. He has been much blamed for interfering with his generals during the earlier campaigns, and the charge is just ; but he was in an almost hopeless position. He had the howling politicians behind him, and before him commanders who showed no real grasp of the situation ; he conceived it his duty to interfere, and he interfered often foolishly, for he was still learning his job. But by-and-by he discovered the true soldiers,—men who had fought their way up by sheer ability,—men like Hancock and Thomas, Sherman and Sheridan. Above all, he discovered Grant.

There can be few romances in military history more striking than the rise of Grant. At the beginning the North had cried out for brilliant generals, people who made fine speeches, people who could be hailed as " young Napoleons." But the Napoleons and the silver-tongues vanished into obscurity, and the North found its salvation in a rough little homely man from the West, who had done well in the Mexican War, but had failed since in every business he had undertaken, and had become a by-word in his family for unsuccess. He never spoke an unnecessary word. He was uncouth in manner, untidy in person, and unprepossessing in appearance, but he was a true leader of men. There were rumours about his habits, and the Pharisees of the North cried out against appointing a drunkard to command the army, declaring that no blessing could go with such a man. Lincoln, you remember, replied by asking what was Grant's favourite brand of whisky that he might send a cask of it to his other generals. I do not think that Grant stands in the very front rank of the world's soldiers, but he was the man for the task before him. He had iron nerve, iron patience, and an iron grip of the fundamentals of the case. Lincoln interfered with the earlier commanders, but he did not interfere with Grant. He knew a man when he saw him.

IV. Grant was the man for the task because he could apply the strategic scheme which the situation required. What was that scheme? In its elements it was very simple, and in substance it was the same as that of the Allies in the Great War. The Southern States formed a rough quadrilateral bounded by the Potomac, the Mississippi, and the sea. One great Confederate State, Texas, lay west of the Mississippi, and North-west Virginia ran up in a long peninsula towards Lake Erie, so that it left an isthmus only one hundred miles wide between the two parts of the North. The first thing was to occupy and hold North-west Virginia, which was done with little trouble. The next was to blockade all the seacoast and prevent oversea imports from reaching the South. The next was to control the Mississippi line, and so not only cut off Texas from the Confederacy but complete the investment of the quadrilateral. After that the sides of the quadrilateral could be pushed in, so that the armies of Lee would be left with less and less ground for manœuvre and supply.

The North was perfectly conscious from the first where her strength lay and what must be the main lines of her strategy. Strategy depends upon geography, and geographical facts cannot be blinked. But in the use of her strength she fumbled for many long days. Strength in war, remember, is not a thing which can be said to exist in the abstract. There may be a potentiality of strength, but till the strength is made actual it is no better than weakness. A country may have an enormous population, but unless that population appears in the shape of trained armies in the right place it is not an element of strength. It may have great wealth, but unless that wealth is used skilfully for the purposes of war it is not strength. The North had the potentiality of strength, but she had to find out how to use it.

One part of the problem was successfully faced from the first. The navy was well handled, and the whole coast-line of the South was rigorously blockaded. That must be set down to the credit of the civilians at Washington. Lincoln broke away from many of the accepted practices of international law, and he and the Supreme Court created precedents which were of great use to the Allies in the late war. The result was that the South was pinched from the first and very soon began to starve. Prices went up to a crazy height. Before the end of the war, coffee sold at forty dollars a pound, and tea at thirty dollars. You could not dine in an hotel under twenty dollars, a newspaper cost a dollar, a pair of boots cost two hundred dollars. Moreover, nearly all the materials of war came from abroad, and if it had not been that the arsenals of the South were well supplied at the start and that great quantities of munitions were captured from the North in the first victories, Lee must very soon have come to a standstill through sheer lack of material. That part of the Northern strength was well applied.

But it was not enough. The South had to be beaten in the field, and it was there that the North fumbled. The main strategic objective was clear, but it is one thing to have a clear strategical objective and quite another to have a clear strategical plan. The two objects to be aimed at were (1) the capture of Richmond, the Southern capital, and (2), as a preliminary, the mastery of the Mississippi Valley. The Northern generals, McClellan and the rest, began with brilliant and ingenious plans for the capture of Richmond, but they were too ingenious, for they dissipated their strength. Five times great armies crossed the Potomac, and five times they were driven back by half their numbers. In 1862 four armies invaded Virginia and converged on Richmond ; in three months Lee had routed them all. On at least two occasions the North was very near patching up an inconclusive peace. It is true that Lee was a man of genius and the fear of his name was worth an army corps, but over-elaborate tactics, which do not use adequately the strength of a people, play into the hands of a man of genius. We must remember, too, that the South was operating upon interior lines and so had the chance of striking rapid blows at the widely separated Northern forces. Even after Gettysburg, when the dark days had begun, she could play that game. You remember Longstreet's swift dash to the West which gave him the victory of Chickamauga and stopped the Federal invasion of Georgia.

A great strategical plan is always simple. Take Moltke's scheme which won the war of 1870 ; take Foch's strategy between July and November 1918. But the North began by flinging away her chances by divergent operations and divided counsels. Then came Grant's capture of Vicksburg, which, along with Admiral Farragut's operations in the lower waters, gave the North the line of the Mississippi. It was Grant's greatest military triumph and a very fine achievement, and it will always remain an admirable example of that most interesting manœuvre when a general cuts himself loose from his base—a movement which Sherman made later in his great March to the Sea. Once the line of the Mississippi was won and Grant was in supreme command, the strategic plan of the North was simplified. The policy of pressing in the sides of the quadrilateral began. Sherman cut the Confederacy in two by marching across Georgia from Atlanta to Savannah, and the war zone was thereby narrowed to Virginia and the Carolinas. Grant with the Army of the Potomac advanced against Richmond. He fought his way southward, till he ultimately forced Lee behind the lines of Petersburg. There began that war of entrenchment with which for four years we ourselves were only too familiar.

Now mark the situation. The South had been blockaded for more than three years. Her troops were ragged and barefoot, with scanty food, scanty munitions, scanty anæsthetics. But they did not give in. Grant did not underrate his enemy. He knew that he could not starve him into surrender, but must beat him in the field. He used all his cards for the purpose and not merely a few. For example, he used the command of the sea. With its assistance in the 1864 campaign he shifted his base and line of communications no less than four times within two months. By the end of March 1865 he had so weakened the enemy's manpower that he forced him to evacuate Petersburg. Lee broke loose, but he could not escape. The net had closed round him, and on April 9, 1865, the greatest soldier since Napoleon, commanding an army which was reduced to little more than a corps, laid down his arms at Appomattox.

The North had ended the war in the only way by which the Union could be safeguarded ; she had won a complete and final victory. She had found the right answer to her three problems as the Allies found the same answer to the same problems in 1918. She had summoned the whole of her available man-power to arms, using for the purpose the legal imperative, and she had learned how to train them so that the initiative of the volunteer was preserved under the discipline of the corporate unit. She had used her navy to hem in the enemy and to starve and cripple that enemy. She had found men to lead her armies who could get the full value out of her greater numbers and better equipment. She had found the right strategical plan and in the end had stuck to it, discarding brilliant side-shows. And when all this had been done she had delivered hammer-blow after hammer-blow till the armed might of the South crumbled in the field.

III

Such is a brief survey of a great struggle of ideals and of heroic men. In that war, fought by your grandfathers, there were nearly all the features of the war of six years ago, in which your fathers and your elder brothers fought and the young men whose names are inscribed on your memorial. If I were talking to a professional audience I could enlarge upon the technical matters in which the earlier contest anticipated the later. You will find the whole philosophy of trench warfare foreshadowed in the struggles in the Wilderness of Virginia. You will find the whole use of cavalry as mounted infantry foreseen. You will find many of our modern weapons of war originating in that four-years campaign. You will find the minor tactics on both sides curiously like those of to-day. But I would direct your attention especially to those greater points of resemblance, which vindicate in the most dramatic form the continuity of human history. You begin with a profound spiritual conflict and a fateful decision. You have at the start quantity opposed to quality, un-disciplined numbers and undirected wealth to smaller but more expert and compact numbers. You have the slow process by which potential strength is made actual, by which the true plan of war is discovered, and the right man to apply it. And, in both cases, at the end you have no easy victory, but that stark contest of human endurance which alone can decide an issue to which men have pledged their souls.

There is, too, a wider philosophic interest common to both wars. Fundamentally America had to fight the battle which all democracies have to face. Democracy as a form of government is subject to a perpetual chal-lenge, not from foreign enemies alone, but from foes in its own household. Liberty demands a close and unremitting guardianship. The leaders of democracy must be prepared to do battle with false causes which profess to fight under the democratic banner. They must be prepared to speak the truth unflinchingly to their peoples, and shun that shallow sentiment and confidence in loud formulas which is their special tempta-tion. They must be ready to make decisions far more difficult than any which can confront an oligarchy or a tyrant. They must be willing for the sake of true liberty to wage war upon licence. America faced the ordeal, and because she faced it manfully and clear-

sightedly she emerged triumphant. It is an ordeal
with which at any time the world may be again confronted. If it should be our fate to meet anew that
fiery trial, may God send us the same clearness of vision
and stalwartness of purpose.

Gentlemen, the day of wars may be over and our
military text-books may for ever gather dust on the top
shelves. But the interest of war cannot cease, for with
all its cruelty and futility it has a power of raising men
to their highest and exhibiting human nature at its
greatest. The Civil War will remain to most of us a
perpetual fascination because of the moral and intellectual elevation of its leaders. It produced two
men of the very first order. On the losing side stands
Lee, one of the foremost of the world's soldiers. Those
of you who study his campaigns will find that the more
they read themselves into his mind, the more they will
marvel at its supremacy. As a man he had an antique
grandeur of character. You remember what Bossuet
said of Turenne, that he " could fight without anger,
win without ambition, and triumph without vanity."
That might be Lee's epitaph, and I would add to it
that he could lose without bitterness. History has few
nobler pictures to present than Lee in the closing days
of the war, fighting a hopeless battle with gentleness
and chivalry, and lifting his broken troops to super-
human heights of achievement. I would set beside
that the picture of the old man in his last years in the
seclusion of a college presidency, striving by every
counsel of wisdom and toleration to heal the wounds
of his land.

The other great figure is Lincoln. That rugged face
has become one of the two or three best known in the

world. He has already passed into legend, and a figure
has been constructed in men's minds, a gentle, humorous, patient, sentimental figure, which scarcely does
justice to the great original. What I want to impress
upon you about Lincoln is his tremendous *greatness*.
Alone he took decisions which have altered the course
of the world. When I study his career, behind all the
lovable, quaint, and often grotesque characteristics,
what strikes me most is his immense and lonely sublimity. There is a story told by John Hay of how
after his death at some negro revival-meeting in the
South the audience was moved to a strange exaltation,
and men called for visions of prophets and apostles.
One young man asked to see Lincoln, and an old negro
rose and rebuked him. "No man see Linkum," he
said. "Linkum walk as Jesus walk. No man see
Linkum." On this I would make the comment which
a great historian has made on a still greater figure.
If the poet is right, and

> " Earthly power doth then show likest God's
>   When mercy seasons justice,"

then the apotheosis of Lincoln would not be the most
extravagant freak of superstition.

To me he seems one of the two or three greatest men
ever born of our blood. You will observe that I am
talking as if we were one household and speaking of *our*
blood, for no drop ran in his veins which was not British
in its ultimate origin. I like to think that in him we see
at its highest that kind of character and mind which is
the special glory of our common race. He was wholly
simple, without vanity or grandiosity or cant. He was
a homely man, full of homely common sense and homely

humour, but in the great moment he could rise to a grandeur which is for ever denied to posturing, self-conscious talent. He conducted the ordinary business of life in phrases of a homespun simplicity, but when necessary he could attain to a nobility of speech and a profundity of thought which have rarely been equalled. He was a plain man, loving his fellows and happy among them, but when the crisis came he could stand alone. He could talk with crowds and keep his virtue ; he could preserve the common touch and yet walk with God. There is no such bond between peoples as that each should enter into the sacred places of the other, and in the noble merchantry of civilization let us remember that, if we of England have given Shakespeare to America, you have paid us back with Lincoln.

VIII

LITERATURE AND TOPOGRAPHY

LITERATURE AND TOPOGRAPHY [1]

LET us first of all distinguish. A taste for topography is not the same thing as a love of the natural
world ; it is not even the same thing as an interest in
landscape. There have been many eminent poets of
nature who have scorned topography, and whose acute
observation is so generalized that it is hopeless to
identify it with particular tracts of the earth's surface.
Where exactly did Keats listen to the nightingale ?
and which of the valleys and woods around London
begot the "Ode to Autumn"? We happen to know, but
the poems do not tell us. Wordsworth has less topography than we should expect, and so terrestrial and
local a poet as Cowper has scarcely any. They condescend upon particulars, as must every poet, but not
upon this class of particular.

The particulars with which topography is concerned
are places—usually actual places, though this is not
essential, for it is possible to create in detail an imaginary
topography—and above all place-names. You give a
concrete habitation to your fancies, and you name the
habitation. You so adjust your background that it
can be made the subject of a map. We shall consider
the full purpose of this later, but one part of it is obvious.

[1] An address to the Working Men's College, London, February 20,
1926.

It is to produce an impression of reality, to link fancy
to solid and nominate earth, and also to get from the
use of sonorous names a certain verbal advantage.
For place-names all over the world are splendid things.
They have rarely been deliberately invented, but have
grown up in the popular mind so that they are as apt
to their subjects as a bearskin to a bear. They may
have the flavour of ancient stateliness, or they may be
harsh mementoes of old passions, or gnarled remnants
of a forgotten humour, or they may reflect the poetry
in the people's heart and sing themselves to music.
But each is a nucleus of association, each comes into art
with a tang of reality, as when a man who has been
walking the hills in wild weather enters a drawing-room.

I

I will begin with poetry, which is the purest form of
literary art, and therefore the best introduction. Now
the poets, with a few notable exceptions, are incomplete
topographers. They are very much alive to the charm
of place-names, but they rarely use them on the grand
scale. It is not their business ; they are concerned to
convey hints and gleams, to open sudden casements, not
to elaborate a landscape of which a plan can be drawn.
The poet looks in the first instance to a place-name to
give him a sounding cadence. There are a thousand
instances in Greek and Latin—the torrent of splendid
vocables in the eleventh piece of Catullus, Virgil's
" nemorosa Zacynthos," Horace with his " infamis scopu-
los Acroceraunia," and that famous falling close, " aut
Lacedæmonium Tarentum " ; or, to come to our own
literature, Milton with the wizard names in " Lycidas " :

" Where the great vision of the guarded Mount
Looks toward Namancos and Bayona's hold ; "

or Matthew Arnold, who had a most delicate ear for this
special magic, with his

" Rejoicing through the hush'd Chorasmian waste,"
and
" The soft Mediterranean breaks,"
and
" Crossing the stripling Thames at Bab-lock-hithe."

Or the poet uses a place-name to give concreteness and
verisimilitude. Take the opening of two dissimilar
masterpieces—Plato's *Republic* (if for the moment we
may rank Plato among the poets whom he decried) and
the ballad of Sir Patrick Spens—Κατέβην χθὲς εἰς Πειραιᾶ
and " The King sits in Dunfermline town." Would they
have been the same if Plato had written, " I was going
for a walk yesterday," or the ballad-maker, " The King
sits in his castle hall " ? I think not. In the first
case the reader's attention is straightway engaged by a
familiar conversational detail ; in the second his fancy
is at once stimulated by a stately name redolent of
Scotland's stormy past. The fashion is too familiar
to need illustration. You will find it very notably
in Latin poetry. Horace does not speak of going to the
ends of the earth, but to the Hyperborean plains and
the " ultimi Geloni." Indeed, in the Silver Latin poets
the thing was carried so far that it became a rather
tedious mannerism, and poetry sank to be the handmaid
of uncouth geography. In our own literature this
particularizing style is everywhere, both in poetry and

prose, and if we wish authority we get it from so unexpected a source as Blake :

. . . " Art and Science cannot exist but in minutely
    organized Particulars,
And not in the generalizing Demonstration of the Rational
    Power,
The Infinite alone resides in Definite and Determinate
    Identity."

It was one of Edmund Burke's favourite devices. An interesting contrast has been drawn [1] between two passages, by Lord Brougham and by Burke, where the feeble abstractness of the one is set against the concreteness of the other. Brougham says :

" In all the despotisms of the East it has been observed that the further any part of the Empire is removed from the capital the more do its inhabitants enjoy some sort of rights and privileges."

Burke says :

" In large bodies the circulation of power must be less vigorous at the extremities. Nature has said it. The Turk cannot govern Egypt and Arabia and Curdistan as he governs Thrace, nor has he the same dominion in Crimea and Algiers which he has at Brusa and Smyrna."

You observe the difference in energy. The place-name, the particular, seems not only to clinch the argument, but to enlarge and dignify it. If you want a good illustration of how a place-name, artfully used, can set the imagination working, you will find it in the opening of Apuleius's *Golden Ass* : " Thessaliam ex negotio petebam "—" I was setting out for Thessaly

[1] By E. J. Payne in the Introduction to *Burke : Select Works I.*, page xxxix.

on business." That word " Thessaly " at once gives the key—Thessaly, the home of witchcraft, the northern land of savagery and wonder. As they say in America, the reader's bell is rung, and he is at once on the tiptoe of expectation.

But if we are to appreciate the notable part topography can play in poetry we must consider the poets who do not merely use it as an occasional grace, but in the fibre of whose method the thing is intertwined, of whose artistic scheme it is an organic part. I will take three poems which the judgment of mankind ranks high— the *Iliad, Paradise Lost,* and half a dozen of the Border Ballads. To the writers of these, local habitations are an essential of poetic thought ; they see the world— even a fairy world—as a concrete place which can be planned and mapped and named ; their characters can as ill do without their territorial connotations as a fighting man can lack a sword or shield. These writers not only use topography far more than other poets, but they use it in a different way ; there is a distinction of kind as well as of degree. Every angler must occasionally present his fly " dry " to a trout ; but the true dry-fly fisherman not only does this more frequently, but in a different way and for a different purpose, so that the whole character of the sport is transformed.

First for the poet of the *Iliad*—Homer or some other. You will find, I think, in this type of poet that he now and then makes a special effort to wrest the last magic from place-names, and has one or two famous passages of thunderous, cumulative topography ; and also that his mind is so interpenetrated by the *genius loci* that everywhere, in his most exalted as well as in his most pedestrian moments, a character cannot enter on the stage without his place of origin attending him like a heraldic blazon. The great example of the first is, of course, the " Catalogue " in the 2nd *Iliad*. It does not affect my argument that the " Catalogue " may, as many have urged, be the work of an inferior poet— not the poet, at any rate, of the " Embassy " or the " Doloneia." In the *Iliad* as we have it to-day I think it hard to deny that the " Catalogue " fulfils a vital artistic purpose—the purpose of setting the stage and preparing and stimulating the reader's mind, and that the work of this Homer is certainly as Homeric as that of any of the other Homers.

" And of them that possessed Lakedaimon lying low in the hollow of the hills, and Pharis and Sparta and Messe, the haunt of doves, and dwelt in Bryseiai and lovely Augeiai, and of them too that held Amyklai and the sea-shore keep of Helos, and that possessed Laas and dwelt around Oitylos, of such was the king's brother leader, even Menelaos of the loud war-cry, leader of sixty ships."

The great surge is sustained, the impetus does not slacken, we are in a world not of fancied figures but of living girded men-at-arms, each shouting the name of his little castle, whether it be Messe of the Doves, or Enispe of the Winds, or Neriton of the Quivering Leaves. We get an impression of a vast background to the stage set at Troy, and of the hurrying of a great multitude thither, a sense at one and the same time of change and of permanence, of motion and of rest.

But, as I have said, it is not only in his set pieces that the poet of the *Iliad* gives rein to his love of topography; the thing haunts every line. Each casual arrival must be identified and blazoned. Sometimes the epithets are only conventional, " high-girt," " deep-walled," " fruitful " ; sometimes they have in themselves the quality of poetry, so that they insinuate a note of gentler music, a flute among the drums of war. Sometimes a complete and unforgettable picture is sketched in a couple of lines. I will give you an instance of this last, which has always delighted me—that son of Teuthras whom Diomedes slays in the beginning of the 6th Book :

" Then Diomedes of the loud war-cry slew Axylos, son of Teuthras, who dwelt behind the strong walls of Arisbe, rich in all livelihood, and was dear to men, for he built his dwelling by the roadside and entertained every wayfarer."

It is all we are ever to know of this lord of Arisbe, but it is enough to make me, at any rate, become his partisan as against the devouring Diomedes, and lament the blow that ended the honest country squire, who had his house beside the road, like an old English manor, and was kind to tramps.

When we turn to *Paradise Lost* we find that Milton has followed and improved upon both aspects of the Homeric method. The poet of the *Iliad* was a topographer, but I doubt if he could have produced a map of the universe as he conceived it. Milton was both topographer and geographer. I can see exactly the kind of map of the world he would have drawn, how he would have portrayed Central Asia and the African coasts. It is quite easy to make a plan of Heaven and Hell and the intermediate regions according to the Miltonic cosmogony, for he gives us the most explicit details about them. His soaring imagination was conjoined with an intellect of such articulating power that he forces the wildest material to take definite and intelligible shape, and transmutes abstract space into concrete place.

Like Homer, Milton essays epic catalogues. The greatest is the roll-call of the Devils in the 1st Book, and, mark you, it is the place-names that matter—not Moloch and Baal and Thammuz so much as the thundering music of their temples :

> " Him the Ammonite
> Worshipt in Rabba and her watry Plain.
> In Argob and in Basan, to the stream
> Of utmost Arnon."

Scarcely less fine is the vision of the kingdoms of the earth shown to Adam in the 11th Book :

> " His Eye might there command wherever stood
> City of old or modern Fame, the Seat
> Of mightiest Empire, from the destind Walls
> Of Cambalu, seat of Cathaian Can
> And Samarchand by Oxus, Temirs Throne,
> To Paquin of Sinæan Kings, and thence
> To Agra and Lahor of great Mogul
> Down to the golden Chersonese, or where
> The Persian in Ecbatan sate, or since
> In Hispahan, or where the Russian Ksar
> In Mosco, or the Sultan in Bizance,
> Turchestan-born ; nor could his eye not ken
> Th' Empire of Negus to his utmost Port
> Ercoco and the less Maritime Kings
> Mombaza, and Quiloa, and Melind,
> And Sofala thought Ophir, to the Realme
> Of Congo, and Angola fardest South ;
> Or thence from Niger Flood to Atlas Mount
> The Kingdoms of Almansor, Fez and Sus,
> Marocco and Algiers, and Tremisen ;
> On Europe thence, and where Rome was to sway
> The World : in Spirit perhaps he also saw

Rich Mexico the seat of Motezume,
And Cusco in Peru, the richer seat
Of Atabalipa, and yet unspoil'd
Guiana, whose great Citie Geryons Sons
Call El Dorado."

I might cite also the vision in *Paradise Regained* of the
Temptation of Our Lord, though it seems to me to be
on a lower level of poetic merit, savouring of Apollonius
Rhodius rather than of Homer.

But, as with the poet of the *Iliad*, it is the way in
which the sense of place interpenetrates Milton's thought
that is the primary artistic miracle. Every phase of
the great argument evokes some stately place-name,
and one recalls another, till the whole earth is laid under
tribute. I am emphasizing here in especial the effect
of the device upon the reader's mind, and not so much
the effect—the tremendous effect—of those superb syl-
lables upon his ear. Let me set forth a few instances:

" Thick as Autumnal Leaves that strow the Brooks
In Vallombrosa, where th' Etrurian shades
High overarch't imbowr : or scatterd sedge
Afloat, when with fierce Winds Orion arm'd
Hath vext the Red-Sea Coast, whose waves orethrew
Busiris and his Memphian Chivalrie."

Paradise Lost, Book I.

" What resounds
In Fable or Romance of Uthers Son
Begirt with British and Armoric Knights ;
And all who since, Baptiz'd or Infidel,
Jousted in Aspramont or Montalban,
Damasco, or Marocco, or Trebisond,
Or whom Biserta sent from Afric shore
When Charlemain with all his Peerage fell
By Fontarabbia."

Paradise Lost, Book I.

" As when farr off at Sea a Fleet descri'd
Hangs in the Clouds, by Æquinoctial Winds
Close sailing from Bengala, or the Iles
Of Ternate and Tidore, whence Merchants bring
Their spicie Drugs ; they on the trading Flood
Through the wide Ethiopian to the Cape
Ply stemming nightly toward the Pole."
                              Paradise Lost, Book II.

" As when a Gryfon through the Wilderness
With winged course ore Hill or moarie Dale,
Pursues the Arimaspian, who by stelth
Had from his wakeful custody purloind
The guarded Gold."   *Paradise Lost*, Book II.

                    " As when to them who sail
Beyond the Cape of Hope, and now are past
Mozambic, off at Sea North-East windes blow
Sabean Odours from the spicie shoare
Of Arabie the blest."   *Paradise Lost*, Book IV.

                         " Not that faire field
Of Enna, where Proserpin gathring flours
Her self a fairer Floure by gloomie Dis
Was gatherd, which cost Ceres all that pain
To seek her through the world ; nor that sweet Grove
Of Daphne by Orontes, and th' inspir'd
Castalian Spring might with this Paradise
Of Eden strive, nor that Nyseian Ile
Girt with the River Triton, where old Cham,
Whom Gentiles Ammon call and Libyan Jove,
Hid Amalthea and her Florid Son
Young Bacchus from his Stepdame Rhea's eye ;
Nor where Abassin Kings thir issue Guard,
Mount Amara, though this by som suppos'd
True Paradise under the Ethiop Line
By Nilus head, enclos'd with shining Rock,
A whole day's journey high."
                              Paradise Lost, Book IV.

" Sea he had searcht and Land
From Eden over Pontus, and the Poole
Mæotis, up beyond the River Ob ;
Downward as farr Antartic ; and in length
West from Orontes to the Ocean barr'd
At Darien, thence to the Land where flowes
Ganges and Indus."
                                   Paradise Lost, Book IX.

Lastly, we reach the ballad-maker, who was almost always drunk with the spirit of place. Consider. He had to hold the interest of his audience by bringing strange things within the orbit of their understanding, and how better could he do this than by emphasizing the familiar things in his tale—the names of crofts and peel towers, and hills and waters, which were within every one's knowledge ? Further, the balladist was an artist, often a profound artist, and he had to lay a spell on the fancy or pluck at the heart-strings by some little sharp detail which stands up like a rock in a cascade to give shape and measure to the fall. There are many ballads of the sheer supernatural where topography would be meaningless, but even in these place-names may be used with cunning effect. Take "The Wife of Usher's Well." I do not know where on earth Usher's Well is ; I do not know if it is anywhere ; but in the ballad it becomes a fixed point in some dim spiritual land. Take the "Lyke Wake Dirge," and note how the names Whinny-muir and Brig o' Dread are used. The balladist gets in a place-name wherever he can. True Thomas is sitting on Huntly Bank when he spies the Queen of Elfland come riding down by the Eildon Tree—terrestrial points, both of them, which you may visit to-day in a char-a-banc. In "Tam Lin," the affair with the Fairy Queen takes place at

(2,709)   13

Carterhaugh, where I have shot partridges. The adventure would not be so impressive if the venue were not named. And you remember the uncanny effect of a single place-name in the ballad of "The Dæmon Lover":

> " I'll show where the white lilies grow
>   On the banks o' Italie."

It is in the riding ballads, however, the stories of actual doings in Sherwood Forest, or in the Cheviots, or in the Debateable Land, that topography is used on the grand scale—naturally, because these ballads deal with men in action in certain physical surroundings which largely determine the drama. Thus "Kinmont Willie":

> " They led him thro' the Liddel-rack
>   And also thro' the Carlisle sands ;
> They brought him in to Carlisle castell,
>   To be at my Lord Scroope's commands."

And "Jamie Telfer":

> " ' Warn Wat o' Harden, and his sons,
>   Wi' them will Borthwick Water ride ;
> Warn Gaudilands, and Allanhaugh,
>   And Gilmanscleugh, and Commonside.
>
> ' Ride by the gate at Priesthaughswire,
>   And warn the Currors o' the Lee ;
> As ye cum down the Hermitage Slack,
>   Warn doughty Willie o' Gorrinberry.' "

And "Lord Maxwell's Good-night":

> " ' Adieu ! Dumfries, my proper place,
>   But and Carlaverock fair !
> Adieu ! my castle of the Thrieve,
>   Wi' a' my buildings there !

Adieu ! Lochmaben's gate sae fair,
    And Langholm, where birks there be ;
Adieu ! my ladye, and only joy,
    For I may not stay wi' thee.' "

We are now—with these examples in our memory
—in a position to determine the precise artistic effect
in poetry of this generous use of particulars in the
form of place-names. All concrete particulars, we are
agreed, have their primary value in producing a sense
of reality. The use of place-names on the grand scale
gives an impression not only of the solid reality of the
world of the poet, but of its spaciousness and its permanence. It produces upon the mind a sense of rest.
When Homer tells us of every little burg and clachan
from which his warriors come we realize that far away
from the feverish plains of Simois and Scamander there
is an intricate human life going on, whether Troy falls
or no. When Milton dazzles us with a torrent of jewelled
names, each with the magic gift of conjuring up further
mysteries, our sense of the greatness of the world and the
majesty of life is enlarged. This artistic effect I should
call especially that of peace. It gives us a world in
which our reason and imagination can abide.

That is one consequence. The other is the opposite
—not a sense of rest, but a sense of movement. We
live our lives under the twin categories of time and space ;
if movement is to be shown, one or other must be
particularized, and since you cannot particularize time
(for people do not have a map of an hour in their memories) it must be space. From Homer to the penny
reciter the best way to give an impression of speed is
by means of a series of place-names, which are like the
posts in a stadium. The movement may be a stately

progress like the Archfiend's in *Paradise Lost*; it may be a mad gallop; but you can get both the stateliness and the speed from judicious topography. It is the secret of all martial ballads, all songs of raids and escapes, from "Kinmont Willie" to Macaulay's "Armada," and Browning's "How we brought the Good News," and Mr. Kipling's "Ballad of East and West." I need not multiply instances, but I would refer you to Sir Walter Scott as an example of a lesser master (in poetry, that is to say) who was an adept at this twofold use of place-names. For the first effect take the mustering of the Scott clan in the *Lay of the Last Minstrel*. Or take the beautiful last lines of the poem :

> " But still,
> When summer smiled on sweet Bowhill,
> And July's eve, with balmy breath,
> Waved the blue-bells on Newark heath ;
> When throstles sung in Harehead-shaw,
> And corn was green on Carterhaugh,
> And flourished, broad, Blackandro's oak,
> The aged Harper's soul awoke ! "

Or take the view of Edinburgh in *Marmion*, or the romantic opening of *The Lady of the Lake*. For the second I give you William of Deloraine's ride in *The Lay* from the time when he fords Teviot and passes the Peel of Goldiland, to the moment when

> " Far beneath, in lustre wan,
> Old Melros' rose, and fair Tweed ran."

II

From narrative in poetry we turn to narrative in prose. The art of prose fiction has a respectable ancestry, but it was a long time before it could divorce itself from poetic traditions and become a transcript and interpretation of the actual world. For ages the vapid offspring of Heliodorus and Longus and Achilles Tatius held the stage, and the story-teller dwelt among the pasteboard groves of artificial pastoral. If *Don Quixote* is the first modern novel it should be remembered that Cervantes set more store by his *Galatea* and his *Persiles and Sigismunda*, romances in the true Heliodorus vein. You find the fashion in the Elizabethans—in Sir Philip Sidney, in Robert Greene, in Thomas Lodge ; and it was not till a century later that fiction in England descended to earth from those insipid heavens, and the English novel was born with Defoe.

Defoe, in his most famous book, is a master of particulars, indeed, but these particulars are not place-names, for Robinson Crusoe's island is outside the map-maker's province. In other books, like *Moll Flanders*, he shows that he realizes what a sovereign aid to verisimilitude can be found in topography. But the great novelists of the eighteenth century were still a little apt to generalize their landscapes. Even Fielding, when he sets Tom Jones on his travels, indicates airily the direction of his movements, but does not condescend to place-names ; while the novelists of manners, from Richardson to Jane Austen, all of them minute particularizers, who build up for the reader visible rooms, houses, streets, villages, are rarely inclined to take pains with the local orientation of their scenes. It is not till Sir Walter Scott that the twofold magic of a concrete nomenclature is discovered. His one predecessor, perhaps, is John Bunyan. The *Pilgrim's Progress* is no doubt an allegory, and its landscape (though you can guess at its prototypes in Bedfordshire and Bucks) is not of the earth but of the spirit ; but none the less his abstractions have "become visible and walk about on roads" ; and in the dream world which he creates the points have all the artistic value of terrestrial names. We can make a picture of the Way in all its length from the Wicket Gate to the River ; we know its stages as if we had travelled them ; the names are allegorical conceptions, but they are turned into place-names as concrete and memorable as any in an English shire—the Slough of Despond, the Interpreter's House, the Hill Difficulty, the House Beautiful, the Valley of Humiliation, Vanity Fair, Doubting Castle, the plain called Ease, the Delectable Mountains, and the Land of Beulah.

One of the features of romance, it has been said, is a quickened consciousness of background. When the great romantic era opened with Sir Walter Scott it was inevitable that the topographical background should be amplified, and in Scott we see for the first time in fiction a specialization in localities. In all his greater novels he particularizes his scene, whether it be the Clyde valley in *Old Mortality*, or Liddesdale and the shores of Solway in *Guy Mannering*, or the Forfarshire coast in *The Antiquary*, or the neighbourhood of the capital city in *The Heart of Midlothian*, or the London streets in *The Fortunes of Nigel*. He does not always stick close to fact ; the landscape of *Ivanhoe*, for example, is hard to place exactly on the map ; but, real or invented, his is a particularized landscape which the reader must carry in his memory if he is to follow the tale. The great masters in the direct Scott tradition, Dumas and Victor Hugo, trod the same path. The ride of D'Artagnan to the sea owes its speed to its artful topography ; and how minutely mapped is the mediæval Paris of *Notre-Dame* and the more modern city of *Les Misérables*. The fashion spread to a class of story which is not generally given the name of romance. Dickens and Thackeray alike portray London more exactly and with more frequent recourse to particulars than any previous writers ; Dickens, indeed, created a country of his own, the south-east corner of England, where to-day over a hundred streets and villages the spell of his imagination has woven memories more vivid than any historic tradition. Anthony Trollope in his Barsetshire novels invented and mapped out a terrestrial province, within the confines of which we can follow precisely the movements of his people. In our own day, to take an instance or two at random, Mr. Arnold Bennett has established the Five Towns in the literary geography of England ; Mr. Neil Munro has made West Highland topography an essential of his two best romances ; and Mr. Wells, in those books which, I take leave to think, are his chief title to fame, has followed Dickens and annexed south-east England, notably the London suburbs and the Channel towns, so that I, for one, can never think of the South Coast without a vision of Mr. Kipps, or see a sluggish Kent stream without thinking of Mr. Polly, or travel the Portsmouth road without meeting the lonely figure of Mr. Hoopdriver.

The novel of to-day which deals with men and women in action, and which cultivates something of the variousness of life itself, is almost always driven to seek aid from a precise topography. Place-names fill its pages as essential items in the background, organically linked to the main drama. The landscape need have no counterpart on a terrestrial map. Mr. Maurice Hewlett

in *The Forest Lovers* devised a land as remote as Broceliaunde, but it was exactly realized, so that the movement of his protagonists can be followed as if in the
pages of Baedeker. I am far from arguing that all
novels must conform to this type. The story of a lonely
spiritual conflict may need only the barest physical
setting ; the highly sophisticated comedy of George
Meredith and Henry James may find an adequate stage
in a drawing-room ; intellectuals can conduct their
dreary business in an anonymous suburb. But the
novel which aims at a convincing picture of the whirl
and march of life in its central aspects, which would
create characters with whom our interest is strongly
engaged, can scarcely disregard topography. It must
have a landscape as a background, and a landscape in
which the points are orientated and named.

I will take three examples of the use of topography
in fiction on the grand scale. The first is Mr. Hardy's
novels. We are not concerned for the moment with
Mr. Hardy as a master-painter of landscape, though no
one in our literature has reproduced the English scene
more faithfully ; nor as the philosophic interpreter of
Nature in its relation to human life, so that a tract of
ground, like Egdon Heath in *The Return of the Native*,
becomes almost one of the *dramatis personæ*. The
aspect of his work to which I would call your attention
is rather that to which he refers in his General Preface
to the collected edition of his novels and poems. His
people, he says, though " typically and essentially those
of any and every place," are " dwellers in a province
bounded on the north by the Thames, on the south by
the English Channel, on the east by a line running from
Hayling Island to Windsor Forest, and on the west by

the Cornish coast." He goes on to say, " in response to inquiries from readers," that " the description of these backgrounds has been done from the real—that is to say, has something real for its basis, however illusively treated." He confesses to the use of many existing names, and when he has invented names he does not contradict the affirmation of " discerning people " that they recognize the originals. But, indeed, we do not require Mr. Hardy's admission. His novels, each a drama of its own locality, are collectively the drama and the history of south-west England. He has created a Wessex of his own, a land of the imagination where the reader can pick his way from town to town and from valley to valley, along ancient roads and rivers, by the aid of the guidance afforded by the writer. It is immaterial that this Wessex is substantially the Wessex of the geographers, and that Mr. Hardy's map can be superimposed upon the map in our atlases and be found in the main features to correspond with it. The point of artistic importance is that a writer who has searched the intricacies of the human heart and sounded the deeps of human passion has summoned place-names to his aid, and has deliberately elaborated and denominated his background.

What is the result ? Not other than that which we found in poetry. Tragedy and comedy walk on a familiar and recognizable stage. Our sense of reality is sharpened ; the romance is heightened because it moves in a concrete world ; we are given a quiet enduring background to the transient fervours of humanity. It is to be noted that Mr. Hardy seeks no illegitimate advantage from this method. When he has to deal with places traditionally famous, which have, so to speak, a ready-made atmosphere for the reader, as a rule he disguises them ; Oxford, you remember, is " Christminster"; Winchester, " Wintoncester "; Shaftesbury, " Shaston"; Wantage, "Alfredston"; Sherborne, "Sherton Abbas." His topography and his nomenclature stand on their own merits, things as English as oak and ash and thorn, whether they be real names like Bubb-Down Hill and Crimmercrock Lane, or happy inventions like " Casterbridge " or " Kingsbere " or " Abbot's Cernal." It is a world in which the mind of the reader can contentedly abide.

My second instance is Mr. Blackmore's *Lorna Doone*. Here you have a narrower area and a more modest purpose. The book is a tale of the life of a moorland farm in the seventeenth century—of a farm rather than of a farmer, for, satisfying hero as John Ridd is, the charm fails as soon as he strays from his native Exmoor. It may be heresy, but apart from Plover's Barrows I do not think that we should be greatly interested in John, or even in Lorna ; and what would the struggle with the Doones be worth if they had not lived in the Doone Valley ? The magic of place interpenetrates the story—the twofold magic, for we have the sense of an antique, homely, enduring manner of life, and we have also at times the sense of swift movement. The story, you remember, begins at Blundell's school in Tiverton when John Fry arrives caked in the mud of the roads ; and presently we are on the Moor watching the firing of Dunkery Beacon, and the place has us in its thrall. The cooking and the cider-making and the shepherding are described so circumstantially that we know every inch of Plover's Barrows, and then romance begins when John, in the cold spring weather, goes spearing loaches up the Lynn water, and finds the Bagworthy stream and climbs the water-slide and has his first sight of Lorna. The scheme of the book is the homely decencies of the Ridds set against the tawdry magnificence and crime of the Doones, but it is still more Plover's Barrows set against the Doone Valley. Before he is a third of the way through the reader has a map in his head and has adopted the countryside, becoming for the time a dweller in the parish of Oare. There is no fumbling, for I do not think that Blackmore's skill in the delineation of landscape has been sufficiently praised ; everything stands out clear and proportionate ; before the end we know roughly the distance of Plover's Barrows from the other places which concern us, we follow the attack on the Doones with an anxious topographical eye, and in the great scene of Carver's flight and death we know, before the author tells us, that if he crosses Black Barrow Down he is certain to come to the Wizard's Slough. The book is a masterpiece in the imaginative use of a detailed landscape.

My last illustration shall be from Stevenson—a romance of the type called " picaresque," where bodily movement, and therefore topography, must play a major part. Now Stevenson is very good at another kind of work, where the *locale* is not mentioned, or only vaguely indicated. Such is the short story " Markheim " ; such is *Prince Otto* ; such, in a sense, is *The Master of Ballantrae,* for though we are told that the scene is laid in the south-west of Scotland, and one or two skilfully chosen place-names are introduced—Durrisdeer, St. Bride's, the Water of Swift—the action does not need them, needs no more indeed than the house, the policies, and a strip of seashore. But in *Kidnapped* the author

gives rein to his love of maps and methodical landscapes.
The journey of David and Alan is not more minutely
treated than the same countryside in the stately pages of
Dr. Johnson and Mr. Boswell. But mark the difference
between a work of record and a work of art. I defy
a reader of the *Tour to the Hebrides*, and still more of
the *Journey to the Western Islands*, to be very clear
where he is, unless recourse be had to the map ; but
Stevenson takes the reader constantly to a hill-top and
gives him a wide prospect, so that he has a map in his
memory. The names, too, are artfully selected. There
is no glut of outlandish geography. We are piloted
across Mull and Morvern, through Appin and the Moor
of Rannoch to Ben Alder, and then south by Breadalbane
and Balquhidder to the shores of Forth, with just the
proper amount of condescension upon place-names, for
each one is a key-point. The effect is not of speed, but
of distance—the fatigue of immense pathless spaces.
When the action shifts in the beginning of *Catriona*
to the environs of Edinburgh place-names are used with
a different purpose ; they are crowded together and the
scale shrinks, in order to suggest an intricate flight in a
closely-settled and closely-watched countryside. I will
give you another specimen of Stevenson's cunning.
David Balfour, you remember, is imprisoned on the Bass
Rock in order to prevent his being present at the trial
of James Stewart at Inveraray ; but he manages to get
off earlier than he had hoped, and rides hard for the
West. Now a dull writer, in order to get the effect of
speed, would have loaded his pages with irrelevant
topography and a minute time-schedule. Stevenson
was wiser ; this, he felt, was no case for a map, and
swiftness must be got by some other means. So he is

economical with his detail. David is set on shore at
Clackmannan Pool on the Saturday afternoon at 2 ;
an hour later he is in Stirling ; at 6 p.m. he is somewhere
about Uam Var, and at 11 reaches the house of Duncan
Dhu. He leaves straightway on foot and reaches Inveraray before the end of the sermon on the Sunday
morning. It is all we want ; we feel that David is
indeed a moss-trooper, as the Lord Advocate said.
Now that journey is to my mind incredible, for no
man, I think, could start on his two legs about 11 p.m.
from somewhere on the east side of Balquhidder, after
having ridden from Clackmannan, and be in Inveraray
before noon on the next day. The feat is as impossible
in the time as the journey of Telemachus in the *Odyssey*
from Pylos to Sparta. It is like the story of Artamines'
single-handed combats, which Major Bellenden in *Old
Mortality* complained " put all pretty men's actions
out of countenance." But artistically it is wholly
right ; Stevenson has not already elaborated this piece
of country, so the reader's credulity is not strained, while
the few selected details are all that is needed to quicken
the fancy.

III

What is the conclusion of our brief survey ? That
in certain forms of literature, and these not the lowest,
a local habitation and a name are essentials for success.
I am not decrying the beauty of *homelessness*. There
are types of art where the purpose is a country " east
of the sun and west of the moon," and where the terrestrial application is of necessity dim and tenuous,
where fancy is free of mundane fetters and spirit creates
its own spiritual landmarks. But for the normal

types, for narrative in verse or prose, above all for the fiction which seeks to move us with something of the emotions of life, there must be a sense of place as well as of character. The writer who is a " kinless loon," who has no roots down in the soil and cannot call any tract of country his own, may be a great artist, but he will fall short of the widest appeal, for the ordinary stuff of humanity is deep in local affections, a devotee, in Edmund Burke's famous words, of " all the little quiet rivulets that water an humble, a contracted, but not an unfruitful field." The writer who has the same prepossession, who can build up in detail his background and dwell lovingly on its contours and its place-names, establishes an instant kinship, and is the more moving and persuasive because he appeals to a most ancient instinct in the heart of man.

IX

THE JUDICIAL TEMPERAMENT

THE JUDICIAL TEMPERAMENT [1]

I PROPOSE to address you with the modesty which
becomes the amateur in the presence of experts.
It is only by a vigorous mental effort that I can realize
that I was once a lawyer. When a man has deserted
the pastoral uplands of the Bar for the low levels of
commerce, when he has ceased to be a manipulator of
the legal mill and has become the crude material which
is ground in it, when in his future relations with courts
of justice he must content himself either with the
insignificant position of the lay client, or the dullness
of the jury box or the witness box, or the garish and
comfortless notoriety of the dock, something is radically
altered in his soul. He has lost his first innocence.
He has embarked upon a career which may be more
profitable and less laborious, but can never be as respectable as that which he has forsaken. But once a lawyer
always a lawyer. Though it is fifteen years since I
ceased to practise I find that I still read the law reports
first in the morning paper, and that fragments of legal
jargon still tend to adorn my dubious literary style.

I propose to address you to-night on a matter which
has always interested me—that which is supposed to
be the fine flower of legal training and that which is at

[1] An address delivered to the Ellesmere Law Society at Oriel College,
Oxford, March 1922.

the same time one of the rarest things on earth, the judicial temperament. I use the word " temperament " advisedly, for I mean more than mind ; I mean the union of mind and character. A man may have a perfect judicial mind and yet be a bad judge, because of defects of temper or character.

The bench is the natural goal of the successful lawyer. It is the most honourable, the most secure, and the most independent position which our society can offer. The law, as Lord Westbury once observed genially in a debate in the House of Lords, " has in its infinite wisdom provided for the not improbable event of the imbecility of a bishop." It has made the same provision for the judge, but only in the extreme resort and after a complicated procedure. The Bench gives a man the right to speak in public without contradiction or inter-ruption, a right not granted at all to the politician, and accorded to the clergy only for a few brief minutes once a week. It provides a compulsory and sympathetic audience for the worst jokes. It offers a secure income, considerable leisure, and, in England, various decorative titles, from the plain knighthood of the puisne to the earldom of the Lord Chancellor who has been long in office. The duties of the post are admittedly of the first importance for the maintenance of order, the con-duct of business, and the continuance of society. Surely the hundred and sixty millions of the people of Britain and the United States should be able to supply at any one time adequate specimens of the judicial temperament to fill the various chairs of justice. It is not so. We have judges witty and dull, learned and unlearned, high-minded and less high-minded, industrious and idle; we have on the whole a most respectable level of intellect and character. But the judicial temperament, the *vera differentia* of the judge, is so rare that I doubt if it appears as often as once in a decade.

I

I begin by propounding to you two of the paradoxes of our civilization. The first is the legislative paradox —that laws are made in their final form by parliaments and congresses—that is, by people notoriously incompetent, with the result that experts have to spend their lives interpreting them. The second is the judicial paradox—that the judge, whose business it is to possess the judicial temperament, is chosen only from successful advocates, who succeed by being unjudicial.

The specific qualities of the advocate are, I think, universally understood. You will find them analysed by a succession of competent authorities from Cicero downwards. The root of the talent is simply the power to persuade—a power which is shared by such diverse characters as saints and company promoters, Abraham Lincoln or Mr. Gladstone and the soap-box orator at the street corner. This power depends upon knowledge of human nature, and it is applied both to the intellect and to the passions of the hearers. The legal advocate must make both appeals or he fails in the highest walks of advocacy. He has to deal with juries of average men, and he must lay his mind alongside theirs and speak their own language. It used to be said of a recent English Chief Justice that he succeeded largely because his mind was more average than that of the average juryman. On that side, the art, whether it be spontaneous or nicely calculated, is based upon an understanding of human nature and the capacity to arouse the more obvious human emotions. It is no more than a superior form of demagogy.

But the advocate has also to deal with the Bench, and there a subtler art is needed. Knowledge of human nature is again the first requirement, but it is a more sophisticated type of human nature. There must, of course, be a certain appeal to the intellect, but advocacy is rarely a cold-blooded impersonal dialectic. The temperament of the judge must be considered. The Bench has its work to get through and it looks to the Bar for assistance, and that advocate will be the best verdict-getter who divines most shrewdly what kind of assistance this or that judge requires. The thing is a fine art, and its greatest practitioners have won by an unholy knowledge of the foibles of the courts in which they practised. It is not, as is sometimes said, the power of making the worse appear the better reason ; it is the gift of so putting a fairly good reason that it will have the fullest effect. With a competent judge a good advocate will have the courage, in spite of the folly of solicitors, to refuse to argue a bad point. He will go straight to the heart of a matter, state it briefly, and then sit down. With an inferior type of judge the better plan may be to snow him under with an accumulation of small points. I was talking the other day to one of the greatest of living advocates, and he told me of a device which he said he frequently found to be effective. If he had a precedent or some evidence seriously against him he was accustomed, after he had interested the court, to express with the utmost emphasis his sense of the magnitude of the snag before him. He said that he usually found that some judge or other would intervene, and say, " Come now, Mr. ——, I don't think this is quite so bad as you make it. I think I see a way of getting round it." For the rest of the argument his case became also that judge's case, for he thenceforth took a personal and proprietary interest in getting rid of the snag.

Advocacy, therefore, is a subtle and varied art, and at its best it will cover an almost infinite range of human nature. But consider what it is. It is primarily a psychological appeal and not the dry light of reason. There is nothing judicial about it ; nay, the judicial is at a discount. That is why the very great advocate is very rarely a great judge, and, if he is, it is because of the possession of qualities which were not revealed in his advocacy. The famous advocates of history are to-day only traditions, like eminent actors, for they have left nothing behind by which we can test their quality. The dazzling repute of Scarlett at the English Bar will not be understood by him who reads the judgments of Lord Abinger. The dæmonic force of Thomas Erskine will not be realized by the student who studies the career of Lord Erskine on the Woolsack. Richard Bethell was the most formidable figure of his day in the courts, and happily a hundred anecdotes remain to attest his wit, but Lord Westbury was not a great Lord Chancellor ; and who could discover in the saturnine Lord Chief Justice the uncanny gifts, the almost Sinaitic terrors of Charles Russell, the advocate ? Judicial office is like the Popedom ; it smothers the preacher of crusades under the extinguisher of the Triple Crown.

II

We reach, then, that rare thing, the judicial temperament, which is something born in a man, which is not to be acquired by the practice of advocacy, and which indeed must be in abeyance during the time when a man in the courts is building up the prestige which carries him to the Bench. It is to this radical difference in the qualities required rather than, I think, to mere blunders of patronage that gross judicial misappointments are due. A man who has acquired sufficient pre-eminence as an advocate to be made a judge can scarcely be a fool. I do not deny that the pure and unadulterated fool has occasionally strayed on to the Bench—men like that Scottish judge in the beginning of last century, Lord Eskgrove, who observed in one of his judgments, "Having thus shown that the pursuer's case is utterly impossible, I will now proceed to show that it is also highly improbable." But these are the rarest exceptions. The ordinary misfits were men like Lord Brougham, who were immensely clever, far too clever, restless, and undisciplined for the prosaic tasks of their calling; or, as I have said, advocates who were only advocates.

To proceed with our analysis—there is one negative quality which we must presume, and that is absence of bias. It sounds simple, but the unbiassed mind is really the rarest of endowments. For consider. An advocate is a human being, a member of society, and no mere debating machine, and in his progress through life he is certain to acquire prepossessions and antipathies. If he is a negative colourless soul, then he is obviously unfitted from the start for true success in

any calling. A man goes to the Bench with political
views, religious views, social views, which, unless he is
constantly on the watch, will colour his judicial work.
The Tory will look askance at the Radical, the High
Churchman will be prejudiced in favour of a particular
doctrine of church government, the teetotaller will
press too hard on drunkenness, the moralist will have a
temperamental shrinking from the grosser forms of vice.
There are countless examples of the commonest, the
political bias. Lord Eldon, great judge as he was,
had it, and the Scottish bench during the Napoleonic
wars gloried in it.   One instance I remember in Scotland.
A certain millionaire took a shooting lodge in the High-
lands, and one of his sons, observing a poacher at night
on the river, promptly shot at and wounded him.   The
case caused great excitement at the time, and it came
on for trial before one who looked exactly what he was,
a Raeburn portrait come to life, the last of the old
school of Scottish judges. But he was not without
prejudices. He was a landowner and a sportsman, and
had a peculiar dislike of poachers. The leading counsel for the erring son was at the time an extreme
Radical and land reformer, who had lately announced
that he would not rest until " God's green fields and
God's clear waters were free to all God's people."   He
was a master of, I think, the most blatantly sentimental
appeal I have ever heard, but he was also an adroit
advocate, and the millionaire did well to brief him.
He knew his judge, and he presented him with an argument which fairly ravished that honest heart. Gone
was the Radical and Henry George-ite, and the advocate
revealed himself as the upholder of the seigneur's right
of pit and gallows. If men and women had rights so

also had the land and the custodians of the land, dominant rights, because they were more vital for the maintenance and cohesion of society. Cursed, saith the Lord, be he who removeth his neighbour's landmark, and the sacrosanctity of private property in land was still the basis of our civilization. I can hear the smooth phrases and see the happy smile of my old friend on the Bench. The millionaire's son was triumphantly acquitted.

There are many other forms of bias—the bias against sexual vice, for example, which makes certain judges entirely unfitted to try certain types of case. After the political, the commonest I should say was the religious. Lord Westbury could not abide a bishop, and was always looking for their heads with a stick like an Irishman at Donnybrook Fair. He it was, you remember, who "disestablished Hell, dismissed the Devil with costs, and took from the Church of England her last hope of eternal damnation." Some judges cherish a passionate ecclesiasticism ; some have a prejudice against the clergy. There was an eminent judge in Scotland, Lord Young, who had a gift of bitter language and a great dislike of Dissent. On one occasion counsel began his speech with, "My Lord, my client is a most eminent and most respected minister of the Free Church of Scotland," and then stopped to allow the words to make a proper impression on the Bench. Lord Young looked down under his grim eyebrows: "Go on, sir, go on. Your client may be a perfectly respectable man for all that."

Now there is nothing to be said against the retention of these prejudices. I believe in every man having a good stock of them, for otherwise we should be flimsy, ineffective creatures, and deadly dull at that. Since a judge is a human being, he must be permitted to have his share in the attributes of mortality. But he must be capable of putting them aside. He must have the power of separating a question from the " turbid mixture of contemporaneousness " with which it is clogged. It is a task which requires supreme intellectual honesty, a complete absence of the " lie in the soul," and it is the first duty of a judge. I think it has been the rule and not the exception in the history of the English and American Benches, and to that I believe is due the high popular esteem in which these benches have so long been held.

III

We now come to the positive qualities. The first and most obvious is the power of interpreting the written word, whether it be in the form of statute or judgment. That is the staple of a judge's duties. The statute law on a subject is contained in Acts often hastily drafted, which in their passage through Parliament have frequently been so mauled as to be unrecognizable by their draughtsmen. Moreover, these Acts show often the bad fault of legislation by reference, so that the judge has to interpret a parent statute *plus* a great progeny of slovenly supplementary legislation. Take the case of the British Revenue Acts ; to settle one point you may have a headachy search through, and a combination of, a dozen statutes. Then there are the many hundred volumes of past decisions which, if they emanate from a higher tribunal, are held to be binding on any judge of a lower tribunal.

Now, judicial interpretation is a most difficult art.

It is easy enough for a quick-witted advocate to find an ingenious reading of a clause or a phrase which supports his case. The judge has a different duty. He has to find out what the legislature or tribunal presumably meant, by deciding what a collocation of words means according to the rules of logic and the uses of the English tongue. Often great subtlety is required, for to decide on the meaning a dozen cross-bearings, as sailors say, must be found from other uses in the same statute or elsewhere. We have all in our minds cases, which in their meticulous balancing of pros and cons, in their elucidation of shades of meaning and *nuances* of atmosphere, in their orderly exposition of the disorderly, have the charm of a difficult mathematical proof, or a chess conundrum, or a piece of very elaborate classical music. Subtlety, of course, may be misplaced and overdone, but a capacity for subtlety is essential if a judge is to be a skilled interpreter, since if the subject-matter be complex a mind which insists on simplifying too greatly may be too blunt a weapon for the job. An axe is, generally speaking, a more valuable implement to man than a razor, but it is no good trying to shave with it.

The next quality is a complement and a corrective to the last. I should define it as common sense, the sense of reality, a rarer and more valuable gift even than the power of nice interpretation. For law, remember, is not a dead corpus of black-letter wisdom. It is an elastic tissue which clothes the living body of society. The test of its value is its applicability to, and its usefulness in, our everyday life. Hence, what may be called the " jig-saw puzzle " view of a judge's functions is radically unsound. A judge must not merely strike a balance between opposing arguments. Nor must he lean too heavily on the assistance of the counsel pleading before him. Indeed, there is a good deal to be said for John Marshall's famous dictum: " The acme of judicial distinction means the ability to look a lawyer straight in the eyes for two hours and not to heed a damned word he says." In the interpretation of statutes and decisions there may be the need of the utmost subtlety ; but the result must always have a genuine meaning, and be more than a mere debating triumph. The conclusion is to be tested by that sense of reality which must be considered to have also guided the law-makers. Under this head, then, what is wanted is robust good sense, which is happily one of the main traditions of the British and American judicatures. We assume that former judges and legislatures were in possession of their wits, and, though the assumption may not always be warranted by facts, it is a sound working basis.

Closely allied to this attribute is another, which might be called the instinct for the spirit of the Common Law. That body of customs and principles which we know as the Common Law and revere as a most precious inheritance is like the British Constitution, an organic thing, the growth of which never ceases. Like the British Constitution, too, it is largely unwritten. Blackstone's great work is an essay on the subject rather than a digest. It is different with the Common Law of Scotland, which is largely enshrined in the works of the great institutional writers who are quoted in the Scottish courts to-day as if they had the validity of statutes— Stair in the seventeenth century, Erskine in the eighteenth, Bell in the early nineteenth. But in England and America the Common Law remains a more fluid thing, of which a man cannot be said to have a final knowledge,   .

but for the principles and spirit of which he may be said to have an instinct, a *flair*. The value of this hinterland of law is that it provides principles of interpretation, a spirit which informs the dry bones and gives them life. The greatest English and American judges have never been content with a mere blind stumbling from precedent to precedent. They have been architects, and have sought to combine the stones into an orderly and shapely building. They have been in a true sense philosophers, and have tried to subsume specific rules under a generic principle. You can see it in all our great judgments, from those of Hardwicke and Mansfield down through Willes and Blackburn to those of our own day. You can see it very conspicuously in the work of Story and John Marshall in the United States, who did not follow Jeremy Bentham's advice " to shut their ports against the Common Law as they would against the Plague."

IV

So much for the work of interpretation. But the judge has also the duty and privilege of construction. He can codify the law and he can also extend it. The former task is performed in those judgments which codify a particular branch. Part of the law of England has been codified by statutes, but a great deal more by elaborate judgments which, if they are the decision of the ultimate tribunal, have virtually the force of statutes. I need only refer, as an example, to the judgment of Jessel M. R. in *Pooley* v. *Driver*, which codified up to date the law of partnership. Lord Eldon is a good case of a judge whose particular type of intellect was specially fitted for this task. It is work which only a full mind and a very clear mind can successfully perform, and only the man with a high sense of public duty is likely to undertake.

Rarer, because infinitely more difficult, is the successful extension of the law. In theory a judge is there to interpret the common and the statute law, and not to make it ; but it was not always so. I am not going to weary you with an argument on that most interesting and obscure matter, the origin of legislative power—Sir Edward Coke's distinction, for example, between *jus dare* and *jus dicere*, and the early seventeenth century view that the Common Law was not mutable by King and Parliament. But I would remind you that in earlier times an Act passed by an English Parliament was merely a caption, a chapter-heading, an empty category, and that it was the business of the judges to provide the contents. The earliest Acts were based upon petitions presented to Parliament and were framed by the judges. After the Restoration we know that the judges habitually attended the sittings of the House of Lords for the purpose of helping in the legislative business, and especially of drafting bills. In a speech delivered by Lord Hardwicke on the Militia Bill in 1756 he said : " In old times almost all the laws which were designed to be public Acts and to continue as the standing laws of this country were first moved for, drawn up and passed in this House, where we had learned judges always attending and ready to give us their advice and assistance. From their knowledge and experience they must be allowed to be the best able to tell whether any grievance complained of proceeds from the non-execution of the laws in being, or whether it be of such a nature as may be redressed by a new law. . . . We have their assistance whereby we are enabled to draw up a new law in such a manner as to render it effectual and easy to understand. This is the reason why in former times we had very few laws passed in Parliament, and very seldom, if ever, a posterior law amending and explaining a former." The practice seems to have been continued up to the middle of the eighteenth century, but now it exists, so far as I know, only in the habit of referring bills to be drawn or settled by judges, where they are estate bills—that is to say, private bills for enlarging the powers of dealing with an estate under a particular family settlement. In Scotland, up to the Union, the judges were the real law-makers, after Parliament had given them a general instruction. You can print half a dozen of the old black-letter laws of Scotland on an octavo page ; the judges did the exposition of details. In Scotland, too, the judges have still the power of declaring that an old law has passed into desuetude and may be forgotten—a legislative privilege which is not enjoyed by their brothers in England.

But alike in England, in Scotland, and in America the Bench has a formative task which, when properly performed, is the highest of all judicial duties. The law, as I have said, should be regarded as an elastic tissue which clothes a growing body. That tissue, that garment, must fit exactly. If it is too tight it will split, and you will have revolution and lawlessness, as we have seen at various times in the history of this country when the law was allowed to become a strait waistcoat. If it is too loose, it will trip us up and impede our movements. Law, therefore, should not be too far behind, or too far ahead of, the growth of society.

It should coincide as nearly as possible with that growth.
So it is the judge's duty to be in touch with contemporary life, to be awake to the emergence of new facts
and forces, and to bring the new facts inside the circumference of law. Now and then statutes may be necessary, but the Common Law is a marvellously adaptive
thing, and it is wonderful what can be done with it by
one who understands it. The classic case, of course, is
Lord Mansfield. During his long tenure of the Chief
Justiceship of the King's Bench modern commercial
life in this country was beginning. The language was
novel, the facts were often new, but behind them lay the
same principles of contract and tort which had grown
up under Plantagenet and Tudor. Mansfield in a series
of masterly judgments created what we know to-day as
Commercial Law. An equally striking case is to be
found in American legal history. John Marshall, when
he began his great career as Chief Justice of the United
States, had the task of interpreting the Constitution
as a practical mechanism for the government of the
country. For the first time in history we have a judge
interpreting a written constitution, and in the fierce
party struggles of the America of his day it needed delicate and firm interpreting. By his famous judgments—
in the *Burr* case, when he dealt with the law of constructive treason, in *Marbury* v. *Madison*, when he
asserted the independence of the judiciary, in the
Dartmouth College case, when he not only established
the sanctity of public contracts but gave to American
development its strong bias towards individualism—he
did perhaps a greater work even than Mansfield. He
laid down not a new code of law, but the groundwork
of a new civilization.

V

We arrive at the last endowment of the great judge—an endowment without which the exercise of the others is apt to be handicapped—I mean the gift of lucid and graceful speech. Without lucidity a judgment will not be understood with that complete accuracy which is necessary in so exact a science as law, and without grace it will not be effectively remembered. Some very great judges have been clear enough, but they have lacked grace, and the result is that they have not had that influence on legal history which they deserved. Eldon is a case in point. He is probably the greatest equity judge, except Hardwicke, that ever lived, but I have yet to meet the man who can read him with pleasure. Take the case of *Wykham* v. *Wykham* (18 Ves. 415), which laid down the distinction between law and equity in the case of contracts—a masterly and epoch-making judgment, but as flat as ditch-water and as ponderous as a tombstone.

It is a fact, I think, that the greatest judges have been usually men of a wide general culture. Such were Hardwicke, Mansfield, Wensleydale, Selborne, Bowen ; such very notably in America was Story. There have been exceptions, such as Sir Edward Coke, but they go to prove the rule. Let it be remembered for the encouragement of classical scholars, that Lord Westbury, that ornament of Oxford, obtained his first chance at the Bar because of a brilliant extempore translation of a passage in Pindar at an Oxford *viva voce* examination. A wide culture will beyond doubt be of inestimable advantage to a man when he comes to the preparation of judgments, for no scholar, born with a love of good English, will content himself with the clumsy jargon which sometimes does duty for legal terminology. I am prepared to maintain that there is a surprising amount of fine literature in the Law Reports. Indeed, I am ready to assert that almost the best prose has been written by men who were not professional men of letters, and who therefore escaped the faded and weary mannerisms of the self-conscious litterateur. As an example I would point to the prose of Cromwell, of Abraham Lincoln, of a dozen explorers like Captain Scott and Captain Boyd Alexander, and of soldiers in the recent war like the Canadian general Sir Arthur Currie. It is the same with the great judges. Mansfield's prose has the massive dignity of the best Georgian manner. Bowen's is often as delicate and careful as an essay of Stevenson's. John Marshall was not, generally speaking, a master of style, as those who have tried to read his *Life of Washington* will bear witness. But he could rise at a great moment to a noble and restrained eloquence, as may be learned from his judgment in *M'Culloch* v. *Maryland*. I have sometimes had an idea of compiling a legal anthology of those judgments which are good literature as well as good law. It would be a fascinating book, and it would put most professional stylists to shame. There is only one rule for good prose, the rule which Newman and Huxley in their different ways enunciated and followed—to set down your exact, full, and precise meaning so lucidly and simply that no man can mistake it. That, and not flowers of rhetoric, has been the aim of the best judges, and small wonder that good prose has been the result.

I am prepared to maintain, too, that in the perfect judicial style there must be both wit and humour on occasion—humour, because unless a man have a sense of the preposterous contrasts of life he will not have the quick eye for reality and the mental perspective which we have postulated ; wit, because an argument is often best and most clearly put in those sharp antitheses which we call witty. There will be many examples of both in my anthology. Some of the finest, such as Lord Macnaghten's judgment in the *Gluckstein* case, are too familiar to quote. So are the best of Lord Bowen's. In looking about for an example which might be new to you I have gone to the Scottish Bench— to Lord Robertson, who succeeded Lord Watson, I think, in the year 1900, as the Scottish Lord of Appeal in the House of Lords. He was a brilliant politician, and was said to have been the only man of his time in the House of Commons whom Mr. Gladstone really feared. His political interests distracted his attention a good deal from the law, but when he chose he was an exceptionally able judge, and he was at all times the master of a perfect style. His manner must have been rather like Lord Westbury's, for he had a refined finicking accent and a dulcet voice. Here is an example of the very dry vintage of his wit. It is taken from his judgment in the case of *The Edinburgh Street Tramway Company* v. *The Lord Provost and Magistrates of Edinburgh* (21 R. 704). The question was as to the value of the tramway undertaking based on a calculation of past and future profits.

" The argument of the defenders was that ' past and future profits ' is merely ' profits ' writ large—for the reason, that time is exhaustively divided into past and future, and that the present is merely an imaginary line between the two. That is, of course, a profound and

impressive truth, but there are times and places for everything, and I should hardly have thought a Tramway Act
exactly the occasion which Parliament would choose for
teaching business men metaphysics unawares—more especially as this statute applies to England as well as to
Scotland."

VI

I have tried to sketch for you very roughly and
summarily what appear to me to be the main features
in that rare thing, the judicial temperament. It may
well seem a combination to which our fallible mortal
nature cannot often attain. My acquaintance with the
Law Reports was never more than perfunctory, and is
now patchy in the extreme, but I am prepared to argue
that at least a dozen of our judges in the past two
centuries have come very near realizing the ideal.
There are two presiding monarchs who have not, I
think, been surpassed—Hardwicke and Mansfield.
After them in England, on the Common Law side, I
should put Baron Parke (Lord Wensleydale) ; Willes,
Chief Justice of the Common Pleas ; Lord Blackburn ;
Lord Bowen ; and I have no hesitation in adding Lord
Halsbury. I once asked Lord Haldane for a corre-
sponding list on the Equity side, and he was clear that
after Hardwicke the list should be Lord Eldon ; Sir
William Grant, Master of the Rolls ; Lord Justice
James ; Sir George Jessel, M.R. ; and Lord Lindley.
If you want judgments as models, I suppose we may
take Hardwicke's *Garth* v. *Cotton* (which you will find
in White and Tudor's *Leading Cases in Equity*), which
no less an authority than Lord St. Leonards thought
the ablest ever delivered ; or, as an example of style,
Sir William Grant's judgment in *Purcell* v. *McNamara*

(14 Ves. 113). I would myself claim as an almost
perfect example the minority judgment of Lord Lindley
in the Scottish Free Church case. That case was one
in which a certain ecclesiastical bias was almost inevitable. I think that the judgment of the House of
Lords was wrong, but I am bound to say that there was
every justification for the majority going astray, since
there cannot have been many cases where the Bench
received less assistance from the Bar. You remember the
point of it. The question was whether the United Free
Church in altering certain ecclesiastical and doctrinal
tenets had forfeited endowments which had been given
while these tenets were held in their unchanged form.
Mr. Haldane—as he then was—led for the United Free
Church, and his argument fell into two parts—one
historical and the other philosophical. The historical
argument was simply that a Scottish church, looking
at the historical growth and the traditional conception
of a kirk in Scotland, must be assumed to have the
right to change its tenets within certain broad limits
and to retain its endowments, unless the instruments
creating such endowments contained specific words to
the contrary. To that argument I believe there was no
answer, and had it been really pressed, the court could
not have resisted it. But Mr. Haldane was not a historian, and he was much more interested in the philosophical argument which was based upon familiar Hegelian
formulas—that identity only exists through change and
difference, that a thing is only a thing because it is also
in some sense its opposite, and so forth. It was a remarkable piece of dialectic and not without a certain
validity, but it was an impossible argument to present
to a court of justice, and it had the most disastrous

effect upon various members of the House of Lords. One, I remember, became fatally confused between the philosophical term " antinomy " and the metal " antimony." Lord Halsbury's masculine intelligence dealt harshly with Mr. Haldane's metaphysics, and the court —wrongly, I think—decided against the United Free Church. It is all the more remarkable that the profound dissenting judgment of Lord Lindley should, in a chaotic atmosphere and with little assistance from counsel, have gone straight to the heart of an intricate subject.

VII

When Lord Westbury fell into disgrace he was replaced on the Woolsack by a virtuous but undistinguished ex-Lord Chancellor, Lord Cranworth. After the appointment he went to Windsor, and the story goes that Queen Victoria took Lady Cranworth for a walk on the terrace after dinner and, laying an affectionate hand on her arm, said, " My dear, do not recent events teach us how much wiser it is to be good than clever ? " Gentlemen, there is much more in that saying than a mere pious reflection, especially in relation to the Bench. Mere cleverness is an ineffective thing in most walks of life, and will certainly not by itself make a great judge. For that, intellect is not the only desideratum ; certain conspicuous gifts of character are demanded. Do you recall a passage in *Weir of Hermiston* where Stevenson speaks of the satisfactory life of a great lawyer ? " As he toiled into the night, he tasted deeply of recondite pleasures. To be wholly devoted to some intellectual exercise is to have succeeded in life ; and perhaps only in law and the higher mathematics may

this devotion be maintained, suffice to itself without
reaction, and find continual rewards without excitement." That is one side of the business—the easy,
happy exercise of the intellect among familiar material.
But there must be more if a man's work is to be a landmark in the history of Law. The Lord St. Leonards
type of judge cuts a considerable figure in the Reports ;
but, valuable as he is, he does not contribute greatly
to the living and organic growth of the Law. For
that, a man with a richer and more various nature is
needed, a man of a wider and deeper experience of human
life. It was a wise saying of the American Mr. Justice
Holmes that " the life of the law is not logic but experience." John Marshall was not a great scholar in
legal matters. His equipment could not for a moment
compare with the wide and profound book-learning of
Story. But his mind became a perfect weapon for
the judicial task because he never lost touch with the
realities of our common life. The great Chief Justice,
jogging in a gig along the sandy roads of North Carolina,
and after the day in court was done playing quoits with
the townsfolk behind the tavern, was in a better way of
judicial education than if he had burned the midnight
oil over his law books. And how much did not his
years as a soldier and a politician contribute to his
success ?

Dr. Johnson, you remember, angrily withdrew Mansfield from the category of mere lawyers. " Mansfield,"
he said, " was not a mere lawyer. When he came to
town he drank champagne with the wits ; he was the
friend of Pope." There is virtue in the distinction.
Mansfield was a scholar, a wit, a man of fashion, a
statesman who might on two occasions, if he had

chosen, have been Prime Minister of England ; and with all these things he was the greatest Chief Justice in our history.   I am inclined to think that to the higher types of mind and character success is open in any sphere, and that it is only the accident of fate which determines their final destination.   I believe that the greatest soldiers have also been great statesmen *in posse*, and that the statesman who steers a country through a crisis could also, with a different training, have led its armies to victory.   With the more exalted type of mind there is no specialization *ab origine*.   The greatest judge is one who might have been great in politics, in administration, in business, or in war.   Which is simply to say that a great judge must be also a great man.

STYLE AND JOURNALISM

STYLE AND JOURNALISM [1]

THE subject which I have chosen for my address this afternoon may sound, I fear, to some of you like a paradox. To many people journalism stands as the exact opposite of literature, and the manner of writing of journalists, which they unkindly call " journalese," as the antithesis of all that is meant by style. To such my title may seem rather of the "snakes in Iceland " type, like a monograph on the railway system of Spitzbergen, or on the grace and urbanity of the Soviet Government. I do not share this view, or I should not be addressing you to-day.

We need waste no time over a definition of style. Let us call it simply the exact and adequate expression in words of a writer's meaning. The business of a writer is to get the full content of his mind across the barrier of personality to the mind of his reader. If that content is trite and barren, the style will be trite and barren also. If it is subtle, the style must be subtle and delicate ; if it is charged with emotion and poetry and imagination, the style must reflect these qualities. It is easy to find writers who excel in rhetoric but fail in lucidity ; there are books, on the other hand, which are clearness itself, but which cannot stimulate or

[1] An address delivered to the School of Journalism in King's College, London, May 19, 1925.

move. The perfect workmanlike style will take on the colour of every mood of the writer's mind, as a clear lake reflects the colours of the sky. If you ask me for examples of perfect workmanlike style, I would take two nineteenth century writers—Thomas Huxley and John Henry Newman. We know from their own confession what they aimed at. They had no other purpose except to make their meaning infallibly clear to the world, and, whatever form that meaning might take, they succeeded. You will find in both passages of noble eloquence and sudden lightning flashes of imagination, but above all you will find a beautiful clarity, so that the dullest is never in doubt as to what they mean. I have called such a style workmanlike, and that is, I think, the proper word. It is like a finely-tempered blade, fit for any use its owner desires. That, and not the more fanciful graces, is, to my mind, the supreme merit of style, and it is the merit which the journalist above all men should strive after, for it is his business to write on every kind of subject and in many manners, and what he needs is not a fancy-dress trinket but a practical tool.

At one time in our history there existed what might be called a canon in style, so that all educated people wrote on a certain fairly high level. The history of English prose is a curious thing. It would be true to say that the late sixteenth and early seventeenth century saw the production of nobler prose than any other epoch in our literature. Then you had the Authorized Version of the Bible and Raleigh's *History of the World*; you had Jeremy Taylor and Bishop Hooker, and presently you had John Milton. Yet, at the very time when these masterpieces were being produced, the ordinary writing of English prose was in a parlous state. The common prose of the period was turgid, crabbed, and uncouth. It was still a weapon confined to the masters, and the plain man could only use it with difficulty. The truth is it was too stately a thing for human nature's daily task. A man could scarcely keep a diary or write letters to his lawyer or his wife in the style of Clarendon or Milton. It was Dryden who first made English prose easy and adaptable. You will see in his wonderful prefaces how its joints are slowly being loosened and suppled. At the end of the century and early in the eighteenth century English prose had become a handy thing—a thing not to be written elaborately like Latin elegiacs, but with a running pen, a thing which had much of the grace of the spoken word. Addison completed the process. He set his countrymen a standard eminently sensible and not too hard of attainment.

Now, notice that as soon as prose is simplified and relieved of the stiff gold brocade of the Elizabethans, journalism begins. You cannot write leading articles and essays and descriptive reports in the style of Jeremy Taylor or John Donne. All through the eighteenth century we have this excellent fixed normal English prose, a canon, as I have said, which every educated man adopted. If you look at the familiar letters which gentlefolk wrote to each other during that century you will find an extraordinarily high standard of clear, easy statement. It is a great thing to have a canon of this sort in carrying on our day-to-day life. The eighteenth century is like a healthy tableland. Its prose has not the soaring peaks of the century before, but it avoids the Elizabethan and Jacobean morasses.

I do not feel that to-day we possess such a canon. Our letters, when we write them at all and do not dictate them, have no doubt merits of their own, but it can scarcely be said that there is a standard of accomplishment below which no educated man or woman falls, and we all of us know very clever people who write abominably. In our literature to-day prose tends to follow a hundred different models, and since it has no canon and each writer desires to make his style the expression of his temperament, we get a great deal of writing which is careless, fantastic, shapeless, and, to my conservative mind, undeniably bad. A scientist may have conclusions of the first importance to expound, but he too often is incapable of writing clear English. A philosopher—well, how many philosophers to-day can write as Hume and Berkeley wrote ? Our historians have advanced in scholarship far beyond the Smolletts and Robertsons and Goldsmiths of the eighteenth century, but in how many cases is their learning obscured by their lack of skill in utterance ? I do not say that we have not excellent writers to-day, but I feel bound to maintain that education does not with us, as it did with the Augustans, presume a gift of vigorous and graceful prose.

If there is a modern canon it is to be sought, I think, in journalism. I believe that English journalism shows at the present moment a higher level of competence than it has ever shown before in our history. We may miss the grace of an Addison or the fiery vigour of a Hazlitt or a Cobbett, but for a body of clear, effective, and urbane prose our journalism need fear no comparison with the past. It is my business to read a good many books in different branches of literature, and I confess that I turn often with comfort from the freakish, stuttering, self-conscious rigmarole of too many modern litterateurs to the clean-cut, efficient prose of a newspaper article.

Whatever journalism lacks it does not lack style, but style in journalism has a specific meaning. It is not, or it should not be, the style of the essayist, the philosopher, the preacher, the historian. Good journalism should be what the French call a *causerie*; it should not be too formal; it should not always be finely dressed; it should have something of the ease and the spontaneity of the living voice. This, I think, applies to every branch of the journalist's profession, from a report or a descriptive article to a leader. The essential virtues of style for these purposes are that it should be clear, that it should be arresting, and that it should be well-bred. It should have in it that which attracts the reader's attention and conciliates his interest, and above all things its meaning should be unmistakable. I am not talking about those base occasions which now and then arise when a writer has to spin out an article in order to fill a certain space, or where an editor, being anxious not to commit himself, is deliberately obscure. I am talking about the profession at its best and most useful, where the aim is to interest and inform, or, it may be, to convince, the reader. For obvious reasons it would be an invidious thing for me to give you examples. But examples lie ready to your hand, and if you wish to find a canon of journalistic style—that undress style which is necessary for this particular task—you will find it almost any day in the columns of our great London and provincial dailies and our best weekly journals.

I am speaking to young men who look forward themselves to practising this profession. I have told you
that the profession possesses at the moment a large
number of admirable practitioners whose work you will
be well advised to study and follow. But I think it
would be more helpful if instead of enlarging upon the
good qualities of style in journalism I were to warn
you against certain dangers. For dangers there are,
pitfalls in style for the journalist quite different from
those which beset the path of the man of letters in his
library. The journalist is compelled to work fast ;
he is compelled to switch his mind from one subject to
another, and constantly to change his mood ; he has
to catch the attention of readers often as hurried as
himself ; he has to be clear and emphatic, and the
subject may scarcely permit of either clearness or
emphasis. Therefore he is in danger of falling into
vices which are, so to speak, the exaggeration of his
virtues. I propose, with your permission, to discuss a
few of these dangers with you in order that you may
beacon them and avoid them. They are perils which
to a large extent lie in wait for every writer, and I know
that they are faults of which I am constantly guilty
myself.

I

The first danger I would warn you against is that of
over-picturesqueness. Picturesqueness is of the essence
of good journalism, but it must be the picturesqueness
which is appropriate to the occasion. I have shrunk
from giving you a definition of style, but at this point
I can scarcely refrain from quoting a great master on
the subject. This is how Cicero defines the good

speaker : " That man has true eloquence who can deal summarily with small things, moderately with moderate matters, weightily with great matters ; who can adapt his oratory to the appropriate ends. Whatever his subject is he will speak becomingly on it—not meagrely when it is full-bodied, not meanly when it is great, not in one way when it demands another, but will keep his style equal and adequate to the subject." Over-picturesqueness sins against this first virtue of propriety, for the writing is too high-powered for the subject matter. You will find this vice particularly, I think, in political journalism. I remember that in 1906, when a Liberal Government first came into power after many years in opposition, Liberal journalists were inclined to model their style upon the Book of Revelation. The most trivial disputes were displayed as a battle between the followers of Light and Darkness, of Christ and anti-Christ. Every Liberal oration was a trumpet-call ; every Conservative rejoinder a muttering from the pit, or the babbling of an idiot. I think this was a vice of style rather than a perversity of mind, for I knew various worthy gentlemen who wrote like that, and they certainly did not take the melodramatic view of their country's politics which one might have gathered from their writings. In the same way, to take an instance from the other side, I have seen honest men write of Imperialism with a falsetto pitch which in the case of one reader, at any rate, produced a violent reaction against the very name of Empire. In the war there were correspondents who, in the search for picturesqueness, offended against every canon of taste and style, and made the unfortunate soldier blush when he read their articles. It is easy to see how the fault arises. A journalist desires to be vivid and arresting. If he really feels enthralled and stimulated by his subject he will probably write well. But if he is feeling tired and bored, he will fall into a mechanical picturesqueness full of outrageous adjectives and irrelevant colour.

It is a fault for two reasons. In the first place it produces a false impression, which is bad journalism. In the second place it will degrade the author's talent, so that he may render himself incapable for ever of true picturesqueness. If you write about a tea-party with a pen dipped in thunder and eclipse, what are you going to do when you have to describe some tremendous spectacle ? If you make a world-shaking crisis out of some trivial incident, how are you going to impress people when the real crisis comes ? If you are perpetually shouting " Wolf ! wolf ! " you will have no voice left when the genuine wolf-pack is after you. If you begin every third leading article with " England stands to-day at the parting of the ways," you have left no more shots in your locker. The picturesque, the apocalyptic, the sublime, should all be found in the journalist's equipment, but they must not be squandered ; they must be kept, to return to Cicero's word, for the " appropriate " occasion.

Now, gentlemen, I am inclined to think that in this respect we have very greatly improved within the last quarter of a century. I do not know if you remember the writings of George Steevens, who was the *Daily Mail* correspondent in Lord Kitchener's advance to Omdurman, and who died of fever two years later in Ladysmith. Steevens happened to be a sound scholar, and he raised war correspondence to a fine art. His book,

With Kitchener to Khartoum, is one of the best accounts of a campaign ever written, for the style is wholly appropriate. He saw clearly, and wrote down exactly what he saw with a minimum of adjectives, and the result is that the reader almost smells the powder. It is the same with other branches of journalism. Foolish picturesqueness should be left to the lower ranks of the politicians. It seems to me that there is a very high degree of moderation and balance and restraint in our better newspapers ; but if you want an example of the vice I recommend to you a little book of Matthew Arnold's called *Friendship's Garland*, published in 1871. At that time the *Daily Telegraph* was a very different paper from what it is to-day. It made a speciality of flamboyance, and there were certain journalists, now almost forgotten, like Hepworth Dixon and George Augustus Sala, who revelled in noisy, high-coloured prose. Against that mannerism Matthew Arnold directs his delicate satire. He praises it with his tongue in his cheek, as " blending the airy epicureanism of the *salons* of Augustus with the full-bodied gaiety of our English Cider-cellar." His friend, Leo Adolescens of the *Daily Telegraph*, gives us many examples of this style, and the Prussian exponent of *Geist*, Arminius, describes it as " middle-class Macaulayese." " I call it Macaulayese," he says, " because it has the same internal and external characteristics as Macaulay's style, the external characteristic being the hard metallic movement with nothing of the soft play of life, and the internal characteristic being a perpetual semblance of hitting the right nail on the head without the reality. And I call it middle-class, because it has these faults without the compensation of great studies and of conversance with great

affairs, by which Macaulay partly redeemed them."
To-day we put a higher value on Macaulay's style, I
think, than Matthew Arnold did, but he has accurately
described the vice to which I am directing your attention. He invents one magnificent example—a sentence
from an imaginary obituary in the *Daily Telegraph*.
" In the Garden of the Hesperides the inscrutable-eyed
Sphinx whispers, with half-parted lips, Mysteries more
than Eleusinian of the Happy Dead." You could not
get a better instance of false sublimity ; it sounds tremendous, but it is fudge.

II

The second fault I would warn you against is the
fault of slovenliness—a fault to which busy men, writing
often in a hurry, are peculiarly prone. It is not exactly
mistakes in plain grammar, like singular verbs and
plural nouns, or mistakes in the refinements of grammar,
like split infinitives and the use of " and which " without
a preceding relative (a mistake which, I may remark in
passing, you will find on almost every page of Thackeray). It is rather a steady undercurrent of inaccuracy,
a frequent misapprehension of the exact meaning of
certain nouns and adjectives, a perpetual lack of care
and precision. The most conspicuous case, of course,
is the mixture of metaphors. The classic ground for
this fault is, I fancy, the journalism of our Indian
Empire. There is the famous case of the gentleman
who, in reporting the death of a mother, declared that
" The hand that rocked the cradle has kicked the
bucket." We do not find anything as good as this in
our own papers, but I have often found a metaphoric
mixture, chiefly when the writer begins with a metaphor

and then has some parenthetical clause and forgets
before the end what exactly his metaphor was.

But that is a form of the fault which can be easily
guarded against. Far more insidious is the slightly
inaccurate use of familiar words. I have noticed in the
last fortnight in papers of the highest repute three
instances which I will give you. The first is the misuse
of the adverb " singularly." When I say that a man
has a "singular" gift I mean that he is the single solitary
man who possesses it. If I say that a football player
is singularly clever, I ought to mean that his cleverness
is unique and that nobody else has anything quite like
it. But you will find in our press to-day " singularly "
constantly used as if it meant only " in a high degree."
This pianist is singularly talented, that statesman is
singularly eloquent, when what is meant is that the
pianist is rather good, and the statesman has made
quite an effective speech. In the interests of the purity
of the English tongue let us protest against this misuse.
A second case is the phrase " it seems evident." As it
stands this is tautology. " It seems " and " it is
evident " have exactly the same meaning. What the
writer wants to say is that it " seems certain " or it
" seems likely,"—something quite different. A third
example is the use of " unique." Now, " unique " is
an absolute word admitting of no degrees of comparison;
it means that something is the only thing of its kind in
existence. You can say that Mount Everest is unique
in height ; you can say, if you like, that Mr. Baldwin
or Mr. Ramsay Macdonald is unique among modern
statesmen in virtue. But you cannot allow phrases like
" Mr. X. is a more unique performer than Mr. Y," when
you mean that he has more originality.

The worst offender, I think, is the word " literally."
When I say that a man was " literally shot to pieces "
I mean to convey that that was precisely what happened in the physical sense ; that the phrase is not
used, as it often is, metaphorically, about some spiritual
or social experience. And yet how often do we read that
" Mr. A. was literally stricken dumb," when the writer
does not mean that Mr. A. suffered an unpleasant
miracle, but that for a few moments he was at a loss for
a reply. The danger comes from the use of meta-
phorical phrases, usually from Shakespeare, which have
become so part of our casual speech that their meta-
phorical origin is forgotten. The other day I read in
a reputable newspaper, in a report of Parliamentary
proceedings, that the Government " literally escaped
by the skin of their teeth." I can only say that I wish
I had been there to see. My imagination boggles at
the picture of the Government beset by a horde of fiery
enemies intent upon their bodily destruction, and only
separated at one moment by less than the breadth of a
hair from death ; or another picture of Ministers vio-
lently assaulted in the face, and in their escape leaving
behind them some indescribably fragile dental covering.

III

The third vice is one which I am afraid is more
common to-day than in the past. We may call it the
vice of abstraction. The interest of the nineteenth
century in theological, philosophical, and scientific
problems brought into journalism a very large number
of abstract phrases, and it is hard to get them out again.
In our own day the development of the cult of psycho-

analysis has introduced a fresh set. Now the worst of abstract phrases is that they are ineffective and obscure. They are ineffective, because it is the concrete detail which really catches the reader's attention, and they are obscure because very often the words are incapable of a precise definition, and their use by writers is merely a cloak for looseness and confusion of thought and intellectual laziness. If you turn to the great English writers you will notice how a man like Edmund Burke, even when writing on some matter of abstract specula-tion, manages all the time to keep his style concrete, and, consequently, his thought clear. The best writing, both in poetry and prose, is full of particulars ; the worst is woolly and abstract. Now it is the special duty of the journalist who wishes to arrest his reader's attention to shun abstractions and vague philosophical phrases. He is not writing metaphysics, where there is a legitimate professional language. He is writing for the ordinary man. Let him, therefore, be chary about all kinds of spurious counters—" isms " and " ologies," inhibitions, complexes, repressions ; and let him say what he has to say in the simple and vivid language of our ordinary life. Unless your object is to avoid the law of libel do not say that a man has a " complex of misappropriation," but that he is a thief ; do not say that he " dabbles in terminological inexactitudes," but that he is a liar. Do not, I beseech you, turn the first sentence in the Scots Shorter Catechism, " Man's chief end is to glorify God," into " The supreme objective of humanity is to further the realization of the Absolute Will," which does not mean so much, if it means any-thing. The English language has a noble concreteness not to be paralleled, I think, by any other tongue, and it is our business to take advantage of what the gods have given us. I am inclined to think that more good writing has been spoiled by sudden lapses into abstraction than by any other fault of style.

IV

The fourth fault is a rather complicated one, which we may call jargon. Every profession tends to develop a speech of its own made up of a number of desiccated phrases which have come to be mere counters and have lost the freshness of the living language. Solicitors, for example, have their jargon, and since they very often do not really try to say what they mean, but simply fit a number of jargon phrases together, their letters are obscure and lead to trouble in the Law Courts. Business men—the great majority at any rate—have invented a very hideous and wooden jargon. Mr. Smith wants to tell Mr. Brown that he has received his letter and would like to talk to him about it. Instead of writing :

" DEAR SIR,—I have your letter of 27th April, and will come and see you about it next Monday at ten o'clock,"

he writes something like this :

" *Re* the above noted matter. We have received your esteemed communication of 27th inst., with regard to which there are certain points which occur to us as relative to the same. Our Mr. Smith will do himself the honour of waiting upon you on Monday, the 2nd prox., in the hope of elucidating certain particulars. It is understood that this letter and the action proposed are without prejudice between our good selves."

Now, that is simply rigmarole. It says nothing which could not have been said in two lines. I noticed the other day that a distinguished city magnate defended this style on the ground that business men had no time for literary tricks. But the trouble is that this kind of writing is full of literary tricks, only they are bad ones, and it is a shocking waste of time as well as an outrage on the King's English. Why are these strong, silent, overworked people so incredibly feeble and verbose in their epistolary style?

You will find, as I have said, jargon in every profession. It is exceedingly bad in Government departments, as any one will admit who has had a controversy with the authorities of the Inland Revenue. It is rampant in blue books and Government reports. It is very common in the Army, as those of you who served in the late war will remember. Jargon is not only incapable of honest brevity, but it is utterly lacking in clearness. The reader has often to think many times before he can understand what the writer is driving at. Journalism, I fear, has developed a jargon of its own, and that jargon is properly called " journalese." It is a specially flagrant vice in journalism, for lawyers and business men and Government officials are not professionally engaged in the use of words, whereas it is the journalist's own craft, and he ought to respect his weapons.

The essence of journalistic jargon is that it uses phrases which may at one time have been fresh and vivid, but which are so staled by long use that all their vigour has departed. The journalist, too, seems to have an affection for a certain kind of word which he regards as a " boss " word, as Mr. Pinkerton in *The*

Wrecker regarded the word "hebdomadary," and drags it in on every possible occasion. Now it is very dangerous to be dogmatic about new words and phrases. If you turn up any volume of memoirs written at the end of the eighteenth or early in the nineteenth century you will find bitter complaints of new words which were creeping into use, and which the complainants thought ugly and vulgar. These words to-day are probably an honourable part of the English language. The young gentlemen from the Universities must have thought Shakespeare a very vulgar innovator in his language, but what would English literature be without Shakespeare's colossal novelties? Therefore I am not going to complain about certain journalistic words, even though personally I do not like them, words such as " glimpse " and " sense," used as verbs. But we are entitled to complain if words are used which have no justification on the ground of convenience, and which are simply cumbrous pedantries, when plain, simple English would be far better. I beseech you, gentlemen, do not say " elect " when you can say " choose," or " actualities " when you mean " facts," and under no circumstances use such hideous and inaccurate Latinisms as " eventuate " and " transpire."

But I think the worst form of jargon is the use of old, stale quotations and echoes of old, stale jokes. The man who first said that somebody was " of the male persuasion " said something funny, but to constantly repeat it gets on one's nerves. Why must every foundation be " well and truly laid " ? Why must we call women " the softer sex " ? Why must we never speak of the body except as " the human form divine " ? Why must we have constant Latin tags, such as *coram*

populo and *cui bono* ? the latter, by the way, nearly
always used incorrectly. Why are we so shadowed
by words like " adumbrate " ? Why are we so obsessed
with the word " obsess " ? Why must any novel incident " give us furiously to think " ? Why, instead of
saying " no," must we say " the answer is in the negative " ? Why must we declare that " the psychological
moment " has come, when we merely mean that there
is a good chance ? Why, above all, must we cumber up
our writing with phrases like " in the case of," " with
regard to," " in these respects," " in such circumstances," and all that adipose tissue of style ? It is a
bad fault in journalism and should be carefully guarded
against ; but it is the vice of many writers who have
not the excuse of a busy journalist. I opened at random
the other day a book of dispatches from an Indian
Viceroy. There was a sentence in which what he meant
to say was, " I am not clear about the causes of the
frontier trouble." What he did say was, " With regard
to the origins of the circumstances which have eventuated
in the unrest in North-West India, I am not yet in a
position to pronounce upon their material significance."
There, in the case of a man of great ability, you have
jargon at its worst.

V

The fifth fault I would have you avoid turns upon
the misuse of similes and synonyms. It is not that these
similes and synonyms are inaccurately used, but that
there is too much of them. You all remember the old-
fashioned sporting journalism, for which I have a certain
weakness. You remember how a prize fight used to be
described. Blood was never blood, but " claret," or

" manly ichor." The mouth was the " box of ivories,"
the stomach the " bread basket," and so on. You
remember the old descriptions of a cricket match, when
the sun was always " Old Sol," and the rain always
" Jupiter Pluvius," and a bat " the willow." I confess
to a sentimental liking for that noisy, preposterous, robust
mannerism, and when it was used by scholars, as it
used to be in the old *Pink 'Un* in the days of Mr. John
Corlett, it was often extraordinarily effective. But it
is not to be recommended as a manner for general use ;
it is too restless ; and when it is applied to other subjects
than sport it is apt to be comic. To-day it survives
chiefly in the passion for unnecessary variation. Up to
a point the instinct is sound. If you are writing about
a well-known man it is awkward to be always repeating
his name. It is legitimate enough in writing about Mr.
Baldwin to call him sometimes " Mr. Baldwin " and
sometimes " The Prime Minister," and sometimes " the
head of the British Government." But if you go on to
describe him also as the " sturdy Worcestershire squire,"
or, as I have seen it done, " our modern Sir Roger de
Coverley," or " that celebrated devotee of my Lady
Nicotine," you become ridiculous. Shakespeare seems
to suffer specially from this trick. How often do we
find him in one short column called " immortal Will,"
or " our greatest dramatist," or " the swan of Avon,"
and given as many endearing epithets as if he were a
pet lamb ?

Now mark how this fault arises. Its source is a
sound instinct : the fear of being clumsy and banal.
But there is no greater clumsiness than is to be found in
these far-fetched synonyms, and no worse banality than
this coyness about a plain name. Sir Arthur Quiller-

Couch has a delightful passage in one of his books, describing an undergraduate's essay on Byron. " My undergraduate," he says, " has a blushing sense that to call Byron Byron twice on one page is indelicate. So Byron, after starting bravely as Byron, in the second sentence turns into ' that great but unequal poet,' and thenceforward I have as much trouble with Byron as ever Telemachus with Proteus to hold and pin him back to his proper self. Half-way down the page he becomes ' the gloomy master of Newstead ': overleaf he is reincarnated into ' the meteoric darling of society ': and so proceeds through successive avatars—' this arch-rebel,' ' the author of *Childe Harold*,' ' the apostle of scorn,' ' the ex-Harrovian, proud, but abnormally sensitive of his club-foot,' ' the martyr of Missolonghi,' ' the pageant-monger of a bleeding heart.' " This kind of thing is as laborious to read as to write, for instead of taking a straight course it staggers from one side of the road to the other. It is like George Meredith's " homing drunkard," incapable of taking two steps in a straight line.

VI

With this I close my Chamber of Horrors. There are many more pitfalls in writing, worse, perhaps, than any I have mentioned—pitfalls of preciosity and affectation ; but these are more likely to beset the leisured man of letters than the busy journalist. The five rocks I have beaconed are those that lie more directly in the course of those whom I am addressing to-day. If we want to give them names let us call them *false picturesqueness*, *slovenliness*, *abstractness*, *jargon*, and *unnecessary variation*.

Now, to make my meaning clear I want to read to you a specimen of good, competent prose, and then to see how it can be spoiled by these various faults I have mentioned. I had thought of taking a passage from the *Pilgrim's Progress*, but there is a slight archaism in Bunyan's style which makes it unsuitable for purposes of comparison. I will take instead a passage from Matthew Arnold. It is not great prose, but it is good prose, honest, workmanlike stuff, conveying exactly what the writer means, and it deals with the kind of topic on which many of you will some day be called upon to write. Its subject is the relation of knowledge of life to poetry, as shown in the contrast between Byron and Goethe :

" Every one can see that a poet ought to know life and the world before dealing with them in poetry ; and, life and the world being in modern times very complex things, the creation of a modern poet, to be worth much, implies a great critical effort behind it ; else it must be a comparatively poor, barren, and short-lived affair. This is why Byron's poetry had so little endurance in it, and Goethe's so much ; both Byron and Goethe had a great productive power, but Goethe's was nourished by a great critical effort providing the true materials for it, and Byron's was not ; Goethe knew life and the world, the poet's necessary subjects, much more comprehensively and thoroughly than Byron. He knew a great deal more of them, and he knew them much more as they really are."

Now let us see how this would be handled in the *false picturesque* style :

" Before a poet dips his pens in ink he should have fleshed his sword in the battle of life ; he cannot retire to his singing bower save with the dust of the arena upon him.

He must have felt the beating of the deep heart of humanity, if the infinite future is to pulsate in his music. The true Hesperides cannot be attained save by an Odyssey more stern than that of Ulysses through the cities and the islands of men, and among the tempest-tossed seas of reality. Byron wrapped himself in his singing mantle and coldly withdrew from the mêlée of common life ; Goethe kept his place in the ranks, shared their hopes and fears, and through humility and discipline attained that beauty which never falls to those who avert their faces from truth. The proud inward-turning eyes of the one dwelt on the narrow orbit of his emotions ; the calm, clear gaze of the other had all life and eternity for its prospect. It is but a hothouse beauty which draws no nurture from the rude winds and the stony soil of the workaday world."

Not perhaps so bad of its kind, but unfortunately it is the wrong kind for this particular topic. Matthew Arnold's plain prose makes the point far more gracefully and clearly.

Now for the second, the *slovenly* :

" It is a truism that a poet should know life before he can write of it ; if he is to reproduce it in his work he must literally be immersed in its tides. If he is forgetful of this truth his work will be singularly poor and uniquely barren. Byron forgot it and it seems evident that his fame is already passing ; Goethe remembered it and so advances from strength to strength. Both writers had the impulse of genius, but Goethe's was fed by thought and watered by knowledge, whereas Byron's was beating its wings in the void."

There you have a riot of slovenliness—the wrong use of " literally " and " singularly " and " uniquely," the tautology of " it seems evident," and the mixture of metaphors at the close.

The third fault, you remember, was *abstractness*. Here is Matthew Arnold in that manner :

" It is obvious that the poet must have an objective sense of reality before he can attain to subjective inspiration, and owing to the complexity and involution of the raw material of his art this knowledge must be quantitatively large and qualitatively profound. Byron and Goethe both began with the primal impulse to create, but Byron's universe of comprehension was narrow and barren and unrelated, whereas Goethe subsumed into his a rich manifold of concrete experience. Not only was this manifold far richer in the case of the German than of the English poet, but it was more highly differentiated, and constituted a more organic part of his intellectual outlook."

It should be noted that in one way that is tolerable prose, since the abstract terms are accurately used and it is reasonably succinct. It would pass in a work of philosophy, but it will not do for journalism, since to nine people out of ten it would be unintelligible. The point can be better made in simpler language.

The fourth fault was *jargon*. Here is Matthew Arnold in the kind of jargon we call " journalese."

" It is the business of a poet to glimpse the immensity of the world and sense the complexity of life, and not to be over-obsessed by his personal outlook. Behold the contrast between Byron and Goethe. The Englishman habitually visualized his own narrow soul ; the German transcended his *ego* so that the world materialized for him. That is the true inwardness of Goethe's greatness, and it gives us furiously to think. In respect of life Byron elected to confine himself to those aspects which flattered his own vanity ; with regard to the other, Goethe took, in the great words of Lord Bacon, ' all knowledge for his province.' The consequence is that while the one is to-day little more

than a chimera *bombinans in vacuo*, the other still with a
large gesture lays his spell upon all who would explore the
avenues of the future. His vision of reality is at once
wider and more authentic and essential."

That is jargon triumphant: worn *clichés* like "obsessed," "visualized," "true inwardness," "gives us
furiously to think," "authentic," "essential"—the
trite quotation from Bacon (who is miscalled)—needless Latinisms like "*ego*" and "*bombinans in vacuo*"
—stale or ugly modern usages like "glimpse," "sense,"
"elected," "gesture," "explore."

Last, I give you Matthew Arnold in the style of
elegant variation. This example sticks very closely to
his text :

" Every one can see that a poet should know life and the
world before he tunes his lyre, and since humanity and the
universe are in these strenuous days matters of some
complexity the work of a modern bard must have behind
it a wide dialectic if it is not soon to be a withered rose
in the garden of the Muses. That is why the poetic web
of Byron, as contrasted with that of Goethe, has so little
of the stuff of endurance. The Pilgrim of the Ages,
equally with the Sage of Weimar, had a strong creative
impulse ; but the German had the ministering angels of
knowledge to bring him largesse, and the Anglo-Saxon
was without such celestial visitants. The Teutonic master
knew life and the world, which are the raw materials of
poetry, far more fully and truly than the British aristocrat."

That is how they do it. A " poet " is, of course, also
a " bard "; his work is " tuning the lyre," or " a rose in
a garden of the Muses," or a " poetic web "; Goethe is
the "Sage of Weimar," the "German," and the "Teutonic
master," Byron the "Pilgrim of the Ages," the "Anglo-
Saxon," and the " British aristocrat."

VII

I would repeat in conclusion what is the golden rule for all writing, whether it be the work of journalist or poet, philosopher or historian. It is to put into words your full and exact meaning as simply as possible. If your meaning is intricate, imaginative, sublime, or merely prosaic, the style in which you write must in each case be appropriate—in other words, it must fully express it. But I would add this warning : before you can apply that rule you must have a meaning to convey. He who has nothing to say may be gifted by Providence with the tongues of men and of angels and yet will produce indifferent matter. I am inclined to explain the merits of the prose of men of action not only by the fact that they have not staled their minds by constant writing, but also because they never take a pen in hand except when they have something vital to say. They always mean a great deal, and that meaning seems to find the appropriate words.

I have tried to make a few suggestions to you which may be helpful in your training for your future profession. That profession is one for which I have a strong respect. It is a profession which is daily becoming of greater social and political importance. It is a profession, too, which I think possesses a very high standard of responsibility and honour. A good journalist is and must be full of loyalties. He has his duty to his country, to his paper, to the traditions of his craft. To these duties and loyalties I suggest that you add another—a scrupulous regard for what is one of the most sacred possessions of our people, the English language and the great canons of our English literature.

XI

CERTAIN POETS

CERTAIN POETS

I

SCOTS VERNACULAR POETRY [1]

THE Teutonic speech of Northern England was brought into Scotland by the first Anglian settlers, and acquired throughout the succeeding centuries certain minor but clearly marked peculiarities. When Scots literature begins, towards the close of the fourteenth century, it is written in a tongue substantially the same as the Northern dialect of Early English, which was the speech current north of the Humber. Gradually a literary language was formed, akin to, but not the same as, the spoken tongue, and this literary language was influenced by Chaucer and the poets of the South. But presently the Midland dialect became the only literary language in England, and the Northern dialect drew further away from it and followed a path of its own. The early Scots writers, like Barbour and Wyntoun, wrote what was virtually Northern English. The *Kingis Quair* of James I., though written originally in Southern English, was northernized by the copyists ; Henryson's language was little affected by the south ; then, as the Middle Scots period develops, we find Dunbar and Gawain Douglas

[1] Introduction to *The Northern Muse: An Anthology of Scots Vernacular Poetry*, Nelson, 1924.

261

and Sir David Lyndsay using a language of their own
—Northern English in stock, with a slight French element, and a strong kinship with the spoken tongue of the
Lowlands, which had developed its own idiosyncrasies.
But to every Scots writer, however robust his patriotism,
his speech was " English," [1] and Dunbar calls Chaucer "of
our Inglisch all the lycht." [2] Gawain Douglas, indeed,
claims to be a " Scottis " and not an " Inglis " poet,
but he confessed himself forced to use some " Sudroun "
words, [3] and his work, though it accepts more from the
spoken vernacular, is in the same tradition as that of
the other " makars," so that Lyndsay could speak of
him as " in our Inglis rethorick the rose." A stout
Scots nationalist like Hume of Godscroft, who lived at
the close of the sixteenth century, might maintain that
he wrote his Scottish mother-tongue, and that he had
" ever accounted it a mean study to learn to read or
speak English . . . esteeming it but a dialect of our
own, and that (perhaps) more corrupt." [4] But his claim
was a mere juggling with words.

Perhaps the process might be thus summarily and
broadly stated. The Scots speech was in its beginnings
the Northern dialect of English, which, as a spoken
tongue, soon acquired minor local differences. When it
came to be written, it was the language of Northern
England, and, though influenced to some extent by
the South, it remained Northern. It was a literary

---

[1] *Cf.* the *Wallace* (IX. 295–297) of Thomas de Longueville :

> " Lykly he was, manlik of countenance,
> Lik to the Scottis be mekill governance,
> Saiff off his tong, for Inglis had he nane."

[2] *The Golden Targe.*
[3] Prologue to *Eneados*, Book I.
[4] Preface to the *History of the Houses of Douglas and Angus,* 1644.

speech, coloured by French and Latin, but it kept its affinities with the spoken vernacular and borrowed from it, being perhaps not much further removed from it than any book language is from that spoken in street and ale-house. As the Midland dialect became the literary language of England, Scots preserved its Northern quality and drew farther apart, developing powers and beauties of its own, though much clogged by an imperfect assimilation of its borrowings. It called itself English, but it was a substantive national speech, and its literature was a national literature, close enough to the common people to be intelligible to them, and yet capable of treating all themes from the homeliest to the highest. Had circumstances been different Scots might have developed into a true world-speech, " perhaps," as Mr. Henderson says, " more than rivalling literary English in fertility of idioms, and in wealth, beauty, and efficacy of diction," or Southern and Northern might have united in one majestic stream.

But the sixteenth century brought a sharp fissure. The chief disruptive agent was the Reformation, which in Scotland not only involved a more violent breach with the past than elsewhere, but put secular literature under a ban and cut at the root of vernacular art and song. It led to a severance with France and a closer contact with England. It made the chief reading of Scotland the Bible—in English ; it gave her the metrical Psalms—in English ; and its great protagonists, like John Knox, had so many English affiliations that they were accused by their enemies of being " triple traitoris quha . . . knappis suddrone." [1] The making of verse ceased to be a pastime of people strongly troubled about

[1] John Hamilton's *Catholik Traictise*, 1581.

their souls, and the few who still practised the art turned, like the poets of the *Deliciæ Poetarum Scotorum*, to Latin, or, like Drummond of Hawthornden, Aytoun, and Alexander, to the courtly muse of Edmund Spenser. The tongue which was spoken at kirk and market went out of literature for a century and more, and when it returned it was no longer as a national speech, but as a modish exercise. Politics, theology, a little law, and less history held the boards in seventeenth century Scotland, and their language was for the best part an ungainly English.

There was a revival early in the eighteenth century at the hands of Allan Ramsay, but its motive was antiquarian. The very men who laboured to expunge all Scotticisms from their prose and polished their Augustan couplets as their serious contribution to letters, turned a curious eye back to their own sixteenth century, and Ramsay's *Tea-Table Miscellany* and *Ever Green* were the consequence. We owe much to this antiquarian interest, for it preserved the old poetry when it was in imminent danger of perishing. Thomson's *Orpheus Caledonius* appeared in 1725 ; and following on the publication of Bishop Percy's *Reliques* came a flood of invaluable miscellanies, such as Herd's *Ancient and Modern Scots Songs* (1769), Pinkerton's two volumes of Ballads (1781 and 1783), Johnson's *Musical Museum* (1787), culminating in Sir Walter Scott's great *Minstrelsy of the Scottish Border* (1802–3). The vernacular had become a book tongue to be studied and annotated ; but when its students had anything to say, they said it in that English which was now the common speech of the literate from Devon to Aberdeen.

But Scots had one season of flowering left to it so

splendid that it is hard to believe that the blossoms were
the product of artificial tending and not the indigenous
growth of the fields. Burns is by universal admission
one of the most natural of poets, but he used a language
which was, even in his own day, largely exotic. His
Scots was not the living speech of his countrymen, like
the English of Shelley, and—in the main—the Scots of
Dunbar ; it was a literary language subtly blended from
the old " makars " and the refrains of folk poetry, much
tinctured with the special dialect of Ayrshire, and with
a solid foundation of English, accented *more Boreali.*
No Scot in the later eighteenth century, whether in
Poosie Nansie's or elsewhere, spoke exactly as Burns
wrote. Perhaps the plain speech of a people can never
be the language of poetry, but a speech so limited and
specialized as the spoken vernacular of eighteenth century
Scotland could scarcely suffice for the needs of a great
poet. Burns, as he was bound to be, was retrospective and
antiquarian in his syntax and vocabulary. He created
a noble poetic diction, but it was a creation, not the
reproduction of a speech still in the ears of men.

A century and a half have passed since Burns wrote,
and the vernacular, confined to an ever-narrowing province, has suffered a further detrition. Old words and
constructions have lapsed from use ; modes of speech
which were current so late as thirty years ago among
the shepherds of Ettrick and Galloway are scarcely intelligible to their successors ; in the towns the patois
bids fair to become merely a broadened and dilapidated
English ; and though the dwellers north of Tweed will
be eternally distinguishable from their neighbours by
certain idiosyncrasies of speech, these idiosyncrasies
will be of voice and accent, and not of language. The

Scots vernacular ceased in the sixteenth century to be a language in the full sense, capable of being used on all varieties of theme, and was confined to the rustic and the parochial ; capable, indeed, in the hands of a master of sounding the depths of the human heart, but ill suited to the infinite variety of human life. Even from this narrowed orbit it has fallen, and is now little more than a robust rendering of colloquial English. The literary Scots which Burns wrote is more than ever a literary tongue, far removed from any speech in common use. It is understood by many, not because it is in their ears from hearing, but because it is in their memories from reading. To restore the Scots vernacular is beyond the power of any Act of Parliament, because the life on which it depended has gone. Thirty years ago I learned in the Tweedside glens to talk a Scots which was then the speech of a people secluded from the modern world ; to-day if I spoke it at a Tweeddale clipping I should find only a few old men to understand me. Scots can survive only as a book-tongue, and it is to that purpose that I would bespeak the efforts of my countrymen. The knowledge of the book-tongue is still fairly common, and if, in the mill of a standardized education, it should ever be crushed out, we shall lose the power of appreciating not only the " makars," but the best of the Ballads, Burns, and Sir Walter Scott— that part of our literary heritage which is most intimately and triumphantly our own.

It follows that the Scots poets since Burns have been retrospective, as he was. They are all of them, from the minor bards of *Whistle Binkie* to Stevenson and Mrs. Jacob and Mr. Charles Murray, exponents of a literary convention and not singers in the speech of

the common day. That is not to say that their art is
not fresh and spontaneous, for art may work through
conventions and yet be free. Poetry, composed with
infinite pains from a thousand echoes, may have the
sound of the natural voice, and to this virtue I think
some of our modern Scots verse attains. It is always
an exercise, the fruit of care and scholarship, and since
the literary tongue is so nobly pedigreed, it will preserve (so long as it has an audience to understand it)
a flavour and a grace which make it the fittest medium
for a Scot to express certain moods and longings. It
will be least successful when it is too antiquarian and
becomes a mere clot of coagulated dialect, or when it
attempts to reproduce phonetically a spoken word which
is too disintegrated for literature. It must always be
in a sense a *pastiche*, but that is not inimical to artistic
excellence. Nevertheless—let us regretfully face the fact
—the *pastiche* is not a growth of enduring vitality, and
it has the further drawback that its appeal is circum-
scribed owing to the lack of any canon of vernacular
Scots. Every shire has its variant. If we call Sir
Walter Scott's version the classic standard, what are we
to make of Burns ? And if the Border speech is metropolitan, is Mr. Charles Murray provincial ?

There is a sentence in a letter of Burns to George
Thomson [1] which seems to me to point a way to the true
future of Scots in our literature. " There is a *naïveté*,"
he wrote, " a pastoral simplicity in a slight admixture
of Scots words and phraseology which is more in unison
—at least to my taste, and, I would add, to any genuine
Caledonian taste—with the simple pathos or rustic

---

[1] January 26, 1793. I owe the quotation to Mr. Gregory Smith's
Scottish Literature.

sprightliness of our native music, than any English verses whatever." He was speaking only of songs to be set to old airs, but the words have a wider application. It is to be noted that in some of the greatest masterpieces of our tongue, in the Ballads, in Burns's "Ae Fond Kiss," in Scott throughout—in "Proud Maisie," in "Wandering Willie's Tale," in the talk of Jeanie Deans—the dialect is never emphasized; only a word here and there provides a Northern tone. I can imagine a Scottish literature of both verse and prose based on this "slight admixture," a literature which should be, in Mr. Gregory Smith's admirable phrase, "a delicate colouring of standard English with Northern tints." In such work the drawbacks of the *pastiche* would disappear; because of its Northern colouring it would provide the means for an expression of the racial temperament, and because it was also English, and one of the great world-speeches, no limits would be set to its range and appeal.

From what has been written it follows that Scots poetry after the sixteenth century has not the width and variety of a national literature, covering all the moods of life and thought. Judged by his scope, Dunbar is its greatest figure. He has been differently estimated; Mr. Russell Lowell thought him a bore— "He who is national enough to like thistles may browse there to his heart's content"; Mr. Andrew Lang was tepid in his praise; Sir Walter Scott, on the other hand, thought him the greatest Scots poet before Burns; and the friends of the late W. P. Ker will remember with what gusto he used to declare, "Dunbar is *my* poet." To me he seems to rank with the Ballads, Burns, and

the Waverley Novels as one of the four of Scotland's
main contributions to letters.   In any case it will not
be disputed that the " makars " alone essayed and succeeded in the grand manner—alone attempted (with
varying success) the full circle of poetic material. Since
their day vernacular poetry has had its wings clipped,
and though it has soared high the latitude of its flights
has shrunk.

Defects have followed from this circumscription of
area, this absorption in too narrow a world.   The most
notable is a certain provincialism of theme, which is
always in danger of degenerating into a provincialism
of thought.   Scots poetry is apt to be self-absorbed, to
become the scrupulous chronicle of small beer, to lack
the long perspective and the " high translunary things "
of greater art.

> " Tiny pleasures occupy the place
> Of glories and of duties : as the feet
> Of fabled fairies, when the sun goes down,
> Trip o'er the grass where wrestlers strove by day."

This in itself is no blemish, and, indeed, a confined outlook could scarcely have been avoided in the literature
of a speech diverted from the larger uses of life and forced
back upon one class and environment.   But it means
that it does not enter for the greater contests of the
Muses, since a cameoist can never be a Pheidias, or a
Teniers a Rembrandt.

From this inevitable provincialism spring two faults
which are the prime weaknesses of Scots verse.   One is
a distressing facility, a preference for easy cadences and
trite epithets and tedious jingles, a lack of the classic
reticence and discipline.   Burns is a supreme example

to the contrary, and he remains a miracle in the Scots tradition. He has the sureness and the rightness of the antique, but much Scots verse is marred by a cheap glibness, an admiration for the third or fourth best, which is due to the lack of a strong artistic canon. It is a defect which is found in popular songs and popular hymns, the price which poetry must pay for popular handling. Scott said that a " vile sixpenny planet " looked in at the window when James Hogg was born, and that planet has not lost its baneful influence. The second defect is sentimentality, which is a preference for the inferior in feeling as the other is a preference for the inferior in form. A study of *Whistle Binkie* and the immense body of minor Scots verse in the last century shows us writers painfully at ease in Zion, who gloat over domestic sentiment till the charm has gone, who harp on obvious pathos till the last trace of the pathetic vanishes, who make so crude a frontal attack upon the emotions that the emotions are left inviolate. Whether it be children, or lost love, or death, or any other of the high matters of poetry, there is the same gross pawing which rubs off the delicate bloom. Heaven is as frequent and as foolish a counter in such verse as in bad hymns, and there is a perpetual saccharine sweetness which quickly cloys. Instead of Burns's " stalk of carle hemp," there seems to be in such writers a stalk of coarse barley sugar.

The misfortune is that these faults are found not only in trumpery verse, but in work of real and often of high merit. Burns is free from them, but they are rampant in Hogg, Tannahill, Allan Cunningham, and most of their successors. They are the result of the provincialism into which the vernacular speech fell, and the consequent "in-breeding" of vernacular literature. But the same cause has produced qualities which may well be held to redress the balance. They are qualities, too, which belong to the whole literature from Henryson to our own day. Vernacular poetry is in a peculiar degree the reflex of the Scots character, and, like that character, combines within itself startling anomalies. It has on one side a hardy and joyous realism, a gusto for close detail, a shrewd observing intimacy with the natural world. Even in conventional work there will come pieces of sharp concrete experience which give it a rude life, and at the best there is a constant sense of the three dimensions of space, of men and women moving in a world riotously alive. The other side is within hearing of the horns of Elfland—a paradox from the point of view of art, but complementary when seen in relation to the national character, which is founded on these opposites. Romance is always at call, an airy, diaphanous romance, so that Scots poetry is like some cathedral of the Middle Ages, with peasants gossiping in the nave and the devout at prayer in side chapels, carved grotesques adjacent to stained-glass saints, and beams of heavenly light stealing through the brooding upper darkness. The Hogg of the *Shepherd's Calendar* can also claim with justice to be a "king of the mountain and the fairy school"; if a "vile sixpenny planet" presided at his birth, so did the dancing star under which Beatrice was born. The combination is found in every literature, but in Scots the transition from the commonplace to the fantastic and back again is especially easy, since each mood has its source deep in the history and character of the race. Romance in the North has always some salt of the pedestrian, and the most prosaic house of life has casements opening upon fairy seas.

II

MORRIS AND ROSSETTI

It is a solemn business to take stock of the idols which once adorned our boyish Hall of the Muses. Some which twenty-five years ago stood in the outer courts we would now move into the *penetralia* ; some would suffer the reverse order of change ; as to others, we wonder how they ever got there at all. Yet, on the whole, in mine I find no very great displacement, and two poets, who even a quarter of a century ago seemed to " date " and who belonged professedly to a " movement " which has long ago spent its strength, seem to me, in re-reading them, to have lost little of their spell.

Few figures more attractive and more individual than William Morris are to be met with in literary history. He had a noble courage, untiring industry, zest for a thousand things in life, and a constant tenderness for weakness and suffering. But his humanity was not of the quickly communicable sort which is needed in the life of politics ; and though he led a busy practical existence, its true stages are to be found in his mind. Swinburne once said of him acutely that he was always more really inspired by literature than by life. In essence he was first a dreamer and then a craftsman ; he walked steadfastly all his days in the direction of his dreams, and his many crafts were only broken lights from the fire of idealism which he nourished within him. Letters were the chief of his crafts, and amid his many businesses he found time for the production of a great mass of verse and prose. At the age of twenty-four he published *The Defence of Guenevere*, the finest fruit of that looking back upon mediævalism which was then the Oxford fashion. In 1867 came *The Life and Death of Jason*, the story of the Golden Fleece ; the invocation is addressed to Chaucer, and there is some attempt at the Chaucerian manner. *The Earthly Paradise* appeared in four volumes between 1868 and 1870—twenty-four tales, half from classical and half from romantic sources, told in a strange land in the West where Northern adventurers find a forgotten colony of Greece. In 1873 he published *Love is Enough*, an elaborately constructed mystery play, and two years later a verse translation of the *Æneid*. Meantime he had found a new inspiration in the Icelandic sagas, and his *Sigurd the Volsung*, which appeared in 1876, re-told one of the greatest of the world's stories in splendid anapæsts. The saga influence was exemplified in the series of prose translations and prose tales which followed. The remainder of his poetic achievement is to be found in his translations of the *Odyssey* and of *Beowulf*, in his *Poems by the Way* (1891), and in the stirring songs which he wrote for his Socialist comrades.

Morris's poetry seems to me to fall into three classes. First in time, and first, too, in perfection of form, come the pieces in *The Defence of Guenevere*. That book inaugurated an epoch, as much as did the *Lyrical Ballads*. None of his contemporaries or immediate successors so pierced to the heart of the Middle Ages—not Rossetti, whose talent was Romanesque, nor Swinburne, who was more Byzantine Greek than Gothic. Out of the *fabliaux* and the *chansons* and Froissart he devised scenes and incidents which for the reader are like narrow windows

opening into a charmèd world. Alone among his books
it has the true and undying magic. Sometimes, as in
"The Blue Closet" and "The Wind" and "Two Red
Roses across the Moon," the verse sways and sighs with
ineffable longing; sometimes, as in "Sir Peter Harpdon's
End" and the wonderful "Haystack in the Floods,"
there is a savage grimness and the ring of iron. There
is no sentimentality, no vapours of the boudoir or the
study. The whole spirit of the Middle Ages is there—its
shuddering bravado, its angry credulity, its mysterious
loneliness, and, like the voice of linnets in a wind, its
adorable April songs. Morris seems to have attained
in his early youth to his highest point in poetic form,
as he did in prose, for no prose cadences of his later
years are equal to those of his undergraduate story *The
Hollow Land*.

The second class embraces *Jason* and *The Earthly
Paradise*. Here the poet is not reconstructing the
Middle Ages; he has, through some kink or fold of
Time, become himself mediæval. These poems have
all the mediæval languor and uniformity of pattern,
nor do they always escape the mediæval prolixity.
Gently, placidly, they unroll themselves at the speed
of more leisured ages. One mediæval quality alone
they lack, humour, for there is none of the Chaucerian
jollity. "The mood," as Professor Elton has said, "is
that of sad old men telling old stories to other sad old
men." They are immensely long, as were the old
romances; *The Earthly Paradise* is twice the length of
The Ring and the Book. The language is a smooth-
flowing crystal stream, there is no rhetoric, and in the
rhythm, "too full for sound or foam," there is something most satisfying and restful. But while it never

cloys, it may grow monotonous, for it has all the mediæval
ennui. The manner is not suited equally well to all
the tales, and "The Lovers of Gudrun" produces an
effect different from the original in the *Laxdæla Saga*.
The figures are scarcely human ; they have not even
the illusion of three dimensions which painting gives ;
they are flat, like the details in a tapestry. Morris has
been called Homeric ; but no wind from the outer world
blows on the puppets of these poems, and we rarely
have even the semblance of life. It is a decoration, not
an epic.

Up to the early 'seventies Morris's inspiration in
landscape had been the shallow green vales of the upper
Thames, where the Windrush and the Evenlode wind
among meadows like the brooks in an illuminated
missal. But now he fell in love with a wilder land,
and his two visits to Iceland in 1871 and 1873, and his
study of the Sagas (for which purpose he acquired the
language) made him the interpreter of the great tragic
poetry and the austere creed of the North. He was
fascinated by the "old Norse nobility of soul," which
could practise virtue for its own sake without hope of
present or future reward, and which built up a cosmogony in which Good must be followed though Good
were destined to fail. In his *Sigurd* he produced a poem
which was his own version of this faith—its gallant
fatalism, its ever present sense of doom, but the great
heart defying it. It is his nearest approach to the epic
mood. The languor and monotony of the Middle Ages
are forgotten, there is a cold wind blowing from the
snows, and the story moves with a fierce, ringing speed.
With *Sigurd* he reached perfection in that simple diction which is fitted both for plain and splendid narrative,

which can kindle at the high tragic moment and yet does not lose its aptness in homely scenes. The work must always remain a fine, a unique achievement, but there is something lacking, something which is present in the broken lays of the *Elder Edda*, and which we can only call magic. *Sigurd* impresses, but does not haunt the mind, as some of *The Defence of Guenevere* haunts it.

Morris can be represented not unfairly by selections. His work, except the earliest, is so much of a piece that its quality can be shown by extracts, and those who like the pattern can have recourse to the complete poems. He stands by himself in the history of literature, for he has little recognizable ancestry. Few things influenced him in English after Chaucer, though he found much that he liked ; nor was he the product of the Greek and Latin classics. One book, his first, profoundly affected his contemporaries, but for the rest he made a world of his own into which no successor has dared to stray. He is rarely quoted or quotable, for his unit was not the phrase or the line, but the picture ; but he has left us a gallery of rare and delectable pictures—a land East of the Sun and West of the Moon, in which we can rest as in a pleasaunce of Spenser's. He did more than any other man, too, to bring the tonic Northern philosophy within reach of his countrymen. Above all, he has dignified the craft of letters by a character perhaps the most generous, simple, manly, and dutiful since Sir Walter Scott.

There are two functions, it has often been said, of poetry ; one, the revelation of the ideal in common things, the other, the imaginative creation of things in themselves wholly ideal, and thereby an adding to the store of poetic material. The first is the way of the large careless masters, while the second demands a nice craftsmanship and a certain degree of virtuosity. It is significant that Dante Gabriel Rossetti, who among recent poets is distinguished by the invention of new poetic genera, was as much painter as singer—was, indeed, apart from Blake, the only figure in our literature who attained to high success in both arts. He became an art student, but finding that the pen could sometimes say what he desired more readily than the pencil, he followed the two crafts simultaneously. The earliest draft of " The Blessed Damozel " was written when he was nineteen, and a number of other poems and sonnets were contributed to *The Germ* and *The Oxford and Cambridge Magazine* ; but his first book did not appear till 1861, a set of versions of *The Early Italian Poets*, republished in 1874 under the title of *Dante and His Circle*. His wife died in 1862, and Rossetti placed most of his manuscripts in her coffin. These were exhumed in 1870, when his first volume of original verse appeared. It contained all his early poems, part of the sonnet sequence called " The House of Life," and many fine pieces like "Love's Nocturn" and "The Burden of Nineveh." His second volume, containing further sonnets and most of the ballads, was issued in 1881, and the *Collected Works* were published by his brother in 1886, four years after his death.

Two things strike at once all who feel Rossetti's power, whether in attraction or repulsion. No English poet of his standing, except Gray, has left so slender a body of verse, and hardly any of it is second-rate or superfluous. Again, it is curiously underivative. There are traces of Elizabethan and Jacobean influence in the rhythms ; Dante has cast a spell over his mind, and he has loved Keats and admired the early Browning ; but he speaks with his own voice, and that voice is new. This novelty appertains both to his matter and to his technique. He wrote of spiritual things in the most definite and concrete sensible imagery. " Like Dante, he knows no region of spirit which shall not be sensuous also, or material." He sees the truth of emotion and thought not in metaphors, but in sharply realized pictures. His style again, whether in ballad or sonnet or lyric, is elaborate, subtle, and strange. He aims at a simplicity which is attained at the expense of infinite art. One of his devices is a bareness which is sometimes Biblical, sometimes almost infantine, lines ending in lapsing monosyllables :

> " The wonder was not yet quite gone
> From that still look of hers."

>   " To be
> As then we were—being as then
> At peace. Yea, verily——"

or a sudden uncouthness which creates a sudden grimness—

> " Even till the early Sunday light,
> When Saturday night is market-night
> Everywhere, be it dry or wet,
> And market-night in the Haymarket."

In the main the simplicity is not simple. It is initiate, sophisticated, deeply pondered, the work of one who muses over his craft and rarely feels the strong self-forgetting impulse of the greatest poetry. But that craft repays careful study, for it has endless intricacies. He can use short words so as to produce an effect of rich elaboration, and he can so handle polysyllables that

they seem homely. He is an adept at the slow spondaic
line, which seems to make a hush in the rhythmical
movement ; and he carried to perfection a fashion which
in lesser men has become monotonous—the long full-
sounding word followed by a strong monosyllable, as
in—

" The wind of Death's imperishable wing ; "

and

" Sleepless with cold commemorative eyes."

Rossetti, if he can scarcely be placed among the
greater poets, had an influence more potent and per-
vasive than many of the great. He intoxicated his
contemporaries, and the effect may be seen in Swinburne and others. There is a ridiculous side to it,
which H. D. Traill caught in his deadly parody of
" Sister Helen " ; but there is also a rare and not easily
defined beauty. He wrote ballads, but he was not a
ballad-maker, lyrics, but he was not a singer ; he is
always the artificer, working with arabesques and
inlays and strange jewels and rich intractable substances.
" The dwelling-place," says Walter Pater, " in which
one finds oneself by chance or destiny, yet can partly
fashion for oneself ; never properly one's own at all,
if it be changed too lightly ; in which every object has
its associations—the dim mirrors, the portraits, the
lamps, the books, the hair-tresses of the dead, and
visionary magic crystals in the secret drawers, the
names and words scratched on the windows, windows
open upon prospects the saddest or the sweetest ; the
house one must quit, yet taking, perhaps, how much of
its quietly active light and colour along with us !—grown
now to be a kind of raiment to one's body, as the body,

according to Swedenborg, is but the raiment of the soul—under that image the whole of Rossetti's work might count as a *House of Life*." [1] It is an image of singular fitness. Rossetti's world is *within doors*. Nature, the outer winds, are only seen or felt through delicately arched, fantastic windows. It is rarely that we have a true landscape seen with observing eyes, such as he gives us in " Spring " :

" The young rooks cheep 'mid the thick caw o' the old :
    And near unpeopled stream-sides, on the ground,
    By her spring-cry the moor-hen's nest is found,
    Where the drained flood-lands flaunt their marigold."

To enjoy Rossetti it is necessary to be clear as to what we demand from him. He works at the greater matters of poetry, but with a narrow purpose. If he does not attain to the last sublimities, he is always winnowed, select, clarified. He can take us, too, to the authentic abodes of magic, as in " The Portrait " :

" Where you might think to find a din
    Of doubtful talk, and a live flame
    Wandering, and many a shape whose name
    Not itself knoweth, and old dew,
    And your own footsteps meeting you,
    And all things going as they came."

He lacks Morris's movement and spaciousness, but the land to which he guides us has perhaps brighter fruits in its fantastic orchards and a stranger palace at the heart of it.

[1] *Appreciations*, p. 214.

III

ROBERT BURNS [1]

It is easy to extract topical morals from Robert
Burns — easy, and on occasion, desirable ; but I
should like to-night to forget that side of his genius,
and to speak to you of him only as a poet. All great
minds are like mountain ranges and fling out spurs into
many countries. In one aspect Burns is the poet of
Scotland, who has summed up the long troubled history
of our land, and has combined all the diverse loyalties
and traditions of Scotsmen. On another side he is the
poet of our common nature who has expounded, as it has
not often been expounded, the greatness and the frailty
of plain humanity. On still another side he is the
reformer who flashed the lantern of his satire into many
foul corners. He appeals to us as patriots, as democrats, as citizens, as fallible men. But it is none of
these things, fine as they are, which make him immortal.
Many have preached the same creed with equal earnestness, with the same sincerity, and their names are to-day
forgotten. Why is it that as years pass the fame of
Burns rises steadily higher and becomes steadily a
more universal thing, so that not Scotland only, but the
whole earth acknowledges his power ? It is because
he was first and foremost a great artist, and though
creeds and philosophies perish a perfect art endures.
I want to speak to you for a little about Burns as a poet.

It is the fashion to call Burns a classic, and he is a
classic in the strictest and truest sense. What does the
word mean ? It does not mean only that his position

[1] A speech to the Edinburgh Burns Club, January 25, 1924.

is accepted by everybody, and that no one but a lunatic decries his genius. It means that he has the same qualities as the great Greek and Latin poets, the universality and the perfection which are beyond the reach of time, and which owe no allegiance to geographical boundaries. He is a classic, as Sappho and Theocritus and Catullus are classics. Literature has many modes and fashions. We have idealists and realists, and romantics and naturalists, and sometimes one mode is in vogue and sometimes another. The exponents of these schools may be great writers, but in most of their work there is what an American critic has called " a turbid mixture of contemporaneousness " ; they make temporary and local appeals, and these appeals go out of fashion. About Burns there is nothing transitory. At his best he attains to the last pitch of perfection, and his work remains a finished thing, as imperishable, as unaging, as the mountains or the sea.

One may well ask how a man struggling with poverty in a remote Ayrshire parish, self-educated, tortured by a temperament too eager for his circumstances, managed to attain this classic quality, which most people believe to be the product of elaborate culture and a nicely balanced soul. It is not for me to expound the ways of genius which blows like the wind whither it listeth ; but there were three influences which I think helped to mould the mind of Burns.

One was that he fell heir to the treasures of old Scottish ballads and songs, which, just because they were the songs of the common people, were free from false literary modes and had the large direct simplicity which is the foundation of the classic. Another was his close kinship with earth. His days were not spent in a library or in an office, but in wrestling with intractable Ayrshire mud, and meeting the buffets of wind and rain. If such a man sang at all his songs would not smell of the lamp. And in the third place the strongest of literary influences upon him were those of English writers of the eighteenth century like Pope and Addison, who, with all their faults, had something of the classic balance and grace. From whatever cause it sprung the fact is beyond question, and I want you to consider a few of the qualities which make Burns all but unique in our literature.

In the first place he has the classic directness of vision and simplicity. He has a great clearness, rightness, and sanity. In his best Scots verse there are no loose edges, no indefinite colours. He is wholly sincere, both in form and matter ; there is no suspicion of false sentiment ; there is never a word too much ; he is the most nobly economical of all the poets. Take, for example, the description of a spate in the "Brigs of Ayr." Every phrase is the result of direct observation, and stings like the whip of an east wind.

If we want to realize Burns's greatness as an artist we must study closely his methods. Take that perfect lyric, "It was a' for our Rightfu' King." Burns composed this from a dozen old rhymes, and there is scarcely a phrase in his song which does not occur in one or other of the originals. But the originals were doggerel, because there was no shaping art in them. Burns unerringly picked out of the patchwork the right words and the right cadences, and blended them into an immortal cry of regret and longing.

I do not say that his inspiration did not sometimes fail him, for his strength was like the strength of Antæus and only endured while he kept touch with his mother, the earth. Sometimes a malign imp prompted him to wander into stilted English, and so we get in the middle of "Ae Fond Kiss," a song as noble and austere as a Greek chorus, the atrocious lines—

> " I'll ne'er blame my partial fancy,
> Nothing could resist my Nancy."

But when he confines himself to his own tongue his instinct is unerring. Many have tried to add verses to his work, and have invariably made a mess of it. You remember the song "O' a' the Airts the Wind can blaw"? All that Burns wrote was two flawless stanzas of eight lines each. But an Edinburgh music-seller was ill-inspired enough to add other stanzas in which the westland winds are implored to bring back to him the lassie " who's aye sae neat and clean." That is the kind of bathos of which Burns was eternally incapable.

The second classic quality is freedom. In that turbid Scotland of the late eighteenth century there were a hundred factions at strife in Kirk and State. There were Moderate and High Flyer, Tory and Reformer, Patriot and Jacobin ; there were traditions of piety and traditions of something very much the opposite ; even the historic loyalties were divided between Jacobite and Covenanter. Burns had the true classic impartiality. He took no side, or rather he took all sides, for he could discern the core of beauty in the most warring opposites. Somehow or other— and Heaven knows how he did it—he had the power to penetrate to the truth, and the truth made him free. The tragedy of his career lay far more in this than in any disposition to drink or casual amours. His

democracy was far greater than that of the professed
democrat. He would have been happier, perhaps, if
he had condescended to compromise and had arrayed
himself among the comfortable battalions of society,
but he would not have been the great poet he was.
He was too liberal for any Liberal ; he was too Tory
for any Tory ; for his devotion was to a liberty on one
side and to a loyalty on the other which are eternally
beyond the reach of partisans. There is a sentence of
the late Sir Walter Raleigh's which puts better than I
can this cardinal truth about his life. " His magnani-
mous recklessness speeded him on his way to death,
but it was the same quality of his mind which, in the
beginning, had lifted him into the light and delivered
him from slavery. He owed a death to the God of
whom music and song and blood are pure ; he paid his
debt early, but he was no loser by the bargain."

The third classic quality in Burns which I would have
you note is joy. For all the grimness of his life, for all
the passion of sadness which breaks out in some of his
greatest verse, the resultant is not sadness. It is joy,
the joy of the conquering artist, the joy of the man who
is determined to make the world realize the beauty and
delight that can be found in life if it be manfully faced.
Who is it to whom Burns speaks most nearly ? Not
the dismal and the disillusioned, not weeping sentimentalists, not the dull and worldly, not the bloodless
and the shirker. It is to lovers, to soldiers, to true
friends, to those who carry the singing heart in the
journey of life. That is why Burns Clubs are in the
right of it ; that is why on the 25th of January men
meet all over the world and celebrate the birthday of
a poet whose course to the ordinary eye would seem to

have been shadowed with clouds, and whose bark went down in wintry seas. We celebrate that birthday because the life on any true computation was triumphant, because Burns attained to the freedom of truth and the freedom of great art, and has bequeathed to the generations above all things a heritage of courage and joy.

IV

CATULLUS

It was the merest accident that the work of the poet who died at thirty and was acclaimed a classic even by his contemporaries did not utterly perish in the Dark Ages. As it is, we have no manuscripts earlier than the fourteenth century ; but the text which has come down to us, though full of mis-spellings and patent errors, is reasonably complete, and a succession of scholars from Joseph Scaliger to H. A. J. Munro have laboured in its elucidation. It is one of the most precious bequests of Rome, for the one hundred and sixteen pieces which survive rank Catullus as the greatest of the Latin lyric poets—perhaps the greatest of antiquity. In his small treasury of verse there is little base metal, for even his exercises in the more frigid Alexandrian moods are saved by his amazing metrical skill. Like Burns, he combined passionate love poetry with stinging satire, and conjugated all moods and tenses of the verbs to love and to hate. The lyric love of youth for the *flagrantes oculos* of Lesbia and the cruelty of disillusion are there ; but so too is the squalid crowd of panders and parasites and bad poets, condemned in burning verse to an immortality of contempt. And often he attains to a simplicity of passion which is beyond praise, since it is the ultimate perfection possible for human speech.

Catullus was a classic in his lifetime, but it is doubtful if the Roman world ever esteemed him quite in our fashion. There was something not wholly consonant with the Roman taste in both him and Lucretius. He was immensely admired, in spite of Horace's sneer,[1] but it was as a satirist and an epigrammatist rather than as a master of every lyrical grace. Martial paid him the compliment of repeated imitation, but only in one aspect of his work, and that not the greatest. To Quintilian he is merely " bitter," as Lucretius is " difficult." [2] Perhaps Martial's contemporary, Sulpicia, whose work is unhappily lost, may have appreciated that other side, for she is said to have taken as her twin models Catullus and Sappho ; and there is a hint of it in Ovid's elegy on Tibullus [3] :—

" Obvius huic venias, hedera juvenilia cinctus
  Tempora, cum Calvo, docte Catulle, tuo "—

for one does not invoke a mere satirist as one whose young brows are garlanded with ivy. But it would seem on the whole to have been for wit and scholarship that his countrymen upheld him, and not for his matchless poignancy and music. He never quite grew up ; he has always, as Mr. Mackail says, the air of " an extraordinarily gifted child," and Rome preferred her poets to have reached maturity.

The best of him is untranslatable. In Swinburne's phrase, he " makes mouths at our speech " when we

[1] *Satires*, I., 10.   [2] Book X., 1, § 96.
[3] *Amores*, III., 9, 61–62.

try to follow him, for he represents the extreme idiomatic perfection of his tongue. Even when the quality is rightly understood there is no exact equivalent in English for the finality of the Latin ; the different genius of the language is the ultimate barrier. Robinson Ellis, whom no refinement escaped, tried it, but the poetry evaded him ; Sir Theodore Martin was too facile ; Sir Richard Burton was more anthropologist than poet ; Grant Allen produced a good version of the *Attis*, though he rendered clumsily the startling change of gender in the opening lines, and laboured under the notion that the poem was " the finest flower of the Celtic genius," whereas it is an elaborate academic *tour de force* ; Mr. Warre Cornish's sound prose is satisfying enough, but no prose can reproduce the effect of verse. The attempts which have come nearest success have been made in the last two years. To Sir William Marris, the Governor of the United Provinces, the translation of Catullus was what the Greek Anthology was to Lord Cromer—a hobby to be taken up at an odd moment, and he has given us a scrupulously faithful and often felicitous version.[1] The Vice-Provost of Eton has crowned a lifetime of Catullan studies by a complete translation [2]—a notable achievement, for Mr. Macnaghten is both poet and scholar.

The prime difficulty of Catullus for the translator is his subtlety. To his contemporaries he was pre-eminently *doctus*, a student of all the Greek metres and an inventor of new harmonies, as learned in prosody as Milton or Mr. Robert Bridges. To appraise him adequately on this side it is necessary to be a master

[1] Oxford University Press, 1924.
[2] Cambridge University Press, 1925.

of the technicalities of his verse, like Robinson Ellis
and Munro. The metre is cunningly suited to the matter
—the melting hendecasyllables in moods of tenderness
and pity, the lilting glyconics of the great wedding
songs, the lingering beauty of the scazon iambics, the
strength of the hexameters, the exotic strangeness of
the galliambics of the *Attis*. His elegiacs have not
the perfection of Ovid's, his hexameters, magnificent
as they are, tend to monotony, and in his sapphics and
choriambics he is surpassed by Horace, but in his own
favourite metres he has no rival. He is subtle, too, in
other things than tune. To illustrate the altered gender
in the *Attis* one must in English vary the pronouns,
which has a far cruder effect than the quiet change of
the terminal letter in the Latin. Take again the XIVth
poem, where Catullus complains that a friend has
spoiled his Saturnalia by a gift of bad poets. The
penultimate line, as Verrall [1] suggests, is probably a
parody of the way in which those bad poets handled
his own hendecasyllables—

" Illuc unde malum pedem attulistis."

But how is the sudden effect of this doggerel to be
given in English ? There is also the subtlety of his
diction. It is as pure as that of Lucretius, but in place
of his noble bareness it has a wooing simplicity. Little
phrases out of ordinary life are always appearing,
colloquialisms are interwoven, the diminutives of
familiar conversation are not wanting. For all the
studied art and the metrical connoisseurship the result
is a triumph of spontaneity. Words and rhythms are

---

[1] *Studies in Greek and Latin Scholarship*, p. 249.

cunningly and magisterially used to produce something as natural as a flower.

It is an interesting exercise to examine one or two translations, for in the process we are helped to an appreciation of the workmanship of the original. I am inclined to think that the Roman was fonder of reading verse aloud than to himself, and that the Roman poet composed more for the ear than for the eye. I think, too, that he read slowly and carefully, pronouncing the words and indicating the rhythm with equal care, so that no delicacy of the poet would be missed. That was possible—necessary, indeed—with a close-textured language like Latin, which admits both quantity and stress. Again, the great lyrics of both Greece and Rome are the very opposite of formless cries. They are built up with cunning art in an elaborate plan which culminates in the final lines. This is as true of Pindar as of Horace, of Euripides as of Catullus. Consequently the place of a word or line in a poem is not haphazard, and inversion, that device of the translator hard put to it for a rhyme, will often be a perversion. We have to remember all this in reading a Latin lyric, and if we are to come near a full understanding we must feel our way humbly towards the author's meaning. A translator, even the best, will often help us to this meaning by bringing us suddenly face to face with beauties which he simply cannot render.

The translator of Catullus has most chance of success with the *Attis* and the few pieces in elegiacs and hexameters. With the *Attis*, because the galliambic metre is extraordinarily rare and a little out of touch with the Latin genius ; we do not quite know how the Romans regarded it, and are therefore free to give our own interpretation. It is a variation in the first four feet of a familiar Greek metre, and gives a strong impression of quivering nerves and ritual excitement. Tennyson's *Boadicea* has roughly the same quality. Sir William Marris uses a variation of the rhymed hexameter, Mr. Macnaghten an unrhymed stress metre with eight accents. It is hard to choose between them, and both are poetry. Mr. Macnaghten has chosen the more difficult path, and if at times he seems nearer to the spirit of Catullus, I find some of his lines difficult to read aloud, probably because an English syllable is now made long and now short without any apparent reason. The elegiacs of Catullus, too, are translatable. Take the fine LXXVIth poem on the disenchantment of love. Mr. Macnaghten does it in Popian couplets, Sir William Marris in the same metre but with more irregular rhymes, which, to my mind, suggest the touch of roughness and impatience in the original. For

" Una salus hæc est, hoc est tibi pervincendum :
    Hoc facias, sive id non pote sive pote "

I prefer (though both are good)—

" 'Tis the one chance and you must struggle through it.
    Impossible or not, you've got to do it,"

to—

" This victory win, this only safety trust,
    Say not you cannot or you can—you must."

The hexameters of Catullus present a more difficult problem. Take the LXIVth piece, a fragment of an Achilleid, which contains the marriage song of Peleus and Thetis. The piece has obvious defects. Catullus cannot tell a story, and he uses his metre with such infrequent variation that it becomes lifeless and dull.

He had a passion for spondees,[1] and could write a line like—

"Qui te lenirem nobis neu conarere " (CXVI. 3).

The fashion induces to monotony in a long poem, but for a few lines at a time he can reach the high-water mark of the Latin hexameter. My criticism of the two translations is that they make the poem as a whole a much brighter and more interesting thing than the original, but that in the great moments they cannot reproduce Catullus's union of exquisiteness with a stiff majesty. Take the famous lines on the dawn wind (270–275)—

> " Hic, qualis flatu placidum mare matutino
> Horrificans Zephyrus proclivus incitat undas
> Aurora exoriente vagi sub limina Solis :
> Quæ tarde primum clementi flamine pulsæ
> Procedunt, leni et resonant plangore cachinni,
> Post vento crescente magis magis increbescunt,
> Purpureaque procul nantes a luce refulgent."

Mr. Macnaghten translates well, but scarcely well enough :

> " Thereon, as Zephyr wakens, when the dawn
> Reaches the portals of the ranging sun
> And ruffles into ridges all the waves,
> And these at first march slowly, while the breeze
> Is gentle, and the ripples softly laugh,
> Then, as the wind grows strong, they crowd apace,
> And floating far reflect the rosy light."

---

[1] Drobisch gives the proportion of spondees in the first four feet of the hexameters of Latin poets thus :—Catullus, 65.8 per cent. ; Lucretius, 57.4 per cent. ; Virgil, 56 per cent. ; Horace, 55 per cent. ; Ovid, 54 per cent. *Versuch üb. die Formen des lat. Hex.*, 140. Cicero's famous spondaic hexameter will be remembered—" flavit ab Epiro lenissimus Onchesmites "—which he bids Atticus make a present of to any of the " younger set." *Ad. Att.* 7, 2.

So with what are, to my mind, almost the noblest of
Latin hexameters, the passage beginning with line 339
of the same poem. Sir William Marris's version runs:

> " Your son shall be Achilles void of fear ;
> Foes know his dauntless front but not his rear ;
> Oft victor in the race shall he outrun
> The fiery footsteps of the flying deer ;
> Run on and draw the woof, ye spindles, run."

It is vigorous and faithful, but it is not—it could not
be—

> " Nascetur vobis expers terroris Achilles,
> Hostibus haud tergo, sed forti pectore notus,
> Qui persæpe vago victor certamine cursus
> Flammea prævertet celeris vestigia cervæ."

With the glyconics we enter on delicate ground.
Take the LXIst piece, the wedding song of Manlius
Torquatus and Junia (or Vinia) Aurunculeia, one of the
great epithalamia of the world. Both translators have
made a beautiful and sensitive thing of it, and, indeed,
there are stanzas of Mr. Macnaghten's which are well-
nigh perfect, both as translation and as poetry—

> " Blossoming brightly now
> As Asian myrtle bough,
> Myrtle, the sweet plaything,
> Which for the dewy spring
> Wood nymphs are watering."

But there is apt to come a moment when Catullus soars
into an artistry where no man may follow him. Such is
the passage beginning with line 82—

> " Flere desine, non tibi Au-
> runculeia, periculumst,
> Nequa femina pulchrior
> Clarum ab Oceano diem
> Viderit venientem.

> Talis in vario solet
> Divitis domini hortulo
> Stare flos hyacinthinus.
> Sed moraris, abit dies :
>   Prodeas, nova nupta."

Now this is the first revelation of the lady's name, and
it comes with a shock of delighted surprise. Moreover,
it is only revealed by degrees ; we are to imagine
the poem spoken very clearly and distinctly, and the
first revelation is only of the first syllable. That
syllable gives the key—" golden "—an idea carried on
by " clarum diem " four lines later. The sounding name
must be kept, but also the connotation of gold, whence
it is derived. In the same way in the second stanza
it is not till the third line that the flower she is likened
to, the iris, is revealed. Catullus keeps the reader
waiting of set purpose. The Vice-Provost of Eton
renders the passage thus :

> " Sweet, you have wept enow,
>   Aurunculeia, how
> Could there be lovelier eyes
> To see from Ocean rise
> To-morrow's bright surprise ?
>
> So in the garth a tall
> Hyacinth, more than all
> Flow'rs the rich owner's pride,
> Blossoms.   But while you bide
> Day passes.   Come the bride."

Charming, but not all of Catullus, for it misses the gold
in Aurunculeia, and the surprise involved in the use of
" *periculum*," and the delay in speaking the name of

the flower. There is no keeping pace with Catullus ; he
is always "making mouths" at us.

There remain the greatest poems of all, which must
be the despair of the translator, for I do not believe that
the English tongue is capable of rendering the best of
the hendecasyllables and the scazons. The scazon,
remember, is a "limping" metre ; it deliberately dis-
appoints the ear in order to produce an effect of play-
fulness, frailty, or pathos. Take the only sonnet in
Latin, the XXXIst poem, *Pæne insularum, Sirmio*, and
the VIIIth, *Miser Catulle*. Both Mr. Macnaghten
and Sir William Marris have good versions, and the
former is resolute to capture all the subtleties. In the
one, for example, he reproduces skilfully the beautiful
echo of—

> " Fulsere quondam candidi tibi soles
> . . . .
> Fulsere vere candidi tibi soles "

as—

> " So bright, so white, the suns that shone before
> . . . .
> So white, so bright, the suns that shine no more " ;

and in the other he catches the true meaning of " *Lydiæ
lacus undæ*, which escapes Sir William Marris—" My
own true Lydian lake "—the point being that Catullus
has come back from Lydia and Pactolus and found in
the Lago di Garda waters not less golden. But both
versions seem to me too smooth and dapper—poetry,
but not Catullus's poetry.

So with the two great love poems in sapphics, the
LIst and the XIth. The first is the piece in which
Clodia first takes the name of Lesbia, because it is a

translation of Sappho's song to a Lesbian girl. In it
Catullus is wholly love's slave :

> " Ille mi par esse deo videtur,
>   Ille, si fas est, superare divos,
>   Qui sedens adversus identidem te
>   Spectat et audit."

In the second he struggles to free himself from the
bondage, and hurls insults at his mistress :

> " Cum suis vivat valeatque mœchis,
>   Quos simul conplexa tenet trecentos,
>   Nullum amans vere, sed identidem omnium
>   Ilia rumpens."

The word " identidem," as Mr. Mackail has pointed out,
is the miracle. Occurring in each in the same place in
the verse, it is like a gift flung in the face of the betrayer.
Mr. Macnaghten renders it " at whiles," but this is just
one of these occasions when complete understanding
cannot achieve complete reproduction. We need something which English does not possess to give just that
flavour of furious sacrilege which is found in the Latin.

As for the hendecasyllables, the tune is not so hard,
but it is in them, where something of the quality of the
lilt can be produced in English, that the difference between the two tongues is most apparent. Mr. Macnaghten makes a delightful thing of *Passer, deliciæ
meæ puellæ*—

> " Sparrow, the plaything of my fair,
>   Whom in her lap she loves to bear,
>   Or with raised finger-tip excites
>   Till wickedly he pecks and bites ;
>   When the bright lady of my yearning,
>   To some dear dainty play is turning,

> Sweet solace for love's pain, I trow,
> Or in the lull of passion's glow,—
> Oh ! might I play with you as she,
> And my heart's burden lighter be."

And his version of the most famous of all, *Vivamus, mea Lesbia,* is not less skilful. And yet—and yet ! All that scholarly art can do has been done, but something eludes us. These old songs, which men have tried their hand at for two thousand years, are still of a pattern and a texture that defy imitation. They are at once precise and simple ; they are finished like gems, and yet suggest the illimitable. We cannot find the equivalent of either the beauty of surface or the beauty of spirit. In English poetry it is hard to join precision and simplicity ; he who would be exact is usually elaborate, and our simplicity is commonly won by a certain vagueness. Again, wistfulness is the hardest of qualities to render in another tongue. There are things in Greek and Latin which admit of perfect translation, but no man will ever translate Callimachus's epitaph on the dead Heraclitus, or the Virgilian "tendebant manus ripæ ulterioris amore," or "sunt lacrimæ rerum," or "fungar inani munere." The exact thrill in the voice of one people cannot be caught by the voice of another.

We must be content to grope our way to an understanding of such a master as Catullus through a minute study of his work, confident that the felicities which we may find are not one half of the felicities which were obvious to a Roman reader. But if we cannot reproduce him in English, we can please ourselves by finding English counterparts. The spirit of poetry is one and indivisible, and the stuff of humanity is the same in all

ages, though accent and custom vary. The same
subtlety of passion which Catullus put into his love
poems may be found in Shakespeare's Sonnets, and our
English version of *Vivamus, mea Lesbia*, that proud
vaunt of youth against age and time, is perhaps the
song which begins—

" O, Mistress Mine, where are you roaming ? "

XII

THE LITERATURE OF TWEEDDALE

THE LITERATURE OF TWEEDDALE [1]

THE literature of a district is not to be taken, it seems to me, merely as the writings of those born within its confines, but should include all prose and poetry, by whatever hand, which derives from that countryside its inspiration. An anthology of the sea would be but a meagre collection if limited to the work of natives of the coast, and those who have written most eloquently of high mountains have as a rule been dwellers in the plains. So I propose in this chapter to bring under review not only the literature produced by the sons of Tweeddale, but that far greater mass in which strangers have paid tribute to the charm of her hills and waters and the magic of her traditions.

I

The story opens far back in the half-world before records in Scotland begin. Till the fifteenth century there is little authentic history in Tweeddale and no authentic literature. But in the early twilight certain dim shapes may be discovered as of figures larger than human in the mists of dawn. The first is the Arthurian Legend.

Many countrysides have claimed the historical Arthur, as the cities of the Ægean contended for the birthplace

[1] From *A History of Peeblesshire*, ed. by J. W. Buchan, Vol. I., 1925.

of Homer.   His period is less doubtful, for he belonged
to the era of darkness which followed the flight of
the Roman eagles.   We do not know how deeply the
Empire had moulded the life of the peoples within the
Walls ; clearly there could not have been, as in South
Britain, a civilization of towns and country houses,
baths and orchards and bustling highways ; but some
breath of the great Mediterranean culture had passed
the Cheviots and influenced the Brythonic dwellers
between the Lennox and the Solway.   They were
Christians after a fashion, and, when the legions had
marched away, they found themselves beset by the
heathen Angles from the North Sea, the Scots of Dalriada,
and the Picts—of whatever race stock these may have
been—from north of the Forth and West Lothian.
For that tangled epoch there are no contemporary
authorities ; the nearest are Gildas, whose *Historia*
was written about 560, Nennius, whose *Historia Britonum*
belongs probably to the eighth century, and the poems
of certain Cymric bards, which are preserved in the
Four Ancient Books of Wales, and may include sixth
century material.   Of these Nennius alone gives any
coherent story.   He makes Arthur a marshal or " Gule-
dig " of the Strathclyde Cymri, a " dux bellorum " who
formed the scattered septs into a nation and twelve
times beat off the invader, so that the land had peace
for many years.   So far Nennius ; a tenth century
chronicle continues the tale, and tells how twenty-one
years later Arthur fell in the battle of Camelon, when
his nephew Mordred rebelled against him.   Much ingenuity has been applied to the identification of the
sites of Arthur's battles, and on the whole those who
place them in the Scottish midlands and lowlands seem

to me to have the best case. With two we are specially concerned. The seventh battle was fought "in Silva Caledonis," which the Britons called Coit Celidon. This is the Nemus Caledonis of Geoffrey of Monmouth, of which Ettrick Forest alone remained in historical times, and the place of battle would appear to have been in Upper Tweeddale, possibly, as Professor Veitch thought, on the skirts of Cademuir. The eighth battle was "juxta castellum Guinnion," which, taking into account the versions of later chroniclers, has been identified with good probability as Stow in Gala, that spot which the Saxons called Wedale or the Vale of Woe. The foundation is too slender for dogmatism, but it may be safely said that on the evidence the shadowy figure of the historical Arthur is of Northern origin, and that some at any rate of his exploits were performed around the springs of Tweed.

More tenuous still is the historical wraith of Merlin. The wizard of legend is familiar enough, but what Cymric bard, if any, was the original of that wild tale is scarcely now to be deciphered from the palimpsest of tradition. Nennius gives the story of Vortigern and the magic tower, but there is no mention of Merlin, who indeed seems to owe most of his attributes to the fruitful invention of Geoffrey of Monmouth. There was probably a bard of that name (Myrddhin in Welsh) who may have been a contemporary of Arthur. There was also a certain Lailoken, a pagan seer, who opposed Saint Kentigern, and, after the last fight at Arthuret, fled demented to the wilds of Tweeddale and wandered, a man possessed, among the birken glades of the Wood of Caledon. This figure Geoffrey of Monmouth blended with the other in his *Vita Merlini*, but some have held that there were two of the name, and called the later,

who was at Arthuret in 573, Merlinus Sylvestris or
Merlin the Wild. He died, says legend, at the hands
of the shepherds of Meldred, a Tweeddale chief, and
was buried under a thorn at the mouth of the Powsail
Burn. Prophecies of this Merlin are extant, and in
the *Book of Caermarthen* are what may be fragments
of his poetry. On such a slender basis rest the cloud-
capped towers of one of the greatest of the world's
legends.

But my concern here is not with history but with
literature, and if, as it seems reasonable to believe, we
can associate the kernel of fact in the Arthur and Merlin
stories with Tweeddale, we can claim for our glens a
noble heritage of romance. We are to imagine the tale
of Arthur carried south by word of mouth, for there
was much traffic among all branches of the Cymric
people. It is blended with other tales—of Wales, of
Somerset, of Cornwall ; Welsh bards make lays of it ;
it crosses the seas to the Cymri of France, and attracts
Armorican elements. The saga grows—the stories of
the Joyous and Dolorous Gards, of Lancelot du Lac and
Guinevere, of the Round Table, of Tristan, are linked
with quite different tales, such as the Holy Grail and the
nature myth of Merlin and Vivien. Under the influence of the Charlemagne cycle Arthur becomes a world-
conqueror who presses to the gates of Jerusalem.
Aboriginal Aryan legends play their part, and the
story draws something from the Irish heroic cycles
and the Tuatha de Danaan, the old nature gods, as
well as from the Northern sagas of Sigurd and Brynhild.
Arthur is likewise a fairy king, and becomes in *Huon de
Bordeaux* the successor of Oberon and lord of all haunted
places. By the twelfth century this cluster of tales,

the *Matière de Bretagne*, has become the most popular in Europe, eclipsing the stories of Troy and Alexander and Charlemagne. The whole folk poetry of the Middle Ages is enshrined in it, and, like a jewel with many facets, the central figure is alike king and priest, conqueror and conquered, lover and warrior, sinner and saint, the champion both of the Christian faith and of those far more ancient beliefs which came down from the dawn of the world. And because he summed up all the wandering aspirations of men he was eternal and could not die. He might sleep in the Eildons or in Brittany or in some isle of the Western Sea, or, as the troubadours sang, in the heart of Etna, but he would assuredly awake and reign again. His kingdom was no longer of this world, but of those spiritual places—Avalon, Broceliaunde, Tir-nan-Og—which men devise as a sanctuary for their dreams. He was Arthur, "rex quondam, rexque futurus," and Merlin's words were true : " Lady, the flesh of me will be rotten before a month shall pass, but my spirit will not be wanting to all who shall come here." The old tale had become at once a faith and a hope.

None has been more potent in the literature of Europe. Its history begins with the bards of Wales and the Books of Hergest, Taliessin, and Caermarthen. Then it passes overseas to the Northern French poets, Chrétien de Troyes and his like ; to Wolfram von Eschenbach and Gottfried of Strassburg in Germany ; back to England with Geoffrey of Monmouth, from whose work sprang the *Bruts* of Wace and Layamon, and a line of romances ending in 1485 with Sir Thomas Malory's great *Morte d'Arthur*. It spreads to Italy and influences Dante and Tasso and Ariosto. It is the matter of the fourteenth century Welsh *Mabinogion* ; and of the

Scottish *Great Gest of Arthur* by the mysterious "Huchown of the Awle Ryale," who may or may not have been Sir Hew of Eglintoun. It was the inspiration of Drayton and Spenser, and Milton meditated an epic on

> " what resounds
> In fable or romance of Uther's son,
> Begirt with British or Armoric knights."

Since then there is no counting the strands in the web the Arthurian tales have woven in the verse and music of the world, from the poems of Tennyson and Matthew Arnold and William Morris to the *Lohengrin* and *Parsifal* and *Tristan* of Wagner. Their incidents and personages have become as familiar as the mythology of Greece, and each new generation reads into them its own philosophy of life. It is strange to reflect that the origin of this stately movement was in all likelihood the moorland battles of a half-savage chieftain and the rhapsodies of a crazy minstrel among the Tweeddale shaws.

The second of the amorphous shades is Michael Scot. For the historical figure there is indeed ample evidence. He was born early in the last quarter of the twelfth century, and died in or about the year 1232 ; he was a Scot undoubtedly, and almost certainly a Borderer ; he could not have been, as Hector Boece states, of the family of Balwearie in Fife, since the Scotts of Balwearie did not come into existence till thirty years after his death, and he therefore cannot be identified with the Sir Michael Scot of Balwearie, who in 1290 was sent on an embassy to Norway. The probability is that in his case " Scot " was a family and not a national name, and, if that be accepted, the natural place of birth would be Upper Tweeddale, where lay the earliest possessions of the great clan of Scott. It is all conjecture, but there is a curious piece of evidence in support. The Exchequer Rolls record in 1265 a payment made by the Crown to one Michael Scot, who had occupied " waste lands in stuth [1] near Peebles." In this case Scot is clearly a surname, and Michael is not the commonest of Christian names. We can say at least that there is a shade more likelihood that Michael was sprung from Upper Tweeddale than from any other Border district.

After that the way is clearer. He studied possibly at Durham, certainly at Oxford and Paris, where in deference to the custom of the age he entered holy orders. Then, after a season at the famous law school of Bologna, he passed to Toledo for the study of Greek and Arabic. In Spain he was busy for ten years translating Aristotle from Arab versions, studying the clear dry Saracenic wisdom, abbreviating Avicenna, and dabbling in that early traditional chemistry which the world called alchemy, and the rudimentary astronomy which it knew as astrology. He was the first, too, to introduce Averröes to the Latin world, that strange philosopher who grafted neo-Platonism upon Aristotle ; and he thereby laid the foundations of a sinister repute for himself, for the sage of Cordova was ill-regarded by the Church. When he entered the service of Barbarossa's grandson, the Emperor Frederick II., he had won European fame as a scholar, and his life at the court of Palermo, which was reported to be the home of necromancy and obscene pagan cults of Astarte and Beelzebub, established his renown as a master of the

---

[1] The form of tenure more generally known as " steelbow," where stock as well as land was rented.

occult. The truth seems to have been that he was no
more than a laborious and intrepid inquirer, but association with Frederick, that ruddy, baldish, short-sighted
monarch who was the most erratic genius of the Middle
Ages—"stupor mundi et immutator mirabilis"—was not
good for the repute of a scholar. His master tried to
find him high office in the Church, but his own honourable scruples stood in the way, and his later years
seem to have been sad and disillusioned, though he
continued to toil at his scheme of publishing a new
Aristotle for the universities of Europe. It is not clear
that he himself took to prophesying, but his name
became linked, like Thomas the Rhymer's, with a vast
number of vaticinations, mostly, no doubt, composed
after the events they foretold. Just before his death
he travelled north again, and may have died in Scotland.
Tradition and Sir Walter Scott place his tomb in Mel-
rose, but Scott of Satchells, writing in the end of the
seventeenth century, will have it in Cumberland, perhaps
in the Cistercian abbey of Holme Coltrame.

No son of Tweeddale, it may fairly be said, voyaged
alone over stranger seas of thought. The historical
Michael was one of the greatest of mediæval polymaths,
—theologian, legalist, mathematician, chemist, physi-
ologist, logician, and linguist. If we can claim him for
our shire, the library of Tweeddale authors must include
a shelf of treatises in difficult Latin, from his translation
of the *De Natura Animalium* to his observations on the
Sphere of John Holywood or Sacrobosco, who may have
studied with him at the parish school of Dryburgh.
But the historical Michael gives place in fame to the
legendary, the lord of the powers of darkness, who
played the part of Merlin to Frederick's Arthur. His

magic repute is as great among the peasants of Italy
as in the Scottish Border, where " auld Michael " used
to be credited with every ancient or incredible work,
from cleaving the Eildons to the riddling of Sandyhill-
neuk, wherefrom the stones may still be seen in Biggar
Moss. He became a figure of pure fäery, riding coal-
black demons to France and entertaining his friends
with dishes brought from the King of Spain's kitchen.
Traces of a nobler conception, the scholar who broke
his heart with forbidden knowledge, may be found in
Giovanni Pico della Mirandola's work against astrology,
in Boccaccio, in Dante, who in the *Inferno* saw Michael's
wasted figure, wearing the tight Toledo girdle, with his
head screwed round over his shoulder

> " Quell' altro, che ne' fianchi e cosi poco,
> Michele Scotto fu, che veramente
> Delle magiche frode seppe il giuoco," [1]

and above all in the *Lay of the Last Minstrel.*

II

With the fifteenth century begins the authentic tale
of the literature of Tweeddale, and the first work on
the list is in its small way a classic and has for its author
a king. James I. of Scotland (1394–1437) has already
his place in English literature by virtue of *The Kingis
Quair,* and I see no reason to doubt that he also wrote
that exercise in a very different *genre, Peblis to the Play.*
The evidence may be briefly set down. John Major in
his *History of Greater Britain,* written eighty-one years
after the King's death, has this passage :

[1] *Inferno,* xx. 115.

" In vernacula lingua artificiosissimos compositos ; cujus codices plurimi et cantilenæ memoriter adhuc apud Scotos inter primos habentur. Artificiosum libellum de regina dum captivus erat composuit, antequam eam in conjugem duceret ; et aliam artificiosam cantilenam ejusdem, *Yas Sen* etc., et jocundum artificiosumque illum cantum *At Beltayn,* quem alii de Dalkeith et Gargeil mutare studue- erunt ; quia in arce aut camera clausus servabatur in qua mulier cum matre habitabat."

If the abominable Latin means anything it is that James, besides writing *The Kingis Quair,* produced a song in an elaborate metre beginning *Yas Sen* (which cannot be identified) and that amusing and elaborate poem *At Beltayn,* which certain poets of Dalkeith and Gargeil (wherever the latter place may have been) tried to parody,[1] and which he composed when he was shut up in a tower where a lady lived with her mother. Now " At Beltayn " are the opening words of *Peblis to the Play;* moreover, in *Christis Kirk on the Green,* which is attributed to James I. in the Bannatyne MSS., there is a mention of the former poem. Such direct evidence as there is, is therefore in favour of the thing being a composition of the early fifteenth century, and almost certainly of James I. Professor Skeat with the weight of his great authority takes another view, and would assign both poems to the sixteenth century, on indirect grounds which I cannot think sufficient. In the first place he seems to me to misconceive the meaning of Major's Latin. Again, the argument from language is a difficult one in the case of a poem the present text of which may have passed through the hands of many transcribers. In any case there are letters extant which

[1] Or perhaps " to make it apply to their own towns."

prove that James knew Scots ; nor is there any substance
in the contention that the use of such a rollicking metre
is unexampled before 1450. As for the argument that
the style of *Peblis to the Play* is unlike that of *The
Kingis Quair*, it is a plea which would deny Falstaff
to the creator of Hamlet, the *Polemo-Middinia* to Drummond of Hawthornden, "John Gilpin" to the author
of *The Task*, and "The Jolly Beggars" to the poet of
"The Cotter's Saturday Night." It may fairly be said
that the probabilities incline to the royal authorship.
Further, as Dr. Gunn has pointed out, James I. had in
all likelihood connections with Peebles. He may have
been brought there as a boy by his father, who often
visited the town, and in later years he was a patron of
the hospice of St. Leonard two miles to the east, where
he may have lodged while hunting—an explanation of
the familiar allusion in the poem to Hope-Kailzie and
Cardrona.

Peblis to the Play is a member of an ancient family
which has left many descendants. In form it derives
both from the old ballad and the alliterative romance ;
in matter it is a rough variant of the Greek idyll and the
Roman bucolic. The same note had already been heard
in Scotland in *Colkelbie's Sow*, it was repeated in
Christis Kirk on the Green, in the *Blythsome Bridal*, in
a hundred songs, in *Habbie Simson* and Allan Ramsay,
in Fergusson's "Leith Races" and Burns's "Holy Fair,"
down to the *Anster Fair* of William Tennant. It is a
Dutch picture of the humours of a country fair, done
with high spirits and jollity and a certain fescennine
realism, which never sinks to the grossness of, for
example, the additional cantos which Allan Ramsay
added to *Christis Kirk*. The metre, which is eight

two-rhymed lines of eights and sixes, with a "bob-wheel," gives a lilting impetus to the piece. The old Beltane Fair at Peebles fell on the first Monday and Tuesday of May, and the poem describes the country lads and lasses preparing for the journey to the town, the girls in their kerchiefs and ribbons, the men with new hats and bows of yew, with pipers strutting before them. It tells of fairings and junketings, and tavern revels, and sudden quarrels, and " dancing and deray " and rustic love-making. The opening stanzas are perhaps the most spirited :

> " At Beltane when ilk bodie bownis
> To Peblis to the Play,
> To heir the singin and the soundis,
> The solace suth to say ;
> Be firth and forest furth they found,
> They graythit tham full gay ;
> God wait that wald they do that stound,
> For it was their Feist Day,
> > They said
> Of Peblis to the Play
>
> All the wenchis of the west
> War up or the cok crew ;
> For reiling thair micht na man rest,
> For garray and for glew ;
> Ane said ma curches ar nocht prest,
> Than answerit Meg full blew,
> To get an hude I hald it best ;
> Be Goddis saull that is true,
> > Quod scho
> Of Peblis to the Play.

* * * * * *

bownis, makes ready to go.　　grayhit, dressed.　　wait, knew.
　　stound, time.　　reiling, bustle.　　garray, haste.
　　　glew, mirth.　　curches, kerchiefs.　　hude, hood.

> Hop-Cailzie and Cardronow
> Gaderit out thik-fald,
> With *Hey and How Rohumbelow* ;
> The young folks were full bald.
> The bagpipes blew, and thai out threw
> Out of the townis untald,
> Lord sic ane schout was thrown amang
> Quen thai were owre the wald
>   Thair west
> Of Peblis to the Play." [1]

The second of what have been called the " Peebles Classics," *The Thrie Tales of the Thrie Priests of Peblis*, is probably to be dated at least half a century later. It belongs to a period before any forestirrings of the Reformation had begun, when men were still loyal to Rome, but when serious folk were talking of reform for patent abuses in both kirk and state.   It has affinities with *The Freires of Berwick*, which has been erroneously ascribed to Dunbar, and it has hints of the later political fervour of Sir David Lyndsay.   Pinkerton assigned it, without much reason, to Dean David Steill, the author of *The Ring of the Roy Robert*, and Sibbald, who dated it about 1540, ascribed it with still less justification to John Rolland.   A reference to the heathen kingdom of Granada would seem to date it at least before 1491.   It

---

thik-fald, manifold.　　　*bald*, bold.　　　*townis*, farmsteads.
　　　　　　　　　　　　　　wald, wold.

[1] The MS. is in the Pepysian Library of Magdalene College, Cambridge.   It is believed to have belonged to Sir Richard Maitland, who lived in the reign of Mary and James VI., and it came to Pepys from the Duke of Lauderdale.   It was first printed by Bishop Percy in his *Reliques*, and then by Pinkerton in the second volume of his *Select Scottish Ballads*, 1783.   It has been edited, with the spelling modernized, by Dr. C. B. Gunn.   The parallel piece, *Christis Kirk on the Green*, is in the Bannatyne MSS. ; it was first printed by Bishop Gibson (Oxford, 1691), and there are many reprints.

is a sententious and highly moral composition, but if the
spirit is in the main that of Gower, it breaks now and
then into a delightful freshness of detail and gusto which
recall Chaucer. Three priests meet on St. Bride's Day,
the 1st of February, and while dining in "ane privy
place" tell each a tale. Friar John relates how a certain king put three questions to his three estates. Of
the burgesses he asked :

"Quhy burges bairns thrivis not to the third air?"

and for answer is given a sketch of the progress of the
successful merchant, a wonderful little version of the
American "three generations from shirt-sleeves to
shirt-sleeves." Of the lords he asked why their order
had decayed in hardihood, and learned that it was due
to the maladministration of justice which impoverished
the nobles and forced them into low marriages for the
sake of money. From the clergy he inquired the reason
why miracles had ceased, and was told that it was due
to the bad appointments in the hierarchy.

"The bishop cums in at the north-window;
And not at the dur, nor yit at the yet."

Friar Archibald follows with a good story of how a
king who, like Rehoboam, took counsel only of the
young and neglected the old, was taught wisdom by a
jester, and Friar William concludes the colloquy with
a grave allegory of Death and the Judgment. I am
inclined to rank these tales high in gnomic literature;
the spirit is wise and tolerant, the details are sharply
realized, and the verse has true ease and vigour.

air, heir.

Here is the setting of the scene :—

> " And, wit ye well, thir thrie they made good cheir ;
> To them there was nae dainties then too deir,
> With thrie fed caponis on a speet with creis,
> With mony other sundry divers meis.
> And them to serve they had not but a boy ;
> Frae company they keepit them sae coy ;
> They lovit not with ladry nor with lown,
> Nor with trumpours to travel through the town ;
> Bot with themself what they would talk or crack ;
> Umquhile sadly, umquhile jangle and jack ;
> Thus sat thir thrie beside ane felloun fire
> Till their caponis were roisted lim and lyre." [1]

The third of the fifteenth century Peebles poems is *The Advice of a Father to his Son*, or *Rait's Raving*, which Dr. J. T. T. Brown has credited to David Rait, who became Master of the hospice of St. Leonard near Peebles in 1427. The piece is among the manuscripts in the University Library of Cambridge, and a version in Old English, along with seventeen other poems attributed to Rait, is in the Ashmole Collection at Oxford. *Rait's Raving* is a composition of nearly two thousand lines, which has the look of a translation, for there is no single idiomatic touch to connect it with Scottish contemporary life. It begins, in the ordinary scholastic fashion, with an analysis of the virtues and vices which attend the senses, divagates thence into moralizations on matters like marriage and trade, and

ladry, common people.   *lown*, low fellows.   *trumpours*, stragglers.
 Umquhile, sometimes.   *jack*, idle.   *felloun*, strong.
  lyre, flesh.

[1] First printed by Robert Charteris, 1603 ; reprinted by Pinkerton, *Scottish Poems from Scarce Editions*, 1792, by Sibbald (in part) in 1801, by David Laing, *Early Metrical Tales*, 1826, and by Dr. C. B. Gunn, Selkirk, 1891.

concludes with a dull version of the Seven Ages of Man. The piece has small poetic merit, being a homily on the text that virtue is the best policy, which is scarcely a fruitful subject for poetry. Its chief interest lies in its *provenance*, if, as has been argued, it is a paraphrase of a Florentine original picked up by Master David on one of the travels which he undertook either under the duties of his Dominican order or as a member of a royal embassy.[1]

III

In Dunbar's "Lament for the Makars" he upbraids Death who

> " has now tane last of aw
> Gud gentil Stobo and Quintane Schaw,
> Of quhome all wightis hes pitie."

This Stobo may have been Sir John Reid, foreign secretary to James III., but of his poetry no line remains. *The Complaynt of Scotland*, finished about 1549, one of the earliest works in Scottish vernacular prose, must have been written by a native of southern Scotland, and may possibly have been the work of Sir James Inglis, the Abbot of Cambuskenneth, who died about 1554 ; which Inglis, as Professor Veitch has argued, may have been an Inglis of Manor. It is all the merest conjecture. It is safer to turn to the heyday of the sixteenth century and the Ballads.

Here it is needless to enter at length upon the vexed discussion as to the origin of our ballad literature. Of no branch of literary art is the peculiar quality more

[1] *Rait's Raving* has been edited, with modernized spelling, by Dr. C. B. Gunn (Peebles, 1918).

easy to recognize, and in none are the sources and
ancestry more obscure. Four main theories have been
promulgated. There is, first, the " communal " school
who maintain that the ballad was born at some primeval
date out of tribal song and dance, as free from specific
human parentage as Melchizedek. It was a work of the
community, a kind of effluence from ancient social life,
as a mist is drawn from a wet hillside. The second
school, which may be called the " popular," do not deny
an original unknown author, but maintain that the ballads
deal chiefly with *märchen* which are common to all
early peoples, and were not the product of a literary
class, but were elaborated and transmitted by ordinary
folk. "Ballads," wrote Andrew Lang, "spring from
the very heart of the people, and flit from age to age,
from life to life, of shepherds, peasants, nurses, of all
the class that continues nearest to the natural state of
man." The third school definitely attributes the authorship to a minstrel class, but minstrels living before the
days of the chivalric romance, folk-singers, who flourished in times antecedent to recorded history. The
fourth school holds that the ballads in their existing form
belong to a comparatively late age, and were the work
of popular minstrels who were the successors of the old
skalds and gleemen, and worked on a literary tradition
which represented the breakdown of the elder tradition
of the romance or fabliau, when they were not composing
lays, like the *chansons de gestes*, called forth by a contemporary event.

The reader may take his choice among the schools.
For myself I find difficulties in them all, but on a survey
of the surviving ballads and such historic facts as are
known about them I incline to the fourth. Both the

" communal " and " popular " theories seem to me to
be a flat contradiction of all we know about the genesis
of poetry. Art—and the ballads are often great art—
does not come into being from popular excitement, but
from the inspiration of a particular gifted individual;
it cannot be syndicated and socialized. The doctrine
of the extreme antiquity of the original minstrel seems
to be contradicted by the facts before us. I am inclined
to the view that, besides the bards maintained by the
feudal lords, there was always a tradition of a rude
popular minstrelsy in the Borders, the songs referred to
by Barbour—

> " Young women quhen thai will play
> Syng it amang thaim ilk day."

In that tradition there were hoar-ancient elements,
reaching back to beliefs far older than Christianity.
As the romantic tradition of the fabliaux died away,
its remnants took popular shape in country tales, which
also embodied the fairy lore of the hills. Out of this
material the ballads were made by "makars" whose
identity has not been preserved; perhaps by some of
those whose names are obscurely enshrined in Dunbar's
"Lament"—"Ettriik" or "Heryot" or "Stobo"—or by
unknown harpers and violers, the predecessors of Nicol
Burne, while some fragments may have come down from
True Thomas himself. I believe that most of the ballads
were made in the sixteenth century by men who summed
up a long ancestry of popular poetry, as in Burns
culminated a long tradition of Scottish vernacular song.
Some of the ballad-makers were men of genius—even
of high genius; and it is possible to detect among the
topical crudities inevitable in popular poetry and the

damaged conventions of the older romances touches of
sharp realism and far-flighted imagination which can
only belong to the individual. A contemporary event
would be celebrated, as chance determined, by a bald
versifier, or by some rude but indisputable poet.

The ballads were the only literature known to the
people. In the old Tweeddale world of little anxious
townships, and constant bickering in the glens, there
were yet seasons of peace and leisure. The clusters of
huts round a peel-tower were not always blazing to
heaven, and the position of the shire, a little aside from
the main route to England, kept its folk for the most
part out of the track of invasion. There were snug
hours in the long winters in ale-house and cottage and
castle hall, when snowdrifts or floods gave security
from troublesome neighbours. There were the revels
at Yule and Hogmanay, and the burgh fairs ; the
clippings and the autumn " kirns," and the rendezvous
at the noontide meal, as described in the *Complaynt of
Scotland*, when the shepherds forgathered to dine off cakes
and curds and cheese, and pass an hour with singing
and playing. Above all, there was the summer time,
when the flocks were driven to the high pastures, and at
the doors of the shielings in the June gloamings young
men and girls danced to the flute and pipe, and some
wandering bard sang of the days of old, of the fairies in
the greenwood and the kelpies in the loch, or of some
great deed of prowess the rumour of which had drifted
across the hills. From such a life the ballads were born.

Of the famous riding ballads Tweeddale can claim
none—she was too far from the troubled Marches.
Nor has she any of the great romantic ballads with which
the neighbouring shire of Selkirk is so abundantly

dowered—" Tam Lin," "The Douglas Tragedy," "The
Dowie Dens," "The Gay Goss Hawk." But of that small
and charmèd circle which deals with the half-world that
is neither of heaven nor of earth—the most marvellous
group of all—Tweeddale in common with all the haunted
Borderland may claim her share. Indeed there is a
tradition, for which I can offer no evidence, that "The
Wife of Usher's Well" has to do with Peebles town.

> " It fell about the Martinmass,
>   When nights are long and mirk,
> The carline wife's three sons cam hame,
>   And their hats were o' the birk.
>
> It neither grew in syke nor ditch,
>   Nor yet in ony sheugh ;
> But at the gates of Paradise
>   That birk grew fair eneugh."

That has the true magic which I long to claim
for Tweeddale. One ballad, indeed, and one of the
first order, is partly ours, since ecclesiastically Megget
parish is joined with Lyne. In May 1530 William Cok-
burne, of Henderland in Megget, was convicted of high
treason and beheaded in Edinburgh. The story may
be read in Pitcairn, and it seems to be the historical
foundation of "The Border Widow's Lament," a poem
which dwells from first to last on the heights of poetry.
No mauling by recitation or interpolation has spoiled
its noble simplicity.

> " My love he built me a bonny bower,
>   And clad it a' wi' lilye flour ;
> A brawer bower ye ne'er did see
>   Than my true love he built for me.

There came a man by middle day,
He spied his sport and went away ;
And brought the King that very night,
Who brake my bower and slew my knight.

He slew my knight, to me sae dear ;
He slew my knight, and poined his gear ;
My servants all for life did flee,
And left me in extremitie.

I sewed his shirt, making my mane ;
I watched the corpse, myself alane ;
I watched his body night and day ;
No living creature came that way.

I took his body on my back,
And whiles I gaed, and whiles I sat ;
I digged a grave and laid him in,
And happed him with the sod sae green

But think na ye my heart was sair
When I laid the moul' on his yellow hair ;
O think na ye my heart was wae,
When I turned about away to gae ?

Nae living man I'll love again,
Since that my comely knight is slain ;
Wi' ae lock of his yellow hair
I'll chain my heart for evermair."

IV

The seventeenth century was for all Scotland a
barren epoch in literature, and in Tweeddale it produced
scarcely a sheaf. There was not even the output of
controversial theology which elsewhere loaded the
presses, and the withered remains of which may still be
found in antique calf on the top shelves of old libraries.
The shire had small part in the strife of King and

Covenant, though Montrose fled through it on his way from Philiphaugh and Cromwell's troopers paid it an unwelcome visit. The ministers, I suspect, were mostly of the "indulged" variety, though there were Covenanters in Tweedsmuir and on the Clydesdale marches. The glens, like all the Borders, were busy trying to adjust themselves to new social conditions, and the old riding lairds were bankrupt or soldiering abroad. It was not the hour for poetry, or for prose save of the controversial kind. But I incline to attribute to the seventeenth century the spirited song "Walifou fa' the Cat," of which the first and only quotable verse is:

> " As I gaed down by Tweedside
> I heard, I dinna ken what;
> I heard ae wife say to anither,
> Walifou fa' the cat.
> Walifou fa' the cat,
> She's bred the house muckle wanease,
> She's opened the awmrie-door,
> And eaten up a' the cheese."

To the same century probably belongs the ballad of "Mossfennan" or "The Logan Lee," which Professor Veitch recovered, with its fine opening:

> " There cam three wooers out o' the west,
> Booted and spurred as ye weel micht see,
> And they lichted a' at Mossfennan Yett
> A little below the Logan Lee."

Lastly, there is the small nosegay of verse associated with the Hays of Yester—the indifferent love song called "John Hay's Bonnie Lassie," said to have been addressed to Margaret, the eldest daughter of the first Marquis of Tweeddale, and the more vigorous "Tweedside," which Chambers attributes to the second Marquis, but for which

Herd, who first printed it, gives no author. The Tweed-
dales, who were still lords of Neidpath, may rank at this
period (about 1686) as belonging in more than name
to the shire. Here is the plaint of Lord Yester, whose
despair does not sound so very desperate, though it is
said that Lady Grizel Baillie's daughter, Lady Murray
of Stanhope, used to draw tears by her singing of it.

> " When Maggie and me were acquaint,
>   I carried my noddle fu' hie,
> Nae lintwhite in a' the gay plain,
>   Nae goudspink sae bonnie as she.
>
> I whistled, I piped, and I sang ;
>   I wooed, but I cam nae great speed :
> Therefore I maun wander abroad,
>   And lay my banes far frae the Tweed.
>
> To Maggie my love I did tell ;
>   My tears did my passion express ;
> Alas ! for I lo'ed her ower weel,
>   And the women lo'e sic a man less.
>
> Her heart it was frozen and cauld ;
>   Her pride had my ruin decreed ;
> Therefore I maun wander abroad,
>   And lay my banes far frae the Tweed."

With Alexander Pennecuik of Newhall (1652–1722)
we reach the humble beginnings of Tweeddale prose.
Pennecuik's father, a scion of the ancient house of
Pennecuik of that ilk, served as a surgeon with the
armies of Gustavus. He himself married Janet Murray,
the heiress of Romanno, and may fairly rank as a
Peeblesshire man, for he practised as a doctor throughout
the shire and lived mainly at his wife's estate. His
chief work, *A Description of the Shire of Tweeddale*, was

published in 1715, and was apparently undertaken as a
consequence of the topograpical enterprise inaugurated
by Sir Robert Sibbald at the command of Charles II.
Pennecuik's joggings about the countryside had given
him great stores of knowledge, he had more than a
tincture of letters, and he sets out his material with
admirable orderliness.   Topography is a form of literature of which I can never have enough, and the homely
details of the *Description* still delight me.   The style
is sufficiently pedestrian, but not without its own
shrewd and graphic touches.   The writer is a true son
of the eighteenth century and indisposed to enthusiasm.
The Cromwellian angler, Richard Franck, could write
eloquently fifty years before of the " glittering and
resolute streams of Tweed " ; but to Pennecuik, as to
the eighteenth century " Person of Quality " who
visited the place, Tweeddale is only a hill, a road and a
water, with no true claim to the picturesque.   Hear
him on the great hills : " This country is almost everywhere swelled with Hills ; which are, for the most part,
green, grassy, and pleasant, except a ridge of bordering
mountain, betwixt *Minch-muir* and *Henderland*, being
black, craigie, and of a melancholy aspect, with deep
and horrid precipices, a wearisome and comfortless piece
of way for travellers."   But on the human side he writes
with decision and gusto :

" The inhabitants for the most part are strong, nimble,
and well-proportioned, both sexes promiscuously being
conspicuous for as comely features as any other country
in the kingdom, would but the meaner sort take a little
more pains to keep their bodies and dwellings neat and
clean, which is too much neglected among them, and pity
it is to see a clean complexion and lovely countenance

appear with so much disadvantage through the foul disguise of smoke and dirt. . . . They are an industrious careful people, yet something wilful, stubborn, and tenacious of old customs. There are amongst them that will not suffer the wrack to be taken out of their land, because (say they) it keeps the corn warm, nor sow their bear seed, be the season wet or dry, till the first week of May be over, which they call *Runchis Week*; nor plant trees, or hedges, for wronging the undergrowth, and sheltering the birds of the air to destroy their corn; neither will they trench and ditch a piece of useless boggie ground, for fear of the loss of 5 or 6 foot of grass, for a far greater increase, which however, with a custom they have of overlaying the ground, which they term ' full plenishing,' makes their cattle generally lean, little, and give a mean price in the market. . . . They are more sober in their diet and drinking than many of the neighbouring shires, and when they fall into a fit of good fellowship, they use it as a cement and bond of society, and not to foment or revenge quarrels and murders, which is too ordinary in other places. And they are of so loyal and peaceable dispositions, that they have seldom or never appeared in arms against their lawful sovereign, nor were there amongst that great number, *twelve* persons from *Tweeddale*, at the insurrections of *Rullion Green* or *Bothwell Bridge*. Of their loyalty they gave sufficient testimony at the fight of *Philiphaugh*, when several of them were killed by *David Leslie's* army, and others the most eminent of their gentry taken prisoners."

His poems are of a lower merit than his prose, and do not compare with those of his namesake, that other Alexander Pennecuik, who died destitute in Edinburgh in 1730, and whose vernacular broadsides give a picture, coarser than Ramsay's but as full of vigour and humour, of the lewd drunken world of the old Edinburgh by-streets. The laird of Newhall follows all the accepted fashions—invitations to a town friend to visit the country, translations of Ovid and Anacreon, inscrip-

tions for his bee-house and his library. Now and then
he forgets his models, and writes "A Panegyric upon
the Royal Army in Scotland," in which Drummelzier's
Tweeddale troops and the vagaries of the local gentry
are amusingly presented, and verses eulogizing or
satirizing his neighbours of Callands or Macbiehill and
the clergy of Linton and Newlands. The few dialect
pieces, such as "The Lintoun Cabal," have small merit.[1]

Pennecuik's chief importance in literary history is
that he is a link with a greater man, for he is believed to
have supplied Allan Ramsay with the plot of *The Gentle
Shepherd*, Sir William Worthy being drawn from one
of the Tweeddale lairds who followed Montrose. With
Ramsay (1686–1756) we enter the world of the aquatint
pastoral, a world infinitely remote both from the old
Sicilian shepherd life from which its first inspiration
came and from the rustic commonwealth at its doors.
But in Ramsay the affectation is not excessive ; there
is a touch—or so it seems to me—of conscious burlesque
in *The Gentle Shepherd*, as if he saw the ridiculous side
of the Damon and Clorinda business ; and his Patie and
Roger, his Peggy and Jenny, wear the true homespun
and have the tan of the hills on their cheeks. I would
fain linger over Ramsay, but indeed his connection
with this chapter is slight, for he was born at Leadhills
in Lanarkshire, and spent his life in Edinburgh, first
as a wig-maker in the Grassmarket and then as a book-
seller in the Luckenbooths. But his masterpiece, *The
Gentle Shepherd*, published in 1725, has, as we have
noted, a Tweeddale *provenance*, and its scene is laid on

---

[1] The best edition of the *Description* is that published at Leith in
1815, which includes also the *Poems*. Some of the latter had already
appeared in *A Collection of Curious Scots Poems*, Edinburgh, 1762.

the northern border of the shire. Often the dialogue, even though in the vernacular, walks on the high stilts of the Augustans or slips into frigid literary devices ; but there are many passages of racy Scots, and above all there is a pleasant atmosphere of homely goodwill and honest country ways. The weak point in the piece has always seemed to me to be the lyrics. Patie sings to Peggie :

> " My dear, allow me, frae thy temples fair,
>   A shining ringlet of thy flowing hair ;
>   Which, as a sample of each lovely charm,
>   I'll often kiss, and wear about my arm."

But Ramsay could do better than that ; witness his other song to Peggy, " The Waukin o' the Fauld," which Mr. Henderson rightly calls " an admirable lyric perfectly faultless in its simplicity."

The Gentle Shepherd had one immediate and lasting effect. It gave to Tweeddale the *aura* of a classical convention. " Pan playing on his aiten reed," as Nicol Burne sang, was now recognized by the polite and literate world as a denizen of the Tweeddale hills, and those green uplands were accredited to the pastoral muse. We see the fashion in Hamilton of Bangour ; we see it notably in the verse of Robert Crawford (1695–1732) who, though the son of a Renfrewshire laird, sang chiefly of the Tweed. His version of " Tweed-side " is pleasant enough in its facile way :

> " What beauties does Flora disclose !
>   How sweet are her smiles upon Tweed !
>   Yet Mary's, still sweeter than those,
>   Both nature and fancy exceed.
> .   .   .   .

> Come, let us go forth to the mead,
>   Let us see how the primroses spring ;
>   We'll lodge in some village on Tweed,
>   And love while the feathered folk sing."

I forbear to quote from his " Bush abune Traquair,"
since that spot, as we shall see, has found a worthier
poet. Later than Crawford, and infinitely better, was
Alexander Geddes (1737–1802), a Banffshire man and a
Roman Catholic, who was chaplain to the sixth Earl
of Traquair. He is said to have written "Linton, a
Tweeddale Pastoral" in honour of the birth of an heir
to his patron's house, but I do not know if it is
extant. He was probably the author of "The Wee
Wifikie," one of the best of Scottish humorous songs,
and he beyond doubt has the credit of "O Send Lewie
Gordon Hame," which enshrines all the glamour and
longing of the lost Jacobite cause.

With the brilliant school of Scottish eighteenth
century prose, which included David Hume and Adam
Smith, Hugh Blair and Principal Robertson, and lords
of session like Kames and Hailes and Monboddo,
Tweeddale has a link in Adam Ferguson (1723–1816),
who for some years was a dweller in the shire. Ferguson
is one of the most delightful figures of his time, and few,
even among Scotsmen, have lived a fuller and more
varied life. Coming from a Perthshire manse, he studied
for the Church at St. Andrews and Edinburgh, and went
abroad as chaplain to the Black Watch, in whose van
he fought at Fontenoy, unclerical broadsword in hand.
For ten years he served with the colours, and then,
resigning the Church, took to tutoring, till he contrived
to secure the chair of natural philosophy in Edinburgh,
a subject of which he knew literally nothing. Seven

years later he exchanged it for that of moral philosophy, which was more to his taste, and ultimately for that of mathematics. During the years of his various professoriates he was a noted figure in the social life of the Scottish capital, was constantly bear-leading young grandees abroad, and published his *Essay on the History of Civil Society*, his *Institutes of Moral Philosophy*, and his *History of the Roman Republic*, which last gave him a solid title to fame. At seventy-two he made the Grand Tour again ; at eighty the old gentleman, clad in furs, " like a philosopher from Lapland," and condemned to a diet of mashed vegetables, left Edinburgh to live at Neidpath Castle, where he fought bitterly with the owls and bats, his co-tenants, and " Old Q.," his landlord. Presently he migrated to Hallyards on the Manor, where he farmed and meditated and entertained the young Walter Scott. At St. Andrews at the age of ninety-three died at long last one who, having fought at Fontenoy, lived to read the news of Waterloo.[1]

A word may be said here on the ministers of Peebles,

---

[1] The classic description of Ferguson is in Lord Cockburn's *Memorials* : " His hair was silky and white ; his eyes animated and light blue ; his cheeks sprinkled with broken red, like autumnal apples, but fresh and healthy ; his lips thin, and the under one curled. A severe paralytic attack had reduced his animal vitality, though it left no external appearance, and he required considerable artificial heat. His raiment, therefore, consisted of half boots lined with fur, cloth breeches, a long cloth waistcoat with capacious pockets, a single-breasted coat, a cloth great-coat also lined with fur, and a felt hat commonly tied by a ribbon below the chin. His boots were black ; but with this exception the whole coverings, including the hat, were of a quaker grey colour, or of a whitish brown ; and he generally wore the furred great-coat even within doors. When he walked forth, he used a tall staff, which he commonly held at arm's length out towards the right side ; and his two coats, each buttoned by only the upper button, flowed open below, and exposed the whole of his curious and venerable figure. His gait and air were noble ; his gesture slow ; his look full of dignity and composed fire."

who during the seventeenth and eighteenth centuries were men of note. Mr. John Hay when he died in 1761 had been minister of the parish for no less than forty-three years—years of constant strife with the Town Council. He was succeeded by Dr. Dalgleish, who was a prolific author. Apart from his contribution to the *Statistical Account*, he published in 1776 *The True Sonship of Christ Investigated* ; it was a work suspected of Arian tendencies and a rejoinder to it was written by a local ploughman, one William Scott, who, it is said, had to sell his cow to meet the cost of printing. He also issued *Addresses and Prayers* in 1801, and four volumes of *Sermons* between 1799 and 1807. His successor, Dr. John Lee, was soon called to a professor's chair, first at St. Andrews and then at Aberdeen. He became Moderator of the Church and a celebrated ecclesiastical leader, and published a variety of sermons. These are now forgotten, but he is still remembered as the original of the delightful figure of Archdeacon Meadows in Hill Burton's *The Book-Hunter*.

With such worthy but uninspired productions we are at the close of the eighteenth century. But there remains one poet to chronicle, one of the most famous of those whom I shall record, though he honoured the shire with only a casual wayside song. I am not pre-pared to accept the view that the name Linkumdoddie was only given to the shieling on the right bank of Tweed opposite the mouth of the Logan Burn after Burns's verses were published, or that the heroine was the wife of a farmer near Ellisland. Wherever Burns got the names—and Willie Wastle is out of the ancientry of Scots nursery rhymes—he makes his scene Tweedside and a well-defined spot there. The poem is a masterpiece of " flyting," unchivalrous, gross, but with a rude magnificence of humour.

> " Auld baudrons by the ingle sits,
>   An' wi' her loof her face a-washin' ;
> But Willie's wife is nae sae trig,
>   She dights her grunzie wi' a hushion.
>
> Her walie nieves like midden creels,
>   Her face wad fyle the Logan Water ;
> Sic a wife as Willie had,
>   I wadna gie a button for her."

V

We now reach that period which ranks as the greatest in Scottish letters, the greatest, too, in English literature save for the age of Shakespeare. Its popular name of the Romantic Revival is no misnomer, for it was born of that stirring of the sense of wonder, that sudden enlarging of horizons and glorifying of foregrounds, which we call in the widest sense " romance."   Like all fruitful revolutions it was in some sense a reaction, a return to what had been overlooked or forgotten.   This was notably true of the Scottish movement, which had its source in the Borders.   The green valleys, clear streams, and softly rounded hills make it a country proper for pastoral, and the classic conventions are less out of place there than elsewhere, for there is a certain Attic graciousness in its landscape.   But the new movement swept away the Augustan conventions and sought inspiration in autochthonous things : the fairy lore which haunted the old Wood of Caledon, the turbulent

baudrons, the old cat.   *loof*, palm.   *dights*, wipes.
    grunzie, nose.   *hushion*, footless stocking.
            walie nieves, huge fists.   *fyle*, foul.

history, and the ballads which had perpetuated a canon
of tragic and comic art far nobler than anything that
had taken their place.   The poet no longer invokes

"Panaque, Silvanumque senem, Nymphasque sorores ";

he is content with greenwood elves and burnside fairies,
with " ladies dead and lovely knights," with the epic
tale of Border war, and the human hearts in hamlet
and castle.   It is a far richer and wider world, and,
though it has its own conventions, it is essentially a
real world, recognizable by the plain man.

The dominant figure is, of course, Sir Walter Scott
(1771–1832).   This is not the place to deal with the
character and work of the chief of Scotsmen—the one
Scot, perhaps, who stands in the small inner circle of
the world's literature ; here we are concerned only with
his Tweeddale connections.   His happiest home was at
Ashestiel within a few miles of the county boundary,
and he had walked or ridden over every acre of our
moorlands.   The shire may therefore claim a part in the
genesis of that Border inspiration which was the strongest formative influence in his genius.   Little of his
poetry, however, is directly ascribable to Tweeddale,
though it is but a matter of hours for the traveller to
pass from the shire to " Yarrow's birchen bower " and the
scene of the *Lay*.   There is only the " Maid of Neidpath,"
written in 1806, a ballad based on a most tragic story,
but not in Scott's happiest vein, for the rhythm is too
light to carry the subject.   Yet it has its fine moments :

" Before the watch-dog pricked his ear,
    She heard her lover's riding." [1]

[1] Thomas Campbell has a four verse ballad, not without merit, on
the same incident.

In the novels Tweeddale has an indisputable share.
The ancient house of Traquair, with its stone bears
at the gate, its avenue, and its stanchioned lower windows, gave him in all likelihood the material for his
picture of Tully-Veolan in *Waverley*. The original of
the Black Dwarf in the novel of that name was David
Ritchie, whom Scott had met when visiting young Adam
Ferguson at Hallyards, and perhaps when he walked
with Skene up Megget and down Manor. The county
town gave its name to one of the best of his comic
characters, Poor Peter Peebles in *Redgauntlet*, and in
the same novel the scene of Pate-in-Peril's escape was
Errickstane-brae on the edge of the shire. Moreover,
one of the novels has its action laid wholly in
Tweeddale, that novel which, but for the pedantry of
his publisher, might have been one of the greatest of
Scott's tragic romances. St. Ronan's Well is Innerleithen, the home of his friend Dr. Wilkie, Marchthorn
is of course Peebles, and Meg Dods, the mistress of
the Cleikum Inn, is almost certainly drawn from Miss
Marion Ritchie, the landlady of the Cross Keys at
Peebles. It is at least possible, too, that Josiah Cargill
had his prototype in Alexander Affleck, who from 1814
to 1845 was minister of Lyne and Megget. This is no
place to quote from what is to all wise men and women
common knowledge, but I cannot resist setting down
Mistress Dods's eulogy of fishermen, which in our land
of many streams might well be a county motto. " They
were pawky auld carles, that kend whilk side their bread
was buttered upon. Ye never kend of ony o' them
ganging to the spring, as they behoved to ca' the stinking
well yonder. Na, na—they were up in the morning—
had their parritch, wi' maybe a thimblefull of brandy,

and then awa up into the hills, eat their bit cauld meat on the heather, and came hame at e'en wi' the creel full of caller trouts, and had them to their dinner, and their quiet cogue of ale, and their drap punch, and were set singing their catches and glees, as they ca'd them, till ten o'clock, and then to bed, wi' God bless ye—and what for no ? " [1]

To the St. Ronan's games at Innerleithen used to come James Hogg over the hills from Yarrow, and sit in the president's chair at the dinner which followed, singing his own songs, and filling the rummers from the punch-bowl, like the Shepherd of the *Noctes*. Hogg (1770–1835) combined several different beings in his burly person. He was, as he said himself, the poet of Fairyland, a remote diaphanous fairyland where few can dispute his title ; he had the true ballad note, and could recapture the spirit of the Middle Ages with its shivering jollity and scoffing credulity ; he had gifts, too, of popular song, and produced the best in that kind since Burns ; in his *Private Memoirs and Confessions of a Justified Sinner* he showed an insight into the psychology of religious mania which would have done credit to a modern realist, as well as an unexpected reticence of style ; he was learned in the theory and futile in the practice of farming, and his first prose work was *The Shepherd's Guide : being a practical treatise on the Diseases of Sheep* ; and he was a rough, hearty, conceited, innocent soul, full of kindliness, thriftlessness, and prickly independence. Sometimes he became the " Boar from the Forest," and stumbled into an ill-breeding rare in the class from which he sprang, as may be seen in many of his letters and his

[1] *St. Ronan's Well*, Chap. I.

deplorable *Domestic Manners and Private Life of Sir Walter Scott*. But Hogg at his worst was an engaging being, as his contemporaries found, to whom much could be forgiven, and he is deservedly esteemed as the special *vates sacer* of his own countryside. He seems to me to have been a fine novelist marred in the making. *The Shepherd's Calendar* is full of superb material, close observation of character, dramatic moments, a rich and often subtle humour, but he never seemed able to shape it to the purposes of art. He knew our county well, tramping its hills to fairs and lamb sales, and as a young man he got his books from a Peebles circulating library. His Tweeddale story, *The Bridal of Polmood*, is of slight interest. Better is *The Brownie of Bodsbeck*, with its fine opening—"' It will be a bloody night in Gemsop this,' said Walter of Chapelhope"—a tale which may fairly be regarded as the classic of that wild triangle of hill between Tweed, Ettrick, and Megget. Tweeddale may claim, too, a share in the *Noctes Ambrosianæ*, since that curious work deals also with the neighbourhood. Professor John Wilson (1785–1854), its principal author, was a great figure in his day, a monarch of literary Edinburgh ; but his work is forgotten now except the *Noctes*, with its immense appetite for life, its horse-play, its feats of guzzling and drinking, and its insatiable rhetoric. Wilson was capable of as bad errors of taste as Hogg, and with far less excuse, and there are moments when the least anæmic reader may find his gusto a little overpowering. The mountains too persistently leap like rams. The chief fault of the book is that the torrential high spirits become monotonous, and the eternal top-note ceases to amuse or arouse. But there are jewels in the pudding-stone, and though

I have never read, and never hope to read, the whole of the work, there are passages to which I often return.

To the same group belongs a writer who produced one isolated song which seems assured of a dim immortality. William Laidlaw (1780–1845), the friend and secretary of Scott and one of the most attractive figures in the Abbotsford *ménage*, was the son of the farmer of Blackhouse on the Douglas Burn, and the scene of his "Lucy's Flittin'" is Glen, on the Tweeddale side of the Blackhouse Heights. Mr. Hepburn Millar thinks that it has been "grossly overpraised," and certainly it is not easy to agree with Professor Veitch that it is "the lyric of the Borders which ranks next to the 'Flowers of the Forest.'" It is one of those Scots poems like "The Land o' the Leal" and "Annie's Tryst" which make a violent assault upon the feelings, but the almost intolerable pathos of which seems to lack the universal note of greater literature. But it has a lovely simple melody, it is written in the purest and simplest Scots, and the only false note comes in the last verse, which was the composition of Hogg. I quote two of the best stanzas :

" 'Twas when the wan leaf frae the birk-tree was fa'in',
   And Martinmas dowie had wound up the year,
That Lucy rowed up her wee kist wi' her a' in,
   And left her auld maister and neebours sae dear.
For Lucy had served in the Glen a' the simmer ;
   She cam there afore the flower bloomed on the pea ;
An orphan was she, and they had been kind till her ;
   Sure that was the thing brocht the tear to her e'e.

Oh, what is't that pits my puir heart in a flutter ?
And what gars the tears come sae fast to my e'e ?

If I wasna ettled to be ony better,
  Then what gars me wish ony better to be ?
I'm just like a lammie that loses its mither,
  Nae mither or friend the puir lammie can see ;
I fear I hae tint my puir heart a' thegither,
  Nae wonder the tears fa' sae fast frae my e'e."

Of the great writers who at that date were the glory
of England we catch fleeting glimpses in Tweeddale.
In 1803 William Wordsworth and his sister made that
Highland tour which was so rich in poetic fruit, and
on their way home passed through the Borders under
the guidance of Scott. " What a pity Mr. Scott is not
with us," was the comment of brother and sister on the
later stages of their journey. To that period belongs
" Yarrow Unvisited "; eleven years later came " Yarrow
Visited " ; and seventeen years on we have " Yarrow
Revisited," when Scott was on the eve of his voyage to
Naples and within sight of death, and " a trouble not of
clouds or weeping rain " shadowed the hills to the eyes
of the poet, his friend. It is idle to praise the three
" Yarrow " poems, which to my mind are the greatest
of Border lyrics, since they enshrine for ever the grace
and mystery and melancholy of the glens and link them
with both the transience and the eternity of man. During the first visit in 1803 Wordsworth transcribed and
sent to Scott the sonnet which he composed after seeing
the devastation wrought by the last Queensberry of
the direct line on the old forest-trees in the gorge of
Neidpath. If it is not one of the greatest of his sonnets, it is a noble outpouring of righteous wrath which
Sir Walter was never tired of quoting, and it has con-
ferred upon the unrevered figure of " Old Q." a sinister
immortality.

" Degenerate Douglas ! O the unworthy Lord !
Whom mere despite of her heart could so far please,
And love of havoc, (for with such disease
Fame taxes him) that he could send forth word
To level with the dust a noble horde,
A brotherhood of venerable trees,
Leaving an ancient dome, and towers like these,
Beggared and outraged ! Many hearts deplored
The fate of those old trees ; and oft with pain
The traveller, at this day, will stop and gaze
On wrongs which Nature scarcely seems to heed :
For sheltered places, bosoms, nooks, and bays,
And the pure mountains, and the gentle Tweed,
And the green silent pastures yet remain."

Wordsworth's companion on this tour, his sister
Dorothy, is to me one of the most wise, pellucid, and
enchanting souls of which literary history has record.
She came to Peebles on a September evening, where she
was made comfortable, she says, in an old-fashioned inn
and given a neat parlour and tea. Next day she continued her journey.

" The town of Peebles looks very pretty from the road
in returning : it is an old town, built of grey stone, the
same as the castle. Well-dressed people were going to
church. Sent the car before, and walked ourselves, and
while going along the main street William was called aside
in a mysterious manner by a person who gravely examined
him—whether he was an Irishman or a foreigner, or what
he was ; I suppose our car was the occasion of suspicion
at a time when every one was talking of the threatened
invasion. We had a day's journey before us along the
banks of the Tweed, a name which has been sweet in my
ears almost as far back as I can remember anything.
After the first mile or two our road was seldom far from
the river, which flowed in gentleness, though perhaps never
silent ; the hills on either side high and sometimes stony,

but excellent pasturage for sheep. In some parts the vale was wholly of this pastoral character, in others we saw extensive tracks of corn ground, even spreading along whole hillsides, and without visible fences, which is dreary in a flat country ; but there is no dreariness on the banks of the Tweed,—the hills, whether smooth or stony, uncultivated or covered with ripe corn, had the same pensive softness. . . . It was a clear autumnal day, without wind, and, being Sunday, the business of the harvest was suspended, and all that we saw, and felt, and heard, combined to excite our sensation of pensive and still pleasure.

" Passed by several old halls yet inhabited, and others in ruin. . . . In one very sweet part of the vale a gate crossed the road, which was opened by an old woman who lived in a cottage close to it ; I said to her, ' You live in a very pretty place ! ' ' Yes,' she replied, ' the water of Tweed is a bonny water.' The lines of the hills are flowing and beautiful, the reaches of the vale long ; in some places appear the remains of a forest, in others you will see as lovely a combination of forms as any traveller who goes in search of the picturesque need desire, and yet perhaps without a single tree ; or at least, if trees there are, they shall be very few, and he shall not care whether they are there or not.

" The road took us through one long village, but I do not recollect any other ; yet I think we never had a mile's length before us without a house, though seldom several cottages together. The loneliness of the scattered dwellings, the more stately edifices decaying or in ruins, or, if inhabited, not in their pride and freshness, aided the general effect of the gently varying scene, which was that of tender pensiveness ; no bursting torrents when we were there, but the murmuring of the river was heard distinctly, often blended with the bleating of sheep. In one place we saw a shepherd lying in the midst of a flock upon a sunny knoll, with his face towards the sky,—happy picture of shepherd life."

VI

Nineteenth century Scotland was no haunt of the
Muses, and the fountains of poetry which were opened
at the close of the eighteenth century died away for the
most part in sands before 1830. There was no master
of vernacular verse to succeed to the tradition of Burns,
no balladist to wear the mantle of Scott and Hogg.
Minor poets there were beyond computation, but little
of their work has survived their lives. The strongest
influence was the Wordsworthian, but it was Wordsworth with a difference. The lonely sublimity of the
Lake poet, his Miltonic gloom, his ethereal melody, his
appeal to the primary and eternal emotions, these were
all absent ; in their place we have an obvious didacti-
cism, nature-worship reduced to a formula, and that
rhetorical simplicity which so quickly becomes monotonous. The new Wordsworthians were mostly men
of a wide culture and considerable powers of mind ;
their feeling for nature was sincere, their meditations
grave and orthodox, their verse scholarly ; but they
were essentially uninspired. In the literature of Tweeddale the chief example of this school was John Veitch
(1829-94), who, born in Peebles, made his way
through that old avenue of talent, the Scottish universities, and became professor of logic and rhetoric
first at St. Andrews and then at Glasgow. No one who
had the honour of his acquaintance could doubt the
depth of his passion for the Borderland : he had its
history and legends in his very fibre, and thrilled to
every mood of its scenery and weather. But he could
not translate this ecstasy into verse, and his essays in

lyric, ballad, and reflective poetry in *The Tweed and
other Poems* (1875) and *Merlin* (1889) convey to the
reader but little of that strong and tender personality.
His reach in this sphere exceeded his grasp, and he
leaves the impression of a soul filled with incoherent
music but unskilled in the practice of the musical art.
John Campbell Shairp (1819–85), the companion of
Veitch on many Tweeddale walks, was like him a notable
scholar, a lover of nature, a Wordsworthian, and a
moralist. Shairp's mind was curiously conventional,
as is shown in his literary criticism, and he had a
bluntness of perception which frequently betrayed him
both in prose and verse into banality. But unlike
his friend, he had moments of true, almost of great,
poetry. Few men have written worse verse than he,
but now and then he can rise to a rare beauty.
To Tweeddale he gave his best and his worst. His
" Manor Water " has little to commend it ; his " Bush
aboon Traquair " is one of the loveliest of Scottish
pastorals.

> " And what saw ye there
>   At the bush aboon Traquair ?
> Or what did you hear that was worth your heed ?
>   I heard the cushat croon
>   Through the gowden afternoon,
> And the Quair burn singing doon to the Vale o' the
>   Tweed.

>   And birks saw I three or four,
>   Wi' grey moss bearded ower,
> The last that are left o' the birken shaw,
>   Whar mony a simmer e'en
>   Fond lovers did convene,
> Thae bonny bonny gloamins that are far awa'.

Frae mony a but and ben,
    By muirland, holm, and glen,
They cam' yin hour to spen' on the greenwood sward ;
    But long hae lad and lass
    Been lying 'neath the grass,
The green green grass o' Traquair kirkyard.

They were blest beyond compare,
    When they held their trysting there,
Among thae greenest hills shone on by the sun ;
    And then they wan a rest,
    The lownest and the best
I' Traquair kirkyard when a' was dune."

Side by side with this literary tradition there existed
sporadically the old habit of popular poetry, the songs
which come out of the emotions, pastimes, and occupa-
tions of everyday life. James Nicol (1769–1819), the
minister of Traquair, is a link between the modish verse
of the Augustans and the true vernacular forms. His
" Where Quair rins sweet among the flowers " is an
exercise in the eternal *motif* of which Burns's " O wert
thou in the cauld blast " is the chief example.

" 'Tis true I hae na muckle gear ;
    My stock is unco sma', lassie ;
Nae fine-spun foreign claes I wear,
    Nor servants tend my ca', lassie.

But had I heired the British crown,
    And thou o' low degree, lassie ;
A rustic lad I wad hae grown,
    Or shared the crown wi' thee, lassie."

Thomas Smibert (1810–54), a Peebles man and a
surgeon, published in 1851 a volume called *Io Anche !*

Poems chiefly Lyrical, which is mainly a set of exercises after approved models; but he is the author of one lyric which bears out the theory that most men are capable of producing a single good poem in their lives. His "Scottish Widow's Lament" is in its modest way a classic, truer and simpler than Laidlaw's "Lucy's Flittin'," without tarnish of false sentiment, and with just those sharp touches of realism which by contrast give poignancy to the dirge-like music, as of an autumn wind.

> " Afore the Lammas tide
>   Had dun'd the birken-tree,
> In a' our water-side
>   Nae wife sae blest as me ;
> A kind gudeman and twa
>   Sweet bairns were round me here,
> But they're a' ta'en awa'
>   Sin' the fa' o' the year.
>
> Sair trouble cam our gate
>   And made me, when it cam,
> A bird without a mate,
>   A ewe without a lamb.
> Our hay was yet to maw,
>   And our corn was to shear,
> When they a' dwined awa'
>   In the fa' o' the year.
>
> .   .   .   .   .   .
>
> Aft on the hill at e'ens
>   I see him mang the ferns,
> The lover o' my teens,
>   The father o' my bairns :
> For there his plaid I saw
>   As gloamin' aye drew near—
> But my a's now awa'
>   Sin the fa' o' the year.
>
> .   .   .   .   .   .

> My hearth is growing cauld,
>   And will be caulder still ;
> And sair, sair in the fauld
>   Will be the winter's chill ;
> For peats were yet to ca',
>   Our sheep they were to smear,
> When my a' passed awa'
>   In the fa' o' the year. "

For the rest there was a multitude of local bards, some of whom published volumes and some whose work lived in the ballad fashion by word of mouth ; but none of them can be said to have left enduring memories. Of this body of verse, minor in the honourable sense, by far the best is a little idyll of which I have not been able to trace the author. I quote it from memory, and I believe that it appeared during the 'sixties in a Peebles newspaper. It is a dialogue between a boy and an old fisherman, and reproduces the simple charm of a vanished world.

JUVENIS.   Canny Fisher Jamie, comin' hame at e'en,
            Canny Fisher Jamie, whaur hae ye been ?
PISCATOR.   Mony lang miles, laddie, ower the Kips sae
            green.
JUVENIS.   Fishin' Leithen Water ?
PISCATOR.   Nay, laddie, nay.
            Just a wee burnie, rinnin' down a brae,
            Fishin' a wee burnie, nae bigger than a sheugh.
JUVENIS.   Gat ye mony troots, Jamie ?
PISCATOR.   I gat eneugh—
            Eneugh to buy my baccy, snuff, and pickle tea,
            And lea' me tippence for a gill, and that's
            eneugh for me.

The Tweedside prose of the century is more considerable than the verse. First come the Chambers brethren, notable sons of the burgh town, which was beautified and enriched by their piety. William Chambers (1800–83) founded the publishing firm which still bears his name, and was a pioneer in the production of good books at a cheap price. He wrote a number of volumes, such as the *Story of St. Giles' Cathedral* (1879), *Stories of Old Families and Remarkable Persons* (1878), and a *Memoir* of himself and his brother (1872), but for us he is chiefly to be remembered as the author of the first *History of Peeblesshire* (1864) since Pennecuik. It is a careful piece of work, written with the enthusiasm of a loyal son of Tweeddale, and, though it may well be corrected and extended, it will always hold its place in topographical literature. His younger brother Robert (1802–71) was the better writer ; indeed, he had a streak of genuine originality and power, which was obscured by his ruthless industry. Few men of letters have adventured in so many provinces. His own *Poems* (1836) are of small value, but he was a most successful editor of poetry, as witness his *Popular Rhymes of Scotland* (1826), his *Scottish Ballads and Songs* (1829), his *Romantic Scottish Ballads* (1844), and his *Songs of Scotland prior to Burns* (1862), while in his *Life and Works of Robert Burns* (1851) he produced the first scholarly edition of a poet who has suffered much from the unscholarly. He was a historian, a biographer, a traveller, a geologist, and in his *Vestiges of the Natural History of Creation* (1844) he produced a book which fluttered the dovecotes of orthodoxy by anticipating some of the theories of Darwin, and was attributed to such diverse authors as Sir Charles Lyell and the Prince Consort. His most enduring work is to be found in his compilations, which, beginning with the *Illustrations of the Author of ' Waverley '* in 1822, included *Traditions of Edinburgh* (1825), the invaluable *Domestic Annals of Scotland* (1858–61), and above all the *Book of Days* (1863–64), the most readable miscellany of popular antiquities in the language. He was also the originator and in part the editor of two admirable encyclopædias, *Chambers's* (1859–68) and the *Cyclopædia of English Literature* (1844). He was pre-eminently a " miscellanist," a man of wide interests, deep reading, and untiring intellectual vigour.

The town of Peebles produced two philosophers who attained to important chairs in the Scottish Universities. Henry Calderwood (1830–97), professor of moral philosophy at Edinburgh, made his first reputation with the publication in 1854 of his *The Philosophy of the Infinite*, in which he attacked Sir William Hamilton's statement that the Infinite is beyond our knowledge. His intuitive system of ethics was anti-Hegelian in doctrine and theological in spirit, as became one who began life in the Church. Few books are dead so soon as those which embody the last fashion but one in speculation, and not many readers disturb to-day the dust on Calderwood's *Handbook of Moral Philosophy* (1872), *The Relation of Mind and Brain* (1879), or *Evolution and Man's Place in Nature* (1893) ; but his volume on *David Hume* in the " Famous Scots Series " may still be read with profit. A greater figure both in thought and letters was John Veitch, whose verse we have already glanced at. Veitch had the noble head of some great Schoolman, and his intellect was of the same strong tough quality. As a philosopher he was a Hamiltonian of the old rock, and, along with that subtlest of metaphysicians, Dean Mansel of Oxford, he edited his master's lectures (1869). His other philosophical works are his *Institutes of Logic* (1885), *Knowing and Being* (1889), and *Dualism and Monism* (1895) ; but to the reader who would taste his precise quality, I would recommend the introduction which he wrote to his translation of *Descartes* (1850–52). His talent for argument and analysis was equalled by few of his contemporaries, but, though the structure he built was solid and well-masoned, there were no views from the windows. As a thinker he lacked that nameless quality which attaches thought to the other instincts of the human spirit, and gives to metaphysics something of the charm of poetry. During his professorial career he saw a change in philosophical modes, and he fought stoutly against the new Hegelian absolutism ; to-day, when that doctrine is in turn out of fashion, we may see a revival of the Hamiltonian relativity. I think that in his later years he lost interest in philosophy and turned happily to that other subject which was included in the duties of his Glasgow chair—rhetoric, the study of literature and poetry. He will probably be longest remembered by his *History and Poetry of the Scottish Border* (1877 ; new edition, 1893), and his posthumous *Border Essays* (1896), which sum up his true working philosophy of life. He wrote sound scholarly prose, which now and then rises to a sober eloquence more poetic than any of his verse. But the subtlety, which was apparent in his technical work, is absent here, and as critic he seems to me to be labouring with blunt tools. He is at his best as an historian of poetic origins, where his strong good sense, clarity of mind, and intense feeling for natural beauty enable him to trace convincingly and delightfully the dawnings of poetry.

Up till now we have seen the literary inspiration coming to Tweeddale mainly by the valley of the Tweed from the Southern Border; but in the best nineteenth century prose the movement is reversed, and the wind blows from the north and the Scottish capital. Dr. John Brown (1810–82) may fairly be included among Tweeddale writers. He was born at Biggar, the son of a Seceder minister, whose portrait in the "Letter to John Cairns, D.D.", is to my mind the best thing he ever did. It was at the farm of Kirklawhill, inside the Tweeddale marches, that the small boy preached that memorable sermon on Jacob's dog :—" Some say that Jacob had a black dog, and some say that Jacob had a white dog, but *I* say that Jacob had a brown dog, and a brown dog it shall be." Throughout his youth he was accustomed to ramble over the Tweedside hills; it was at a Tweedside kirk that he first heard Dr. Chalmers; and his letters, written when he had gone to live in Edinburgh, are full of accounts of visits to Callands and to his friend, Dr. Craig, at Innerleithen. It is idle at this time of day to praise a style which recalls now Lamb, now Thackeray, but is pre-eminently the reflex of his own stalwart, whimsical, and infinitely compassionate soul. To the end he was more a child of the green uplands between Tweed and Clyde than of his beloved capital, and the three volumes of *Horæ Subsecivæ* are full of Tweeddale memories—of famous physicians like Dr. Andrew Brown of Dolphinton and Dr. Reid of Peebles; of historical matters, as in the essay on "The Black Dwarf's Bones"; or of landscape, as in the fine paper on "Minchmoor." Except for "Marjorie Fleming," I suppose he is most famous for his chapters on dogs, and two of the chief of those classic beasts came from Tweeddale. It was at Macbiehill that the immortal Rab worried sheep and would have been hanged but for the intercession of the Howgate carrier, and Wylie, the "wee fell yin," who volunteered for service each market day in Edinburgh, came from Haystoun glen, from the cottage of Adam Cairns, the herd of the Newbie "hirsel," where, as the author tells us, he once assisted in burning the water, after "having been on every hilltop from Muckle Mendic to Hundleshope and the Lee Pen, and having fished every water from Tarth to the Leithen."

It was from the Edinburgh side, too, that Robert Louis Stevenson (1850–94) first approached Tweeddale. He came there for his health in his early teens, and has recorded that one of his first literary efforts was an endeavour "to do justice to the inhabitants of the famous city of Peebles in the style of the Book of Snobs."[1] He came again at the age of thirty-two, when, in search of health, he spent a July at Stobo manse in disastrous weather. To this period belongs the letter which he wrote to Sir Edmund Gosse, in which he portrays his imaginary friend, Mr. Pegfurth Bannatyne—a passage which cannot be mentioned without quotation:

"Old Mr. Pegfurth Bannatyne is here, staying at a country inn. His whole luggage is a pair of socks and a book in a fishing-basket, and he borrows even a rod from the landlord. He walked here over the hills from Sanquhar, 'singing,' he says, 'like a mavis.' I naturally asked him about Hazlitt. 'He would never take his drink,' he said, 'a queer, queer fellow.' But he did not seem further communicative. He says he has become 'releegious,' but he still swears like a trooper. I asked him if he

[1] *Memories and Portraits*, p. 61.

had no headquarters. ' No likely,' said he. He says
he is writing his memoirs, which should be interesting.
He once met Borrow ; they boxed ; ' and Geordie,' says
the old man, chuckling, ' gave me the damnedest hiding.'
Of Wordsworth he remarked, ' He wasna sound in the faith,
sir, and a milk-blooded, blue-spectacled bitch forbye.
But his po'mes are grand—there's no denying that.' I
asked him what his book was. ' I havenae mind,' said he
—that was his only book ! On turning it out, I found it
was one of my own, and on showing it to him, he remembered it at once. ' O aye,' he said, ' I mind now. It's
pretty bad ; ye'll have to do better than that, chieldy,'
and chuckled, chuckled. He cannot endure Pirbright
Smith—' a mere æsthatic,' he said. ' Pooh ! Fishin' and
releegion—these are my aysthatics,' he wound up." [1]

There are many references to Tweeddale throughout
Stevenson's books ; in his poetry, for example :

> " By Lyne and Tyne, by Thames and Tees,
>   By a' the various river-Dee's,
>   In Mars and Manors 'yont the seas."

Our shire and the Pentlands gave him that vision of
the " hills of sheep " which was one of the two or three
types of landscape which to the end haunted his fancy.
The fragment *Heathercat* has a Tweeddale background ;
it was by one of our green drove roads that David
Balfour in *Kidnapped* journeyed from Kirk Essendean to
find fortune and Alan Breck, and the drovers in *St. Ives*,
Sim and Candlish, conducted the escaping French pris-
oner. But it is in *Weir of Hermiston* that he draws the
shire and its people with a master hand, and that noblest
of unfinished romances may well be accounted the true

---

[1] *Letters of Robert Louis Stevenson*, 1900, i. pp. 243–244.

classic of our countryside. Like all good artists he borrowed lavishly and from many quarters, and it may be that in the scenery of *Weir of Hermiston* there are suggestions from the Lammermuirs and the Moorfoots and Glencorse in the Pentlands ; but no one who knows the land intimately can differ from Sir Sidney Colvin's view that the natural identification is with " Upper Tweeddale, with the country stretching thence towards the wells of Clyde." His rides and walks as a boy had fixed the landscape in his memory, and far off in the Pacific at the close of his days his heart returned to it. No other man's verse or prose has so embodied its lonely and subtle peace :

" The road to Hermiston runs for the great part of the way up the valley of a stream, a favourite with anglers and with midges, full of falls and pools, and shaded by willows and natural woods of birch. Here and there, but at great distances, a byway branches off, and a gaunt farmhouse may be descried above in a fold of the hill ; but the more part of the time the road would be quite empty of passengers and the hills of habitation. Hermiston parish is one of the least populous in Scotland ; and, by the time you came that length, you would scarce be surprised at the inimitable smallness of the kirk, a dwarfish, ancient place seated for fifty, and standing in a green by the burn-side among two-score gravestones. The manse close by, although no more than a cottage, is surrounded by the brightness of a flower garden and the straw roofs of bees ; and the whole colony, kirk and manse, garden and grave-yard, finds harbourage in a grove of rowans, and is all the year round in a great silence broken only by the drone of bees, the tinkle of the burn, and the bell on Sundays. A mile beyond the kirk the road leaves the valley by a pre-cipitous ascent, and brings you a little after to the place of Hermiston, where it comes to an end in the backyard before the coach-house. All beyond and about is the great field of the hills ; the plover, the curlew, and the lark cry there ; the wind blows as it blows in a ship's rigging, hard and cold and pure ; and the hilltops huddle one behind another like a herd of cattle into the sunset." [1]

VII

Attempts to capture the *genius loci* in a definition are rarely fortunate : it is wiser to point to its literature as the embodiment of a thousand subtle and vagrant traditions. But there is that in the situation and history of Tweeddale which marks it out from other Scottish shires. It is of the Borders, but the nearest point of the Borders to midland and metropolitan Scotland. It was on a highroad, but not the chief highroad to England, and therefore, though always in the main march of Scottish history, it was saved from the worst devastation of the mediæval wars, and permitted to cultivate its soul in peace. It lies in the very heart of the great hill system which stretches from Galloway to the Lammermoors ; it is the most truly upland shire in Scotland, for no part of its land falls below a high elevation. Hence, though it has been in the centre of national life from the far-away days of Arthur and Merlin till a century or two ago when it contributed Mr. Secretary Murray to the confusion of the Jacobite cause, and though its sons shared in every great struggle, from Bruce and Wallace to Montrose and Prince Charlie, it could always withdraw itself securely into its hills, and the life in its remote glens went on unchanged, whether Flodden was lost or won. It has been both a cockpit and a sanctuary, a battleground

[1] *Weir of Hermiston*, Chap. V.

for the nation and a little kingdom to itself. Lastly, though highland in character, it has valleys of a lowland richness, its hills are for the most part green and gracious, and a classic charm dwells in their outline which softens the stern gothic of the Borders.

It is a land which, alike in history and configuration, unites and harmonizes opposites, and it is perhaps not fantastic to see this bold harmony reflected in the character of the men it bred and the literature it inspired. If it has produced no one masterful inspiration, it has shared fully in all the moods of thought and feeling which are Scotland's contribution to letters. It tempers the wild Border vigour with a nameless grace of its own ; it is friendly alike to classic and romantic ; it is in its modest way an epitome of Scottish literature and life. As I look back upon the long record I seem to see some power at work, some emanation from the changeless hills and waters, laying its spell upon the generations. I see the procession of its lovers, gentle and simple ; Stevenson roaming the moors as an eager child ; John Veitch, as I remember him, striding up Cademuir in an autumn gale ; the bards of the burgh town set to their glees at their winter suppers of kippered salmon and strong ale ; Sir Walter Scott on his pony riding from Megget to Manor, and Hogg with his gusty voice ruling the St. Ronan's games ; the simple old Georgian world which paced on horseback along the rough roads, and sat by the fire in the village change-house, and travelled with beasts from Falkirk Tryst to Northumberland, and slumbered peacefully of a Sabbath through the two hours' sermon in the little whitewashed kirks; Dr. Pennecuik jogging about the shire with physic in one pocket and a note-book in the other ; Yester with his love-songs ; the minstrel of a summer night at the shieling door repeating the tale of Otterburne ; the Master of St. Leonard's hospice in his *scriptorium* inditing his dull moralities ; James, poet and king, hunting in Eshielshope, and halting his horse in Peebles street to admire the humours of the Beltane Fair ; a hundred forgotten pipers and violers, playing lilts for the folk to dance to, and sending children quaking to bed with tales of warlocks and fairies ; True Thomas listening in the greenwood for the bridle bells of the Queen of Elfhame ; the hungry face of the boy Michael Scott setting out to pursue strange knowledge overseas ; and at the end Arthur marshalling his men in some glade of the Wood of Caledon, and Merlin singing his wild songs in the morning of the world.

XIII

THOUGHTS ON A DISTANT PROSPECT OF OXFORD

THOUGHTS ON A DISTANT PROS-
PECT OF OXFORD [1]

I

EAST of Magdalen Bridge, between Cherwell and Isis, a ridge of upland runs for ten miles to the north-east, and culminates in the bold eminence of Brill, which dominates the flats of Buckinghamshire as the Hill of Cassel commands the levels of Flanders. From the crown of this ridge, above the village of Old Marston, may be had the only view of Oxford which is the same as that of our grandfathers. There is no sign of the hideous periphery of raw brick ; the grey stone spires and turrets rise over woods and meadows within their cincture of mild hills just as they appeared to Dr. Johnson when he came this way of an afternoon. To a dweller on this ridge, the city is seen not as an unrelated vision at the end of a railway journey, but in the natural setting which first gave it significance. East and west is the waterway of the Thames ; from the south over the Berkshire downs come the roads leading from Winchester and the Channel ; down the Cherwell valley is the approach from the north, and over the distant Cotswolds the roads from Wales and the west ;

[1] *Blackwood's Magazine*, October 1923.

while across this very ridge runs the highway from the
Capital. The avenues of history are there before the
eye, and it would be strange if such a dweller, having
nothing of Oxford in sight but what is ancient and
beautiful, did not amuse himself with pictures of her
past.

Two books have lately been published which are
potent aids to such reflections. Mr. Albert Mansbridge,
in his *Older Universities of England,* has enlarged the
Lowell Lectures which he delivered last year in America.
He has come to the consideration of his subject at a
later age than most of us, and therefore his eye is clearer
and his judgment more mature. He approaches Oxford
after a study of England and the English people, and no
man has a better understanding of the English tradition
than the founder of the Workers' Educational Association. He has the sense of history in every fibre, and
rejoices in all things long-descended and continuous.
Because it has been his business to deal with hard facts
he judges shrewdly, because he has the historic imagination he judges tenderly, and because he is something of
the prophet and dreamer he judges truly. He sees the
older universities as embodying a high purpose which is
still in process of fulfilment ; their ancient organism is
still young ; and whatever the future holds for them in
the way of development is to be found in embryo in
their past. Above all he sees them not as fortuitous
growths, but as rooted in the life of England, a mirror
in each age for the vices and virtues of the land, as
toughly and intimately national as the village church
and the borough hall. He has given us a picture of
their development which is at once a vivid piece of
historical painting and an acute study of English

society. Mr. Falconer Madan's little volume, *Oxford outside the Guide-Books*, contains the notes of a very learned and witty scholar on the delicacies of Oxford history—the key-points for historical reconstruction, the quainter survivals, the *nuances* of old social life, jocosities which have not lost their flavour. *Lætus, hilaris, jucundus*, he re-creates the past for the benefit of the present. Both Mr. Mansbridge and Mr. Madan give us a " prospect " of Oxford, a panorama of her stages, though the latter also takes us by the hand and invites us in his agreeable company to poke into dusty nooks.

II

The dweller on the ridge of which I have spoken, if he indulge in picture-making, will not concern himself with prehistoric Oxford, when the hills were a tangle of exotic forest, and the valleys vast quagmires, and the elephant from Shotover, who descended to drink at the Cherwell, met his death from an early and aggressive type of Don, the machairodon or sabre-toothed tiger. The shameless pun is Mr. Madan's, but the bones of the luckless elephant were dug up the other day in Magdalen deer-park. But if he takes some date, say, in the fourth century of our era, for his prospect, he will look over a strange landscape. The Cherwell will be some hundreds of yards broad, and the Isis, half a mile wide or more, will be seen sweeping in a broad silver band from the corner of Wytham hill. Most of the two vales will be swamp and lagoon, but at the junction of the streams will be a mass of trees running northward, where is the spit of gravel which is now the site of Oxford. On that spit there is no sign of life, except perhaps the smoke of a hunter, who has landed from his coracle to cook the wild-fowl he has taken among the floating driftwood and matted isles of the Isis. But on the ridge behind there are habitations. Clearings have been made in the Stowood forest, and on the promontory at Beckley there is a Roman villa, where the road from Dorchester to Bicester is carried on a causeway across Otmoor. This, however, is a mere side-path, and the great Roman highways, Akeman Street and Ermine Street, are many miles distant. The Romans knew too much about malaria to go near a swamp, and preferred for their dwellings the dry uplands of Cotswold.

A century later the Romans have marched away, and the briars have grown over Beckley villa and their woodland altars. Presently we have the Saxon invaders on the ridge, giving names to the clearings, like the " field of Ella " and the " stone town." If we take up the same viewpoint in the eighth century we shall see a change in the triangle of hard ground below at the junction of Cherwell and Isis. In the course of the centuries a ford has been discovered where now stands Folly Bridge—a double ford, for the road leads first across the main stream of Isis, and then, turning sharply southward, across a second channel at the foot of Boar's Hill. Men have begun to make their homes on the patch of gravel above the clay, for it is comparatively dry and healthy, defended by the marshes on east and west, and affording outlets to the south and north. A street of rude huts lines what is now St. Aldate's, and to the east of it rises a cluster of thatched roofs which is the new nunnery of St. Frideswide, the lady whose doings are depicted in a window of the Latin Chapel in Christ Church Cathedral. The place is called

Oxenaforda, and is already a large hamlet, fast growing into a town, for it is the key to the Upper Thames, and therefore of importance to both Mercia and Wessex.

Presently it is a city, duly walled and becastled, with its four streets of wooden houses intersecting crosswise at the place called Quatuor Furcas or Carfax, and the churches of St. Michael at the north and south gates and the churches of St. Peter to bless the eastern and western approaches. She suffers heavily at the Norman Conquest, so that at the time of the Domesday survey she has a population of only 1,000 to her 732 houses; but she soon recovers, and begins to play her part in the history of England. On a snowy night in the year 1142 the Empress Maud escapes in white from the castle over the frozen river; in the palace of Beaumont outside the North Gate King Richard Cœur de Lion and King John first see the light, and royalty frequents the neighbouring palace of Woodstock. She is a busy little city, with her many trade guilds, and—sure proof of commercial prosperity—a flourishing Jewry which has the audacity to mock at the processions in honour of St. Frideswide, and even to smash up crucifixes. The Court has a weakness for the place, and grants liberal charters, and the Mayor has the right to act as Assistant Butler at Coronations. Meantime on the ridge on which our observer is stationed much has been happening. It is nearly all Crown land on which the hamlets have rights of feeding their herds of pigs—a chain of huge forests, Shotover, Stowood, Bernwood, with enclaves in them which are the holdings of various Norman houses. There is also church land there, and cells and chapels rise among the oak-woods, while at Beckley is a hunting lodge of the King's, and a great deer-park covering all the northern slopes of the hills and running down into the broad green swamp of Otmoor.

Some time in the twelfth century our observer, if he be a prescient man, will have scented a change. The roads are beginning to be thronged by a new type of traveller as part of the immense vagabondage of mediæval England. Turbulent disputatious lads are drifting towards the city from all quarters, begging their way, sleeping hard and faring rough, and talking of matters beyond the ken of the foresters and charcoal-burners on the ridge. The Oxford merchant, per-ambulating the High, begins to see at a street corner or in a church porch groups of hungry and ragged youths listening to an elder man who is speaking to them in strange tongues. The squire of Stanton or Marston finds that he cannot get his corn to the mill because of the mob of truculent boys who crowd the gates. It is the first rude beginnings of the University. The Englishman, unable to journey to Paris or Bologna, is making for himself schools at home, and as early as 1117 one Theobald of Étampes boldly dubs himself a *Magister Oxenefordiæ*. Soon these scholars have made themselves a guild, and hired rooms for lectures, and provided little hostels for their rude lodging, with signs over the door like an eagle or a brazen nose. The teachers, too, become a *societas*, and in another century colleges have been founded, and the University with its constitution and faculties is in being, with its head-quarters in the little building which we call the old Congregation House, under the north-east corner of St. Mary's Church. The city grows enormously popu-lous, rather to her disgust, for she does not welcome this herd of noisy, unprofitable students, who are perpetually quarrelling and hiving off to new homes. The respectable burgess prefers the old ways of solid merchandizing and an occasional visit from the Court. But the University has more powerful friends than the city, and at the great trial of strength in 1354, following the Town and Gown riot on St. Scholastica's Day, it is the University that wins, and the Corporation of Oxford is compelled to swear an annual oath to respect the University's privileges.

The mediæval student must have been a strange figure to the country folk on the ridge, and not less to their masters, the lords of the little manors. The foresters knew him as a ubiquitous poacher and breaker of pales ; the dwellers by the roadside as a resourceful mountebank and mummer, when he caroused in the pot-houses with Henry Pimpernel and old John Naps of Greece. In term and vacation alike he had a rough life of it. He shared an attic with several others, sleeping under a ragged coverlet, with the winds of heaven blowing through a glassless window. His food was execrable, and his academic gown was literally his chief garment. He was up before dawn, reading by the first light in the libraries, and his study of a night was done by the aid of a candle-end. Pestilence was always in the air, in the food he ate, and the water he drank, so that he was liable at any time to be cut off in his hardships. He was no pale retiring bookworm, but a robustious and aggressive person, who wore arms and rejoiced in a row. If we look at the old Benedictine buildings at Worcester College, or stand in a winter's morning in Merton Library, we can reconstruct the surroundings amid which his life was lived. We must picture, too, the narrow High Street with a gutter in the centre, the little halls that crowded its south side, the noisy Northgate Street, where corn was vended, the Beaumont Fields where archery or football or pike-staff play went on of an afternoon.　When he walked out he was obliged to have a companion for defence in case of trouble with the townsmen—a custom which at Brasenose survived far into the nineteenth century, for it was rigid etiquette that undergraduates should walk out of college in pairs and arm-in-arm.　His mind may have been well nourished, but his belly was often empty, for he would break his fast on a crust begged from the buttery, and his dinner at 10 a.m. might be no more than a thin broth.　Oxford in those days might be but a barren fount of culture, but she was an assiduous nurse of character, and her gates were open to all, gentle and simple, rich and poor, who were willing to submit to her stony regimen.

By the sixteenth century the view from the hilltop has changed ; to keep the spire of St. Mary's company there are the towers of Magdalen and New College.　The young Elizabeth is hurried by way of Beckley to her captivity at Woodstock, and long after returns a Queen, to be welcomed on Shotover by the city magistrates. Lord Williams of Thame has made very free with church lands, and the priory of Studley is a thing of the past.　But the great forests still remain, though empty now of wolves and bears, and the game-warden in one of them is a certain Milton, whose grandson is destined to be a famous poet.　Down in the Oxford streets there have been many changes : new colleges have been built, including Wolsey's noble fabric of Christ Church ; and the University is so far above the city that already when men speak of Oxford they think only of the seat of learning. The new humanism has made ground, though far more slowly than at Cambridge, and soon the religious quarrel has been decided against the ancient Church. There is a difference, too, in the undergraduates, for slips of nobility and gentry have begun to matriculate there, instead of going as pages and squires to great houses. The raffish young gentleman appears, soon to be putting his manhood to trial in the Spanish Main, and there is a set who cultivate the unacademic Muses, and presently migrate to town to add to the number of the " University wits " and lead a merry and short life of plays, madrigals, and drinking bouts. Over this epoch hangs the bright influence of Gloriana, for it was the code of Elizabeth that gave the colleges their major share in University government—reforms carried out by Leicester in the intervals of less reputable business ; and the great Queen loved to attend a disputation in St. Mary's till the hour of candle-lighting. Her famous words have often echoed in other hearts : " Farewell, farewell, dear Oxford ! God bless thee and increase thy sons in number, holiness, and virtue."

It would be hard to say that the seventeenth century saw an increase in virtue, but it was the most stirring period in Oxford's history, since she was swept into the main march of the nation's destiny. The beginning was peaceful enough for a dweller on our ridge, who was not greatly concerned with theories of Church and State. When he descended to market he would hear tales of the wonderful Doctor Laud, the head of St. John's, who was giving the University the statutes which endured for two hundred years ; but our countryman left politics alone till they sought him out and upset his easy days. The outbreak of war brought the King to Oxford, and there were parliaments in her halls, and presently a Court resident in the colleges. Since the Cotswolds represented the Royalists' first line and the Chilterns that of the Parliament, our ridge, filling an intermediate position, became a battleground. In October 1642 Charles entered the city in triumph after Edgehill, and thereafter every month brought forth its sounding incident. Boarstall Castle under the Brill upland was besieged, and presently Oxford was an armed camp, and soon a beleaguered city, with the trenches at the back of Wadham, and across St. Giles's, and east of Magdalen Bridge. Our countryman was in the way of seeing brave sights—a grave young man, who was the Marquis of Montrose, riding north one March morning to conquer Scotland alone ; Rupert and his horse swinging over Magdalen Bridge bound for a raid in the Chilterns ; the Parliament army on Bullingdon Green ; the June day when Essex marched by way of Stowood to Islip and Woodstock, and the evening of the same day when Charles slipped between him and Waller and galloped for Burford and the West. A month later came news of Marston Moor, and then the plague, and after that a great fire, and melancholy fell upon the city round which the clouds were gathering. Next year she was closely beset, with Cromwell at Wytham and Fairfax at Marston ; and the year after, when the Royalist army was scattered, Fairfax and Rupert met at Unton Croke's manor-house of Marston, just under our ridge, and negotiated terms of surrender. The dwellers on the hills saw the Prince march out with flying colours, and thanked Heaven that they would be vexed no more with the din of cannonades and visits from light-fingered soldiery. As they resumed their journeys to the town on market-days they may have seen the seventy evicted members of Christ Church foundation trooping sadly from the college, and the stout-hearted wife of the Dean, who refused to move, deposited in a chair in the middle of the quadrangle.

The rest of the century was peace, save for the quarrels of James with the Magdalen fellows, and it was notable for the activities of the unpopular Doctor Fell, who got Wren to build Tom Tower, from which the great bell of Oseney rang every night for distant country-folk to set their clocks by. The Laudian discipline had gone to pieces during the Civil War, which for Oxford was one prolonged Eights Week. Tutors were courtiers and boon companions ; undergraduates spent their days in faction fights, or, like the famous Lord Shaftesbury, in rowdy coursing matches. Up on our ridge the age saw the passing of the great forests. In the unquiet times of war there were few verderers and wardens left, so the deer were hunted by all and sundry, and trees felled by passing troops and by the adjacent villages. Before the end of the century the hills were largely cleared, out of Shotover and Stowood were carved farms of rough pasture, and the woodlands were now to be measured by acres instead of miles. From the Cherwell banks a man looked up no longer at ridges dark with oak and ash and thorn. The wilds of Old England had begun to shrink.

The dawn of the Augustan age found Oxford still suffering from the indiscipline of the Stuart period, an indiscipline which affected both dons and undergraduates. It is easy to paint too dark a picture of eighteenth century Oxford, but the fact remains that for the first fifty years there was a curious deadness and earthi-

ness in the place. Oxford had forsworn herself ; she
had accepted the Hanoverian régime against her conscience for the sake of the loaves and fishes, for it is to
be noted that, while Whig Cambridge produced forty-two
non-juring Fellows, Tory Oxford could only show fourteen. The place shrank in numbers, for it was becoming
a rich man's resort, where young gentlemen lived as if in
a hunting-box, and the small yeoman class were getting
scarcer. The poor man was now the exception instead
of the rule. It was an indecorous age. The Fellows of
Balliol resorted habitually to a low tavern over against
the college to drink with draymen and tinkers, " and
by perpetual bubbing add art to their natural stupidity
to make themselves sots." The Vice-Chancellor in the
interests of order was compelled to " walk " himself,
and found the Proctors in a disreputable ale-house.
Merton Walks and Magdalen Grove and Paradise
Garden were the dubious haunts of youth of an afternoon, and there were taverns and coffee-houses for the
evening which no authority put out of bounds. It
was a snobbish era, when noblemen and gentlemen-
commoners strutted in fancy robes, and a man's clothes
cried out his rank. The Oxford " smart " has been
drawn for us by Nicholas Amherst—a being who spent
what time he could spare from the adornment of his
person on the neglect of his duties, who damned his
father as " an old country putt," drank all day in the
taverns, and contended for the favour of some " toast,"
probably the daughter of a local tradesman. To be sure
there was another side. Charles James Fox at Hertford
read hard at mathematics, and devoured Dante and
Ariosto in the intervals of gaming and flirting, Blackstone at All Souls was clarifying the law of England,

while Dr. Johnson found Pembroke a nest of singing birds. There were the Wesleys, too, and the " Holy Club," and there were dozens of quiet people who worked hard and lived reputably. But the atmosphere was bad ; the serious student, like Mr. Gibbon of Magdalen, found " his time lost and his expenses multiplied," and the authorities made a dead set against the Methodists, with the quaint approval of Dr. Johnson. " I believe that they might be good beings, but they are not fit to be in the University of Oxford. A cow is a very good animal in a field, but we turn her out of a garden."

One curse of eighteenth century Oxford was her sham politics—a sentimental Jacobitism, which even at the end of the century Dr. Routh found flourishing in Magdalen, a thing begotten of bumpers of port and misapplied Scripture texts. Oxford had no right to the sentiment, for her service to the forlorn cause was only of the lips. For one moment the Government took it seriously, and sent a troop of horse to keep order, but presently its hollowness was understood, and the University was left in peace to drink the health of Prince Charles Edward. It was a very easy loyalty which came in with the wine and fled at the first sight of arms, and was rightly despised by the poor gentlemen of the North who were facing the fire of King George's soldiery. But it led to endless disorders. The Tories were for the most part the democracy of the colleges, but there were plenty of Whigs, mostly scions of the ruling families ; so Fellows wrangled in their common-rooms, and party bands of mohawks paraded the streets and celebrated Jacobite festivals. Merton and All Souls were the Whig strongholds, and Hearne talks of " abominable riots at All Souls," where a Whig club dined on woodcock,

" whose Heads they cut off in contempt of the memory of the B. Martyr." Not till the third George came to the throne did this folly cease.

Up on our hill the prospect has changed. The line of grey roofs from Magdalen to New College is now enriched with the pinnacles of All Souls and the fine dome of the Radcliffe Camera. The road from the city is appreciably better, though still far from good, and the citizens wander farther afield. Up the hill of a summer afternoon comes Dr. Johnson, on a visit from Town, to drink tea at Elsfield with his friend Mr. Francis Wise of Trinity, and get very much out of breath on the walk home. There are field-naturalists and antiquaries among the College Fellows, who see the hoopoe on Otmoor, and verify the botanical discoveries of Mr. Gerard of the Herball in Stowood, and write monographs on village churches and " British " remains. A little earlier Mr. Thomas Hearne might have been met with, the testy Jacobite sub-librarian of Bodley's, who would set out from St. Edmund Hall of a morning and walk thirty miles with a volume of Cicero in his pocket. Mr. Hearne was the eighteenth century counterpart of the present Provost of Oriel, for he once covered—or so he says—the eight miles between Dorchester and Oxford in an hour and a quarter. Also the undergraduate is beginning to discover the neighbouring countryside. In Jacobean times, when he was not engaged in more doubtful recreations, he would spend his summer days in " tumbling in the Hay, watching frogs swimming, telling stories under a Hay-mow." But now he is beginning to forsake the idyllic for the athletic. He goes down to the river in cap and gown, changes, and rows to Nuneham. He fishes, like Mr. Jeremy Bentham.

He is permitted to shoot over their lands by neighbouring squires, and, if he is not, he poaches.   He rides races
on Port Meadow, and he hunts assiduously in the slow
fashion of his century.   If he can cover the distance he
may don the blue and ermine of the Beaufort Hunt, or
he may go north to Warwickshire and Mr. John Warde.
The Bicester, which he calls the " Burcester," is a god-
send to him when that famous pack is started, and many
a winter afternoon the dweller on our ridge must have
watched an undergraduate party jogging homewards
from a run with Lord Abingdon's Rycote Hounds.

We are now getting very near our own day, for the
view from our hill has not altered for two hundred years,
and the only change in the hill itself is that the old rough
pasture has given place to better farming.   Men coming
up at the beginning of the nineteenth century by the
London road found no houses till they reached the Cape
of Good Hope Inn and saw Magdalen Tower rise like a
dream beyond the Cherwell.   But the railway, though
the University fought hard against it, came in time,
and with it the new *rentier* population which has spilled
itself into red-brick suburbs to the north and east.
Boar's Hill, twenty years ago as rustic as Wytham, is
now, like the peak where Browning's Grammarian was
interred, citied to the top and crowded with culture.
As for the changes in the academic life, they may be
followed in Mr. Mansbridge's pages.   The open fellow-
ships at Oriel, and the foundation of an Honours school,
were the beginning of an intellectual revival, which is
part of the history of England.   The University administration was revised by Royal Commissions, and the
old régime of study has been broadened to cracking
point.   The discomforts of the Middle Ages have been

gradually expelled, till they only survive nowadays at the railway stations. "Only one error," Mr. Mansbridge says truly, "can destroy the life of scholarship, and that is committed by men who not only fear to embark on unknown seas, but who hold back because of the comforts and rest of the shore." There was little of such holding back in nineteenth century Oxford, and some old ghost from the past, if he returned to life, might well rub his spectral eyes and declare that of all that he knew and loved, whether in buildings or customs or ideals, nothing remained.

III

Yet the ghostly judgment would be hasty, for the marvel of Oxford is not that so much has changed but that so much is changeless. Just as the prospect from our little hill has not altered in substance for centuries, so has Oxford, seen in perspective, remained the same in essence since her dim beginnings. Bracken still springs up, if permitted, in the quadrangle of All Souls, a survival from the wooded ridge of gravel which was before the city, and the thing may be taken as a parable : spray still washes her foundations from immemorial seas. It is not only that the past tends to jostle the present, and the hoar-ancient to make fantastic inroads on the modern. The Chancellor's Court has still the odd civil jurisdiction given it by Henry the Eighth, a jurisdiction asserted as recently as 1886. Till 1827 every Bachelor of Arts took an oath never to be reconciled to one Henricus Symeonis, a gentleman who in the thirteenth century killed an Oxford student, and every undergraduate swore never to hear or deliver

lectures at Stamford. There is still an outdoor service
at Magdalen on St. John's Day, a relic of the times of
the peripatetic teacher. Up till 1830 at New College
two choristers proclaimed that dinner was ready in
mixed Latin and Norman-French.[1] Queen's still cele-
brates each Christmas the deliverance of her alumnus
from the Shotover Boar, and once a century may be
seen the spectacle of the respectable Warden and
Fellows of All Souls hunting the roofs with lighted
torches for an imaginary mallard. There is still the
May morning Latin hymn on Magdalen Tower, and at
the Sunday evening service in Christ Church a special
verse is still sung after the anthem which dates from the
residence of King Charles in the College. The list is
endless, but similar survivals will be found in many
parts of our ancient land. The true legacy of the past
to Oxford is not in such incrustations, but in something
deeper and more essential, something in the inner citadel
of her soul.

A soul is a difficult thing to dogmatize about, and
Oxford has at many times been unmindful of her traditions. But, as one surveys her long progress, it would
seem that two principles were never altogether forgotten.
The first was her duty to what we may call in the largest
sense scholarship, the single-minded pursuit of learning
for its own sake. Just as a philosopher's first service
is to truth and not to popularity, so a university is
pledged in the first instance to the quest of scholarship
and not of utility. There is a sound instinct in the
Cambridge toast—" God bless the higher mathematics,
and may they never be of use to any one." It is the

[1] This pleasant fashion has been revived, I understand, at the
annual Gaudy.

duty of the older universities to produce minds—to
manufacture not ammunition wagons but guns to fire
off ammunition. Their business is not with a narrow
vocational training but with the humanities ; they are
guardians of the broad central culture of mankind.
Matthew Arnold was right in claiming that Oxford has
never sold her soul to the Philistines—who to-day, I
take it, are represented by the " practical " man, who
is so childishly unpractical, and the Chambers of Commerce, who demand a ready-money value in every study.
Not hers the quest of the immediate advantage and the
obvious end. She does not, and ought not, to provide
the final technical training for any calling, and it will
be an ill day for her if an ignorant clamour ever drives
her to forget her prime duty and scatter her energies
in competition with new specialized seminaries. Her
task is to provide that stable foundation of mental and
spiritual training on which alone specialism can be
built.

If the first principle of her being is to some degree
exclusive, the second is inclusive. She is a University
for the whole English nation, and not a preserve of a
class. It was only in the last century that the avenue
of approach to her was made strait and narrow. Pre-
Reformation Oxford was chiefly the home of poor men,
and great figures like Robert Grosseteste and William of
Wykeham and Thomas Wolsey sprang from the humblest
stock. The statutes of her colleges gave the preference
to such as were " honourable, good-living, peaceable,
humble, and indigent," and right on through the seventeenth and eighteenth centuries the boy from the village
could make his way there if he had the will. He might
be a humble sizar or servitor, but he had his chance, and

names like those of Johnson and Whitefield, Isaac Newton, Bentley, Porson, and Whewell witness that the older Universities then offered a career to merit. It is curious to reflect that it was the Liberal reformers of the nineteenth century who closed this door, by laying the emphasis on an " efficiency " which was beyond the reach of the poor. There were honest men who objected to these changes, as there were honest men who objected to the First Reform Bill, on grounds which were neither stupid nor reactionary. About the 'eighties of last century Oxford had become a middle and upper-class preserve to an extent unknown in her past.

Just as the physical city is best seen from a hilltop which shows it in its proper setting, so the spiritual Oxford can only be truly understood when considered in regard to her setting—which is the people of England. The people of England have begun to awake to a sense of their heritage. Extra-mural teaching carried the ideal of Oxford into the industrial centres, and a body like the Workers' Educational Association made explicit a popular demand of which Oxford must be the final realization. Of these and kindred movements, the most hopeful, perhaps, of our day, Mr. Mansbridge has written eloquently and wisely. The latest Royal Commission has confirmed the old Universities in their spiritual autonomy, and strengthened them, we may believe, in their ancient ideal of a scholarship which obeys no other law than that of its own being ; but in endowing them with State funds it has emphasized the fact that they are of right the possession of the whole nation. As to how the poor man may best enter upon his inheritance there may be many views, but at any

rate his title has been established. In this there is no
revolution ; indeed there is a reaction, a return to an
old creed which had been forgotten. Mediæval Oxford
owed her strength to the fact that her roots struck deep
into the life of every parish and township in the land,
and the Oxford of the future will win her power from
the same source. She is not a sanctuary of gardens
in which a privileged class may prolong for a little their
happy youth ; but, like Bunyan's House Beautiful, an
inn " for the relief and security of pilgrims," to which
all roads should lead, as they once led to Rome.

INDEX

378 Index

Index

PRINTED IN GREAT BRITAIN AT
THE PRESS OF THE PUBLISHERS